SOJOURNERS IN THE WILDERNESS

Religious Forces in the Modern Political World
General Editor: Allen D. Hertzke, The Carl Albert Center,
University of Oklahoma at Norman

Religious Forces in the Modern Political World features books on religious forces in politics, both in the United States and abroad. The authors examine the complex interplay between religious faith and politics in the modern world, emphasizing its impact on contemporary political developments. This new series spans a diverse range of methodological interpretations, philosophical approaches, and substantive concerns. Titles include:

God at the Grass Roots: The Christian Right in the 1994 Elections
    (1995) edited by Mark J. Rozell, American University, and Clyde
    Wilcox, Georgetown University
Let Justice Roll: Prophetic Challenges in Religion, Politics, and Society
    (1996) edited by Neal Riemer, Drew University
*When Sacred and Secular Mix: Religious Nonprofit Organizations and
    Public Money* (1996) by Stephen V. Monsma, Pepperdine University
*The Right and the Righteous: The Christian Right Confronts the
    Republican Party* (1996) by Duane M. Oldfield, Knox College
Religion and the Culture Wars: Dispatches from the Front (1996) by
    John C. Green, Bliss Institute of Applied Politics, University of
    Akron; James L. Guth, Furman University; Corwin E. Smidt, Calvin
    College; and Lyman A. Kellstedt, Wheaton College
*Beyond Missionaries: Toward an Understanding of the Protestant
    Movement in Central America* (1996) by Anne Motley Hallum,
    Stetson University
The Christian Democrat International (1997) by Roberto Papini,
    Trieste University, translated and with a foreword by Robert Royal,
    Ethics and Public Policy Center
*A Conscience as Large as the World: Yves R. Simon Versus the Catholic
    Neoconservatives* (1997) by Thomas R. Rourke, Florida International
    University
Everson *Revisited: The Past, Present, and Future of Religion and
    Education* (1997) edited by Jo Renée Formicola, Seton Hall
    University, and Hubert Morken, Regent University
*Sojourners in the Wilderness: The Christian Right in Comparative
    Perspective* (1997) edited by Corwin E. Smidt, Calvin College, and
    James M. Penning, Calvin College
*God at the Grass Roots, 1996: The Christian Right in the American
    Elections* (1997) edited by Mark J. Rozell, American University, and
    Clyde Wilcox, Georgetown University

Sojourners in the Wilderness

The Christian Right in Comparative Perspective

Edited by
CORWIN E. SMIDT
and
JAMES M. PENNING

ROWMAN & LITTLEFIELD PUBLISHERS, INC.
Lanham • Boulder • New York • Oxford

ROWMAN & LITTLEFIELD PUBLISHERS, INC.

Published in the United States of America
by Rowman & Littlefield Publishers, Inc.
4720 Boston Way, Lanham, Maryland 20706

12 Hid's Copse Road
Cummor Hill, Oxford OX2 9JJ, England

British Library Cataloguing in Publication Information Available

Library of Congress Cataloging-in-Publication Data

Sojourners in the wilderness : the Christian right in comparative
  perspective / edited by Corwin E. Smidt and James M. Penning.
     p. cm.—(Religious forces in the modern political world)
  Includes bibliographical references and index.
  ISBN 0-8476-8644-2 (cloth : alk. paper).—ISBN 0-8476-8645-9
(pbk. : alk. paper)
    1. Conservatism—Religious aspects—Christianity—Comparative
studies. 2. Conservatism—History—20th century. 3. World
politics—1945– . 4. Church history—20th century. I. Smidt, Corwin
E., 1946– . II. Penning, James M. III. Series.
BR115.P7S61212   1997
320.5′5′097309045—dc21   97-18546
                                              CIP

ISBN 0-8476-8644-2 (cloth : alk. paper)
ISBN 0-8476-8645-9 (pbk. : alk. paper)

Printed in the United States of America

♾ ™ The paper used in this publication meets the minimum requirements of
American National Standard for Information Sciences—Permanence of Paper
for Printed Library Materials, ANSI Z39.48–1984.

Contents

Tables

Foreword

This book is a product of the Calvin Center for Christian Scholarship (CCCS), which was established at Calvin College in 1977. The mission and purpose of the CCCS is to promote and enable creative and rigorous Christian scholarship that addresses important theoretical and practical issues.

Corwin Smidt and James Penning approached the CCCS in the fall of 1995—they wanted to call together a group of top-flight scholars to meet prior to the 1996 general election and discuss and analyze the Christian Right. They wanted to broaden the base of discussion on the topic through comparative methods. The participants would examine the Christian Right in the contemporary United States by comparing it with past right-wing religious movements and movements in other nations.

With new angles of vision—after comparing over time and place—the scholars' conversation about present-day America was enriching. However, as scholars know, a good consultation does not necessarily mean a good book. To achieve this goal, Smidt and Penning worked very closely with the authors to transform their spoken papers into the essays we present here. We believe this book to be a lively and worthwhile contribution to the ongoing conversation on the role of religion and politics in the United States. As Smidt and Penning suggest in the conclusion, much work must yet be done, especially in merging the concerns of empirical and normative analyses. For now, the conversation is well-advanced by this book. The CCCS of Calvin College is delighted to have the opportunity to make this contribution.

Ronald A. Wells
Director, CCCS
Grand Rapids, Michigan
February 1997

Introduction

Corwin E. Smidt and James M. Penning

Over the past two decades, scholars and journalists alike have written much about the Christian Right. As the political fortunes of different candidates and parties wax and wane, so too do assessments of the strength and vitality of the Christian Right. This pattern of interpretation is clearly evident in assessments of the 1992 and 1994 federal elections. Following the election of President Bill Clinton in 1992, most analysts tended to dismiss the Christian Right as a continuing force in American politics; in fact, one major analyst marked its demise as early as 1988 (Bruce 1988). Yet, only a few short years later, the Christian Right was seen to play an important role in shaping the outcome of the 1994 congressional election, helping the Republican Party capture both houses of Congress (Green et al. 1995; Kellstedt et al. 1995).

It is this enduring nature of the Christian Right and its periodic, if not continuing, political importance that prompts the assessments in this volume. Certainly, the Christian Right has been the subject of a great deal of scholarly analysis, but the movement has not been adequately studied in a truly comparative framework—across time, faith communities, and the varied institutional contexts of different state systems. No adequate understanding of the contemporary Christian Right movement in American politics is likely to emerge until analysts fully understand: (1) how it exhibits both new and continuing qualities compared with earlier manifestations of Christian Right movements in American society; (2) the level to which organizations tied to the movement have been able to mobilize resources, exhibit differentiation and innovation, recruit skilled leaders, and demonstrate political "sophistication" among its rank-and-file members; (3) the opportunities and constraints evident in efforts at mobilizing segments of different religious communities within American society; and (4) the "opportunity structures" associated with different state systems that help shape and modify the vitality and influence of the Christian Right within such systems.

The chapters in this volume are organized to address these different issues. Almost all of the chapters contained in this volume are drawn from papers presented at the Conference on the Christian Right in Comparative Perspective held at Calvin College on 4–5 October 1996, sponsored by the Calvin Center for Christian Scholarship. The aim of this conference was to present recognized scholars, operating out of different disciplinary frameworks and faith perspectives, who would provide a balanced assessment and critique of the Christian Right through comparative analyses.

The first two chapters place the Christian Right in historical perspective, revealing how today's Christian Right exhibits both continuity with and change from its earlier manifestations. In the first chapter, Michael Lienesch describes how the Christian Right draws upon a "set of precedents" established in the early twentieth century's emerging fundamentalist movement—one that provided a set of "protest repertoires, mobilizing networks, master frames, and opportunity structures" upon which conservative Christians could later emulate and follow. Lienesch's analysis reveals important aspects of continuity across time in the Christian Right. On the other hand, in chapter 2, Matthew Moen reports how the Christian Right has changed dramatically since the early 1970s, particularly its rhetoric, agenda, goals, tactics, and approaches to public policy.

Moen's chapter also provides an important bridge to the analyses contained in the next part of this volume, which analyzes the organizational structure and political strategy of the Christian Right. Mary Bendyna and Clyde Wilcox compare the organizational structure and activities of the older Moral Majority with those of the more recent Christian Coalition in chapter 3. Their analysis reveals how in building their organization the leaders of the Christian Coalition sought to learn from the Moral Majority's mistakes. Bendyna and Wilcox suggest that, while the Christian Coalition may have avoided many of these earlier mistakes, it may have made several important tactical errors of its own. In chapter 4, attention turns to the structure of the most visible, and arguably the most important, organization of the Christian Right today—the Christian Coalition. Here, Laura Berkowitz and John C. Green compare county chapters of the Christian Coalition within the state of Ohio. Their study reveals that these county organizations are not monolithic in nature, varying considerably in terms of strength, activity, and visibility. Berkowitz and Green identify five organizational categories, and to characterize the various Christian Coalition chapters, they tie differences across these five categories to the nature and level of grievances, resources, and opportunities.

Chapters 5 through 8 focus on the opportunities and obstacles faced by the Christian Right as it seeks to mobilize different religious communities within American society—evangelical and mainline Protestants, Roman Catholics, African Americans (largely "Black Protestants"), and Jews. In chapter 5, John C. Green, Corwin E. Smidt, Lyman A. Kellstedt, and James L. Guth argue that the Christian Right has successfully mobilized increasing numbers of evangelical Protestants to the Christian Right over the past several decades, whom it has largely drawn into the Republican Party. As a result of this mobilization, the authors contend that "the Christian Right has contributed directly to the ascendancy of evangelicals in the Republican coalition." On the other hand, the authors assess that the Christian Right has been far less successful in its efforts to win support among mainline Protestants and, indeed, may have become a negative referent among many mainline congregants. Nevertheless, the authors argue that, overall, the impact of the Christian Right on the GOP has been more positive than negative in increasing electoral strength.

In chapter 6, R. Scott Appleby examines the Christian Right's prospects for mobilizing Roman Catholics in the United States. While certain organizations of the Christian Right, particularly the Christian Coalition through its formation of the Catholic Alliance, have sought to more fully incorporate Roman Catholics within their ranks, Appleby suggests that important constraints exist within the Catholic community that are likely to limit the success of any such efforts.

The same is true within the African American community. In chapter 7, Allison Calhoun-Brown argues that, despite the fact that many African Americans share similar doctrinal beliefs with white evangelical Protestants, such similarities are not likely to translate easily into an alliance that bridges the two racial groups. While the groups may share similar conservative religious doctrines and conservative views on various moral-cultural issues, such issues are not interpreted in the same way by black and white religious conservatives, and the communities clearly part company on their perceptions of the appropriate role of government in addressing social ills. Still, the chapter does note that some potential opportunities for the Christian Right within the black community are emerging.

The prospects are far less encouraging in any effort to create a broader alliance with various segments of the Jewish community. In chapter 8, Kenneth D. Wald and Lee Sigelman review the stark differences in political attitudes and behavior between Jews and born-again/ evangelical Christians and see "little prospect of any but the most fragmentary cooperation" between the two communities. Despite the fact that the Christian Right continues to persevere in its efforts to woo Jewish voters, and, regardless of the fact that many Jews and evangelicals share a similar sense of dismay over certain changes in American cultural life, Wald and Sigelman contend that most Jews believe that the Christian Right has forged the wrong answers to such issues.

The next part of this volume analyzes the Christian Right in other geographic areas by comparing it to the U.S. Christian Right. J. Christopher Soper compares the Christian Right in England (chapter 9), Dennis R. Hoover compares Canada and the United States (chapter 10), while Anne Motley Hallum focuses upon the Christian Right in Central America (chapter 11). These analyses reveal that, while the Christian Right tends to draw upon similar constituencies across these different settings, the success that the Christian Right experiences in each setting is clearly shaped by the institutional structures of the state and by the historical experiences of the people. These chapters in particular help to shed light on why the Christian Right is likely to exhibit greater vitality in the United States than elsewhere.

The last two chapters of the volume are more evaluative in tone and focus. Here the comparison is largely between the ideals and norms of democratic theory and the degree to which the Christian Right fulfills such expectations in reality. In chapter 12, Mark J. Rozell assesses the extent to which the Christian Right in the United States may be exhibiting greater democratic "maturity" today than in the past. Still, Rozell's analysis raises the prospect that such maturity may constitute a double-edged sword, since accepting compromise and building coalitions with secular organizations may well risk a loss of enthusiasm among rank-and-file Christian Right members. In chapter 13, Ted G. Jelen focuses on how the Christian Right "poses risks for both Christianity and democracy," while the activity of Christian Right members "provides enormous opportunities" for both as well. Rozell and Jelen provide even-handed analyses of the Christian Right; each defends, yet also criticizes, the Christian Right in terms of its democratic implications.

We conclude the volume by analyzing the general conclusions drawn from the studies and suggesting future directions of research on the Christian Right.

References

Bruce, Steve. 1988. *The Rise and Fall of the New Christian Right*. New York: Oxford University Press.

Green, John C., James L. Guth, Lyman A. Kellstedt, and Corwin E. Smidt. 1995. "Evangelical Realignment: The Political Power of the Christian Right." *The Christian Century* 112 (July 5–12): 676–79.

Kellstedt, Lyman A., John C. Green, James L. Guth, and Corwin E. Smidt. 1995. "Has Godot Finally Arrived? Religion and Realignment." *The Public Perspective* 6 (June/July): 18–22.

Part 1

The Christian Right in Historical Perspective

1

The Origins of the Christian Right: Early Fundamentalism as a Political Movement

Michael Lienesch

For all our fascination with the Christian Right, and despite the deluge of articles and books that have been written on the topic by scholars over the last two decades, few have seriously tried to place the movement within its historical perspective. As a result, the story of the creation and early development of the Christian Right, while relatively recent, seems distant and disconnected from our own times. Moreover, to the extent that scholars have found the beginnings of Christian conservatism in the emerging fundamentalist movement of the early twentieth century, their descriptions have tended to be highly stereotypical. Thus, according to *The National Experience* (Blum, Morgan, Rose, Schlesinger, Stumpp, and Woodward 1993, 655–56), among the most respected of college-level U.S. history textbooks, early fundamentalism was (1) an attempt of traditional people to fend off modernity and maintain "the ways of the 'good old days' "; (2) a protest of the farm against the city and the South against the North, the product of "rural hostility to urban culture"; (3) an attack on evolutionary science, an emotionally charged campaign that "seized on science as an archenemy"; and (4) a lost crusade, which culminated when William Jennings Bryan took the stand at the Scopes trial, revealing "an invincible ignorance of modern learning," which "cost the fundamentalists their argument and . . . lost them their cause."

Like much conventional wisdom, this view is not wholly correct. In

3

fact, a substantial body of scholarship (Marsden 1980; Sandeen 1970; Szasz 1982; Wills 1990) suggested that early fundamentalism can better be seen as (1) a modern movement, mobilized by innovative means of communication and methods of organization; (2) an urban movement, led by educated elites from the cities of the North; (3) a pragmatic movement, in which opposition to evolution was less an emotional symbol than a rational strategy; and (4) a successful movement, arguably one of the most effective and enduring of modern political movements, whose presence has been a permanent feature of U.S. politics throughout the twentieth century.

As is usually the case with conventional wisdom, the accepted view contains an element of truth. But the real story is more complex and paradoxical than either its conventional or revisionist versions would suggest. Thus, the first fundamentalist movement may best be described as (1) modern and antimodern, applying modern means and methods to antimodernist ends; (2) urban but with rural roots, created to ease the transition from the country to the city, and to reconcile southern values with northern ones; (3) strategic as well as symbolic, with evolution emerging as a means to maintain the movement, while at the same time creating enemies and encouraging emotions that fundamentalists could not control; and (4) successful on some counts and unsuccessful on others, with its most important outcome being the transformation of fundamentalism itself.

The important point about this characterization of early fundamentalism is that it describes much of later Christian conservatism as well. For the first fundamentalists provided a set of what Sidney Tarrow (1994) has called protest repertoires, mobilizing networks, master frames, and opportunity structures that later Christian conservatives have emulated and followed from that time till now. In addition, this first fundamentalist movement initiated a regularly recurring cycle of protest (Tarrow 1994) that has typified what we have come to call the Christian Right in the twentieth century. Thus, any attempt to study the Christian Right must begin with an understanding of its origins in early fundamentalism.

Modern Antimodernism

The roots of American fundamentalism lie in modern revivalism. A creation of the turn-of-the-century city, reformed revivalism provided what Tarrow (1994, 31), following Tilly, called the "repertoire of contention," the set of means and tactics for mobilizing protest that made fundamentalism possible. Its origins can be traced to Dwight L. Moody, the Chicago shoe salesman-turned-evangelist, who transformed the old-time revival meeting into the modern crusade, in which thousands would gather in music halls or sports stadiums to hear sermons preached by world-renowned revivalists and to sing songs led by professional musicians and mass choirs (McLoughlin 1959). Bankrolled by prominent businessmen, operated according to modern management methods, using up-to-date techniques like the statistical conversion card, Moody's revivals attracted audiences of the churched and unchurched alike, breaking down denominational boundaries and introducing a more ecumenical approach to religion (Harrington 1959). Abandoning the theological text for a more popular style of preaching, Moody and his lieutenants—who included A. C. Dixon, Reuben A. Torrey, James M. Gray, Arthur T. Pierson, A. J. Gordon, William J. Erdman, and C. I. Scofield, all of whom would become prominent fundamentalists—preferred to talk about contemporary concerns, using business terminology and modern metaphors (Marsden 1980). Professional songleader Ira Sankey sang sentimental solos and led the assembled in popular hymns that critics denounced as "music hall songs" (McLoughlin 1959, 234). The message was modern; the techniques were sophisticated. Far from the old-time religion, modern revivalism was designed, in the words of William McLoughlin (1959, 281), "to make the old-time religion seem new."

In creating institutions, early fundamentalists began to find a common identity, discovering similarities among themselves and distinguishing their differences from other evangelicals. Throughout the late nineteenth century, Bible conferences began to meet regularly, bringing together evangelical conservatives from different denominations (Cole 1931). Styled on these meetings, prophecy conferences mobilized growing numbers of Christian dispensational premillennialists who came in the thousands to hear powerful preachers predict the imminent Second Coming of Christ (Sandeen 1970). Also appearing at this time were the conservative Bible institutes: Moody in Chicago, the Boston Missionary Training School, Minneapolis's Northwestern Bible Training School, the Bible Institute of Los Angeles, and similar schools in Denver, Philadelphia, New York, Toronto, and other cities (Gasper 1963). These institutions, in turn, provided support, including financial support, for the evangelical social service organizations that seemed to spring up everywhere at the close of the century: Sunday schools, missionary alliances, student volunteer agencies; organizations to publish and distribute Bibles and Christian literature; charities, healing homes, and rescue missions (Marsden 1980). With the founding of evangelical publishing houses, a growing number of religiously conservative newspapers and magazines came into circulation (Cole 1931). Moreover, alliances began to form, as activists and leaders from different parts of the country came into contact with one another, and the conferences, institutes, and social service agencies grew connected into a nascent network. In these institutional interconnections, "the outlines of a broad fundamentalist alliance were emerging" (Marsden 1980, 118).

With the publication of the famous *The Fundamentals*, fundamentalism gained not only a canon but also a modern means of mass communication. Inspired by a sermon preached by the evangelist A. C. Dixon, the southern California oil millionaire Lyman Stewart provided a fund of three hundred thousand dollars to underwrite publication of a series of accessible volumes of the best traditional teaching about the Bible. Dixon was recruited to act as editor, and he and his editorial committee persuaded some sixty-four authors to write the ninety essays that would eventually comprise the twelve volumes. The project, which was international in scope, transcended both denominational and doctrinal differences, establishing the essential elements of fundamentalist faith. Equally important was that it introduced a modern means of mass communication, creating the first of what would become many Christian conservative mailing lists by sending volumes free of charge "to every pastor, evangelist, missionary, theological professor, theological student, Sunday school superintendent, Young Men's Christian Association and Young Women's Christian Association secretary in the English-speaking world, as far as the addresses of all these can be obtained" (*The Fundamentals* 1910, 1:1). Ten thousand recipients responded with letters of appreciation. Over the next several years, one hundred thousand more wrote to request copies of issues they had missed, and with the demand for past issues, publication ran to over three million copies. All told, *The Fundamentals* served as a catalyst to the creation of fundamentalism, not only announcing its articles of belief but also creating what Jeffrey Hadden (1987, 12) called its "communications infrastructure."

The founding of the World's Christian Fundamentals Association (WCFA) in 1919 transformed fundamentalism into an organized movement. Inspired by a formidable group of founders that included Dixon, Torrey, and William Bell Riley, the purpose of the organization was to provide centralized control over the proliferation of fundamentalist conferences, institutitions, and publications. Meeting in Philadelphia in late May 1919, the organization was an instant success, as delegates from forty-four states and most of the Canadian provinces filled the Academy of Music and flowed over into the city's largest theater and several of its biggest churches. The Philadelphia meeting was only the beginning, because in its wake, conferences convened in more than one hundred cities, organizing fundamentalists at the local level (*School and Church* 1919, vol. 2). In addition, ministers participated in a speaker circuit that began in Philadelphia and connected the local conferences, so that efforts would not be duplicated or time wasted (*School and Church* 1919,2). By late 1919, letters from across the country attested to the system's success in creating a national network and connecting it to a grassroots constituency (*School and Church* 1920,2). According to one scholar, no similar organization had ever been as effective. The WCFA, argued Milton Rudnick (1966, 52), "was the first, the most comprehensive, and the most enduring organization of its kind."

Yet, while fundamentalism was institutionally a modern movement, it was ideologically a movement against modernism. In the idealistic aftermath of World War I, liberal church leaders had announced the creation of the Interchurch World Movement, an organization designed to bring together the diverse denominational efforts of Protestant mission and benevolent boards into a common campaign of evangelical revival and social reform (Marsden 1980). Closely connected to organizations like the YMCA and the Federal Council of Churches, supported by liberal seminaries, and funded by business progressives like John D. Rockefeller Jr., the Interchurch Movement was considered by many conservatives to be part of a conspiratorial plan on the part of theological modernists to capture the churches. As the modernists mobilized, conservatives countered with their own movement. In fact, in creating the WCFA, the first fundamentalists became emulators as well as enemies of their modernist counterparts. Imitating the modernists' interdenominationalism, they decried the modernists' excessive ecumenism. Establishing an organization with a strikingly similar structure to the Interchurch Movement, they denounced it for its centralized control. Relying on the support of wealthy patrons, including the president of Union Oil Company, the first fundamentalists derided the liberals' dependence on Rockefeller and his Standard Oil millions. In short, fundamentalism was an almost perfect antitype to modernism. Taken together, the movements manifest the two sides of what Ferenc Szasz (1982) called "the divided mind" of early twentieth-century Protestantism.

Thus, early fundamentalism can best be seen as an example of modern antimodernism. Building on a revised form of religious revivalism, the fundamentalist movement combined innovative institutions and changed methods of communication and sophisticated organizational techniques, all in support of orthodox religion and traditional political values. In the process, it provided a prototype for Christian conservative movements throughout the twentieth century. Moody would be succeeded by a long line of revivalists from Billy Sunday to Jerry Falwell and Pat Robertson; radio and television would supercede the speaker circuit; early mail lists would give way to computerized address banks, the WCFA to the Christian Coalition, and enemies such as the Interchurch World to the ACLU and NOW. The changes should not be underestimated, but the basic repertoire has remained the same—Christian conservatism in the twentieth century has been a modern antimodernist movement.

The City and the Country

The first fundamentalist movement was a product of the city. It was in the industrial cities of the North that fundamentalists created the mobilizing networks that would provide control, coordination, and continuity for their movement (Tarrow 1994). Leadership was centered in a few metropolitan areas: Dixon in Chicago and Baltimore, Gray in Chicago, Torrey in Chicago and Los Angeles, Gordon in Boston, Pierson in Philadelphia, Riley in Minneapolis, and John Roach Straton in New York (Sandeen 1967). At the founding of the WCFA, representatives from the New York-Boston-Philadelphia metropolitan areas were particularly prominent. Indeed, among the American authors of *The Fundamentals*, almost all were northerners, and most of them lived in large cities. Strong institutional support came from Bible institutes located in these big cities (Sandeen 1967), particularly the Moody Institute in Chicago (where Gray served as dean), the Bible Institute of Los Angeles (led by Torrey), and Northwestern in Minneapolis (Riley's headquarters). Membership in the WCFA was concentrated in the North and West, as seen in its choice of early convention sites: Philadelphia (1919), Chicago (1920), Denver (1921), and Los Angeles (1922). Sandeen (1967, 83) confirmed the movement's origins: "Fundamentalism originated in the northeastern part of this continent in metropolitan areas and should not be explained as a part of the populist movement, agrarian protest or the Southern (sic) mentality."

Among the leaders of the movement, academics and intellectuals were well represented. There was a tendency among early fundamentalists to stress academic credentials, with authors almost always going out of their way to display their degrees, titles, and institutional affiliations. Even taking into account a certain degree of exaggeration, the credentials were frequently impressive. Included among the authors of *The Fundamentals*, for example, were Princeton theologians Charles R. Erdman and Benjamin B. Warfield, along with Oberlin's George Frederick Wright, one of America's most respected geologists and a leading proponent of theistic evolution. It should be said that *The Fundamentals* were more representative of the movement in the prewar period than after the war, and that a clearly detectable element of anti-intellectualism did appear in fundamentalism after 1919. Nevertheless, even in the late 1920s, fundamentalists were following closely the developments at Princeton Seminary, where the New Testament scholar J. Gresham Machen was engaged in a fierce intellectual fight in defense of orthodoxy (Marsden 1980). At the very least, it can be said that early fundamentalists were respectful of scholarship and considered themselves to be "competent and learned people" (Rudnick 1966, 39).

Early fundamentalism also included a surprising number of urban professionals. While most leaders were ministers, lay leaders, who included not only church-connected professionals such as religious publishers, mission workers, and educators, but also those in secular occupations such as attorneys, doctors, and public officials, held a very visible station. Typical of these was Philip Mauro, a successful lawyer and Manhattan socialite, who became well known among fundamentalist audiences for his personal testimony, the story of how he found himself turned by an unseen hand from a line of well-dressed playgoers in front of a Broadway theater toward a dark and dirty rescue mission, where his soul was saved among the city's most destitute poor (*The Fundamentals* 1911,4). Within the mainline churches, where fundamentalists styled themselves a movement of the pews against the pulpits, lay organizations were especially strong. Ironically, the fundamentalist base of support among middle-class professionals was indistinguishable from that of the modernists. Both, concluded Sandeen (1970, xii), had their strength "in the cities and in the churches supported by the urban middle classes."

Yet, in spite of its urban setting, fundamentalism did retain strong rural roots. The movement was the product of a period of dramatic expansion in America's urban population, and in many ways it existed to ease the transition from the countryside to the city. Borrowing from the big-city revivalists, fundamentalists saw themselves as meeting the needs of a transitional population, a new middle class attempting to retain the traditional values of the farm and small town amid the opportunities and temptations of the city. Fundamentalist sermons often included welcomes and warnings to those who were newly arrived in the cities. Fundamentalist songs frequently contained images of sons or daughters lost to the lure of big-city lights, along with nostalgic images of farm families and small-town communities. Fundamentalist leaders emphasized their rural roots: Straton, for example, liked to preach to his Manhattan congregation about his small-town Indiana boyhood. Southern backgrounds seemed particularly common: Riley grew up in Kentucky; J. C. Massee came from a farm in Georgia; Curtis Lee Laws, the Baptist publisher who coined the term *fundamentalist*, was from rural Virginia. As one student (Herman 1980, 27) observed, "these leaders retained many of the ideas and attitudes of the South in their ministries in the North."

Over time, southern connections would emerge more clearly. In its first four years, the WCFA crossed the continent, moving from city to city along a line from east to west. By 1923, when it made the conscious choice to hold its fifth annual meeting in Ft. Worth, Texas, the organization was prepared to turn south. In part, the change was inspired by a shift of strategy, as leaders sought to move beyond the church denominations, most of which had their headquarters in the North, and into the broader public realm. Although the South was foreign territory to many fundamentalists, it was seen as welcoming, with some leaders predicting that as many as ninety percent of southerners would be sympathetic to the movement. At the same time, the South seemed to be more backward and, therefore, more tractable, since modernism was not as strong in the region, and thus southern conservatives could anticipate some of the modernist initiatives that had already appeared in the North. Southern leaders like Texan J. Frank Norris were also seen as energizing forces. It was only at Ft. Worth, however, where they were warmly received in 1923, that fundamentalists seemed to realize the potential to transform their movement from an organization of preachers and intellectuals centered in the cities of the North to a mass movement of what one called "thousands upon thousands of the plain, common people of the South" (*Christian Fundamentals* 1923:5:15). Sandeen may be overstating the case slightly, but he is right in saying that fundamentalism came late to the South, and then only as the product of conscious choice. "Fundamentalism," he concluded (1967, 321), "was not a sectional controversy but a national one, and most of its champions came from the same states as their modernist opponents."

All told, it is best to consider early fundamentalism as a transitional movement, the product of a long period of industrialization and urbanization, in which rural and small-town populations found themselves moving from the country to the city. The situation is strikingly similar to more recent versions of Christian conservatism. The cities of the early twentieth century tended to lie along the northern industrial crescent, while those of the late twentieth century can be found along the southern urban rim. But the social stresses remain quite similar for those who find themselves in transit. Thus, Grant Wacker (1984) argued that some of the strongest support for the New Christian Right of our own time comes from constituents from farm and small-town backgrounds who have moved to the suburbs and cities seeking education and employment opportunities. In spite of the stereotypes of backwoods bumpkins, the Christian Right, then as now, has mobilized a more complex constituency, a mobile middle class in transition between the country and the city, people searching for certainty in a changing culture.

Evolution: Strategy and Symbol

At its inception, fundamentalism had little to say about evolution. To the extent that leaders of the movement were concerned with highlighting issues and creating what Tarrow (1994, 122) called "frames of meaning," they tended to define these in theological terms. Thus, their earliest focus was on what was commonly called the "higher criticism," the historical and interpretive school of biblical scholarship that had originated in Germany in the mid-nineteenth century and that flourished in many mainline seminaries at this time. Believing this critical approach to the Bible to be an attack on the timeless truths of scriptural text, early fundamentalists saw themselves as debating issues of interpretation, not theories of evolution, and contending with biblical scholars rather than scientists. While Charles Darwin's ideas had been discussed several decades earlier at the time of the popularization of his works, those discussions had all but disappeared by the turn of the century. Occasional references to Darwinism, most of them critical, can be found in fundamentalist writings of the early 1900s. But as Szasz (1982, 107) surmised, for most fundamentalists before the 1920s, "evolution was not an issue."

In fact, many fundamentalists considered themselves to be theistic evolutionists. As Marsden (1980) has shown, fundamentalists thought of themselves as scientific thinkers. Relying on an epistemology that was the product of Baconian and Common Sense realist premises, they tended to think that statements of truth had to be tested and proven, and that empirical evidence provided the best proof. Far from being antiscientific, or even skeptical of science, they considered themselves to be advocates of the scientific method, although admittedly of a very literal version. Thus, those like George Frederick Wright could cite archaeological evidence as testimony that modern science provided proof of scriptural truths. Writing in 1910, in one of the early volumes of *The Fundamentals* (1910, 2), Wright went so far as to argue that the Bible and Darwin were completely compatible, and that scientific discoveries could be counted on not only to confirm but also to reinvigorate Christian religion. By 1912, he was beginning to express reservations about the evidence of evolution (*The Fundamentals* 1912, 7). Yet, as late as 1920, evolution seemed to be at best a secondary concern, and certainly not a cause, even among its most ardent critics. Ronald Numbers (1992, 39) summarized, "Fundamentalists may not have liked evolution, but at this time few, if any, saw the necessity or desirability of launching a crusade to eradicate it from the schools and churches of America."

Antievolutionism was not a creation of the fundamentalist movement. With World War I, however, antievolutionism moved to the fundamentalist agenda. At its beginning, fundamentalist reaction to the war was ambivalent and divided, with responses ranging from patriotism to isolationism and even pacifism, but by its end almost all fundamentalists had come to see the conflict as a challenge to American culture (Marsden 1980). With increasing U.S. involvement, intellectuals began to explain the German war effort as a product of German philosophy, pointing in particular to ideas of the "survival of the fittest," which were usually associated with the German philosopher Friedrich Nietzsche (Szasz 1982, 107). Prominent in popularizing these views in the United States was William Jennings Bryan, who resigned as Secretary of State as a protest against U.S. war policy and took up a personal crusade against Nietzsche's "might makes right" philosophy (Wills 1990). Fundamentalists' assumptions about German philosophy seemed to apply equally to German theology, so that, over the course of the war, Nietzscheism and modernism conflated in the minds of many fundamentalists, with evolution as the common denominator (Marsden 1991). Even so, it was Bryan who brought the issue to the public forefront in a series of speeches beginning in 1921.

Within fundamentalism, the issue of evolution emerged as the product of pragmatic politics. Among leaders of the movement, Riley seemed most enthusiastic about Bryan's efforts, in part because he himself had been dubious about Darwinian theory for some time. Of more immediate importance to Riley, however, were strategic considerations involving the impact of the evolution issue on the fundamentalist movement. In 1922, following a series of defeats suffered by fundamentalists at several mainline church conventions, Riley began an active antievolution campaign, encouraging members to bring the issue before their denominations by calling for investigations of the influence of evolutionary ideas on church colleges and seminaries (*Christian Fundamentals* 1923, 5). At the same time he announced the creation of the Minnesota Anti-Evolution League, which was created to reach beyond the church denominations and to build bridges between fundamentalists and other citizens concerned about the use of Darwinian textbooks in public schools and universities (*Christian Fundamentals* 1923, 5). Most important, responding to growing grassroots sentiment, Riley sought to bring together fundamentalist and antievolution forces under the auspices of the WCFA, calling on Bryan at the organization's 1922 convention to lead a lay movement of millions designed to bring about state legislation outlawing the teaching of evolution in the schools (*Christian Fundamentals* 1923, 5). For Riley and other leaders of the movement, evolution was a godsend, allowing them to encourage demoralized followers, build their base of support by constructing ties to other constituencies, respond to growing grassroots pressure for antievolution legislation, and maintain control over a movement that seemed to be spinning out of their control. As to Bryan, Szasz (1982, 115) has contended "fundamentalists were trying to use him for all his worth."

After 1923, however, evolution increasingly took on symbolic status within the movement. With modernists carrying out successful campaigns to assure control of the churches, and with liberal opponents of antievolution legislation blocking bills in the state legislatures, fundamentalists saw that their most effective efforts would come in shaping public opinion. Consequently, they created a campaign to bring the issue to the broader public, taking the offensive in pamphlets, speeches, and a spectacular series of public debates in which fundamentalists like Straton argued against evolutionists like Charles Francis Potter before packed auditoriums and extensive radio audiences (Gatewood 1969). In moving beyond the churches into the broader culture, fundamentalists were forced to transform their message, redefining evolution as a social and political threat, a menace not only to Christianity but to American civilization itself (Marsden 1980). Tying together atheism, modernism, and the emerging specter of bolshevism, and attributing all of these to evolutionary theory, they declared themselves to be at war with evolution (Mattison 1983). Charges of conspiracy became common, with much ado made about the "Protocols of the Wise Men of Zion," the notoriously anti-Semitic forgery that purported to reveal the plans of "international Jews" to destroy Christian culture. Throughout 1924 and early 1925, fundamentalists made their case with increasing intensity, warning that events had taken on eschatological significance, foretelling the end of civilization. Thus, when the case of *State of Tennessee vs. John Thomas Scopes* convened in the summer of 1925 amid this apocalyptic atmosphere, it was only predictable that the trial would be seen in stark and symbolic terms, as "the meeting of the great forces of skepticism and faith" (Szasz 1982, 118).

Early fundamentalists' use of evolution served both strategic and symbolic purposes. But this choice came at a cost, as the debate created enemies and emotional forces that the fundamentalists could not control. Strategic and symbolic purposes cannot be separated easily or simply, and ideological issues have a tendency to take on a life of their own.

In the case of contemporary Christian conservatives, the issue of abortion has followed a similar course. As described by A. James Reichley (1985), abortion was one component of a conscious strategy designed by conservative political strategists Paul Weyrich, Howard Phillips, and Richard Viguerie to bring together southern fundamentalists and northern Catholics. Reichley suggested that, as an organizing tool, the issue was extremely effective. Yet, he also argued that abortion soon took on symbolic significance, becoming a kind of a litmus test for many in the movement, creating deep divisions between activists like those in Operation Rescue and more pragmatic movement members. In the case of abortion, as with evolution earlier, Christian conservatives have combined strategic and symbolic concerns. The result has been a complex and sometimes contradictory mixture, a politics of both strategy and symbol.

Success, Failure, and a Transformed Fundamentalism

In the minds of most early fundamentalists, the outcome of the Scopes trial marked a victory for their movement. Not only did Bryan win the case, but with his victory—and even more with his sudden death five days later—fundamentalism inherited a set of opportunities, or what Tarrow (1994, 82) called "opportunity structures," that seemed to promise sweeping fundamentalist gains. Certain that his performance on the stand did not constitute a defeat, Bryan emerged from the trial determined to carry on the crusade by introducing antievolution legislation in several additional state legislatures (Levine 1965). Following his death he became a martyr to the movement, and others took up the cause, announcing campaigns to drive evolution from each of the states (Ginger 1958). By 1927, more than a dozen states were considering restrictive legislation (Shipley 1925). Moreover, with the Tennessee verdict, schoolbook publishers rushed to amend their textbooks, avoiding any possible litigation by deleting references to evolution or replacing them with less controversial terms like "development" (Wills 1990, 113). In short, as Numbers (1996, 23) has recently shown, fundamentalists were not defeated at Dayton, but "emerged victorious on both the legal and pedagogical fronts."

The extent of this victory, however, should not be overstated. Bryan's death left the antievolution crusade without a clear leader at a critical moment in its history. As others—including Riley, Straton, and the California minister Paul Rood—sought to assume Bryan's mantle, the movement became increasingly disorganized and divided. After 1925, liberal opponents, who had been frightened by the trial and the growing power of the fundamentalist forces, began to organize more effectively. With the opposition organizing, and without the personal and political skills of a Bryan, legislation in several states began to falter. By the late 1920s, Tennessee, Mississippi, and Arkansas had passed antievolution laws, but elsewhere bills were stalled or defeated (Larson 1989). Even so, as Numbers (1996) described, fundamentalists responded not by surrendering but by shifting their strategy, turning from statehouse to schoolhouse, and applying pressure on state textbook commissions, school boards, and teachers. The result was a quiet but resounding victory, as the now-controversial concept of evolution all but disappeared from science teaching in U.S. schools. Wrote Wills (1990, 113), "Just as the lawyers and journalists left Dayton, laughing and congratulating themselves that they had slain fundamentalism, the teaching of evolution was starting its decline in America, one from which it would not recover until the 1960s."

Nevertheless, Scopes can also be viewed as a crushing defeat for fundamentalism, creating a stereotype of Christian conservatives as (in Clarence Darrow's terms) "bigots and ignoramuses," from which they have never entirely escaped (Marsden 1980). Yet the ramifications of the trial are more ambiguous and troubling. For by pitting fundamentalism against liberalism, and by defining these two great forces in such dualistic terms, it transformed them into enduring enemies. The result, seen even today, is that any combination of evangelical moralism and progressive politics has become exceedingly difficult. The trial, concluded Wills (1990, 106), "sealed off from each other, in mutual incomprehension, forces that had hitherto worked together in American history."

To all appearances, the fundamentalist movement seemed to enter a phase of reaction and retreat after 1925. With no single leader of national standing able to assume Bryan's place, and with the focus of the antievolution fight shifting to state and local settings, the movement became increasingly decentralized and disorganized. Throughout the the late 1920s, new leaders and new organizations arose, including Rood's Bryan Bible League, George Washburn's Bible Crusaders of America, Gerald B. Winrod's Defenders of the Christian Faith, with its squads of "flying fundamentalists," and Edgar Clarke's Supreme Kingdom, which was organized along the lines of the Ku Klux Klan (Marsden 1980). Discredited by the extreme positions of many of the new groups, embarrassed by the criminal behavior of some leaders (notably Norris, who in 1926 shot and killed a political enemy), and fighting a social tide of cynicism and political passivity, fundamentalists found themselves defeated in their denominations and losing legitimacy in the eyes of the public (Wilcox 1992). Having lost control of the movement, Riley reluctantly resigned the leadership of the WCFA in 1929, turning the organization over to Paul Rood, who announced that the future of fundamentalism lay in evangelical efforts (Russell 1976). By the eve of the Great Depression, fundamentalism had, in the words of Marsden (1980, 192) "beat a bitter retreat."

Yet, in retreating, early fundamentalists were also regrouping. On its face, fundamentalism in the 1930s and 1940s would appear to be a marginalized movement. Distracted by the Great Depression and denied power by the New Deal, mainstream organizations like the WCFA lost membership, while smaller groups, many of them embracing extreme positions, seemed to proliferate. Fundamentalist firebrands like Winrod, William Dudley Pelley, and Gerald L. K. Smith were very visible on the political scene, contenting themselves with uncovering conspiracies and denouncing Democrats, often in harshly intolerant terms (Ribuffo 1983). Yet, within the movement as a whole, other changes were taking place. Working through local congregations and local pastors, founding and supporting their own colleges, publications, and service organizations, and preaching their message to millions of new members, fundamentalists in the 1930s were beginning to build the infrastructure of a revitalized movement. The defeats which fundamentalists experienced in the denominational conflicts of the 1920s moved them to establish their own institutional structures. Says Joel Carpenter (1980, 75), fundamentalists "responded creatively to the trends in contemporary popular culture and made a lasting place for themselves in American Protestantism."

Conclusion

Although most Americans, apparently including many scholars, consider early fundamentalism to be a figment of the forgotten past, it remains very much a part of contemporary politics. In addition to providing a set of precedents—repertoires, networks, frames, and opportunities—for future Christian conservatives to follow, the movement also set into motion what Tarrow (1994, 153) called "a cycle of protest": a predictable cyclical pattern in which conflict arises, constituencies are created, innovative forms of contention are introduced, issues are identified, participation becomes organized, and sequences of intensified interaction between protesters and public officials are produced, leading to reform, repression, and sometimes revolution. By the end of the 1920s, one such cycle had run its course, and the regrouping that would mark the 1930s and 1940s had already begun. "Fundamentalism," concluded Marsden (1991, 61), "was not disappearing but realigning."

What followed was the continuing cyclical pattern of Christian conservative politics that we have come to associate with the Christian Right. Appearing and disappearing throughout the twentieth century, a series of Christian conservative crusades have adopted the precedents and carried on the pattern set by the first fundamentalist movement. In the late 1940s and early 1950s, a reformed fundamentalism found political focus in opposition to communism, leading to the creation of Christian anticommunist groups like those led by Billy James Hargis, Fred C. Schwarz, and Edgar Bundy, which allied themselves with the John Birch Society, fought fluoridation, and eventually supported Barry Goldwater in his unsuccessful presidential bid (Jorstad 1970). In the late 1970s, inspired by a resurgence of religious and political conservatism, a broad coalition of fundamentalist, evangelical, and charismatic conservatives came together around a set of family issues—opposition to abortion, the Equal Rights Amendment, gay rights, pornography—to create the New Christian Right (NCR), with Jerry Falwell's Moral Majority its most visible organization (Liebman and Wuthnow 1983). Since then, as the movement has matured, the NCR has followed as many as four transforming "waves," culminating in the Christian Coalition of the late 1990s (Moen 1995). Today the Christian Right arguably may be drawing to the end of its present cycle, and beginning the process of realignment and rebuilding that the pattern requires. The movement, said Ralph Reed (1994, 201), "is carving new contours into the coming shape of American politics."

Throughout the twentieth century, the Christian Right has been a movement of both continuity and change. While relying on past precedents, Christian conservatives have proven remarkably successful at adapting to new technologies, seizing on timely issues, and responding to shifting political pressures. And it is this capacity to combine continuity with change that makes it all but certain that the Christian Right will continue to play a prominent part in American politics in the twenty-first century as well.

References

Blum, John M., Edmund J. Morgan, Willie Lee Rose, Arthur M. Schlesinger, Jr., Kenneth M. Stampp, and C. Vann Woodward. 1993. *The National Experience.* 4th ed. New York: Harcourt Brace Jovanovich.

Carpenter, Joel A. 1980. "Fundamentalist Institutions and the Rise of Evangelical Protestantism, 1929–1942." *Church History* 49: 62–75.

Christian Fundamentals in School and Church. 8 vols. 1921–28. Minneapolis, Minn.: Northwestern Bible and Missionary Training School.

Cole, Stewart G. 1931. *The History of Fundamentalism.* New York: Harper & Row.

The Fundamentals: A Testimony to the Truth. 12 vols. 1910–15. Chicago: Testimony Publishing Company.

Gasper, Louis. 1963. *The Fundamentalist Movement.* The Hague: Mouton & Co.

Gatewood, Willard B., Jr., ed. 1969. *Controversy in the Twenties: Fundamentalism, Modernism, and Evolution.* Nashville, Tenn.: Vanderbilt University Press.

Ginger, Ray. 1958. *Six Days or Forever? Tennessee v. John Thomas Scopes.* Boston: Beacon Press.

Hadden, Jeffrey K. 1987. "Religious Broadcasting and the Mobilization of the New Christian Right." *Journal for the Scientific Study of Religion* 26: 1–24.

Harrington, Carroll Edwin. 1959. The Fundamentalist Movement in America, 1870–1920. Ph.D. diss., University of California, Berkeley.

Herman, Douglas E. 1980. *Flooding the Kingdom: The Intellectual Development of Fundamentalism, 1930–1941.* Ann Arbor, Mich.: University Microfilms International.

Jorstad, Erling. 1970. *The Politics of Doomsday: Fundamentalists of the Far Right*. Nashville, Tenn.: Abingdon Press.

Larson, Edward J. 1989. *Trial and Error: The American Controversy over Creation and Evolution*. New York: Oxford University Press.

Levine, Lawrence W. 1965. *Defender of the Faith: William Jennings Bryan, The Last Decade, 1915–1925*. New York: Oxford University Press.

Liebman, Robert C., and Robert Wuthnow, eds. 1983. *The New Christian Right: Mobilization and Legitimation*. New York: Aldine Publishing Company.

Marsden, George M. 1980. *Fundamentalism and American Culture: The Shaping of Twentieth-Century Evangelicalism, 1870–1925*. Oxford: Oxford University Press.

———. 1991. *Understanding Fundamentalism and Evangelicalism*. Grand Rapids, Mich.: Eerdmans.

Mattison, Elvin Keith. 1983. *A Movement Study of Fundamentalism between 1900 and 1960*. Ann Arbor, Mich.: Xerox University Microprints.

McLoughlin, William G., Jr. 1959. *Modern Revivalism: Charles Grandison Finney to Billy Graham*. New York: Ronald Press.

Moen, Matthew. 1995. "The Fourth Wave of the Evangelical Tide: Religious Conservatives in the Aftermath of the 1994 Elections." *Contention* 5: 19–38.

Numbers, Ronald L. 1992. *The Creationists*. New York: Alfred A. Knopf.

———. 1996. The Scopes Trial as History and Legend. Unpublished ms.

Reed, Ralph. 1994. *Politically Incorrect: The Emerging Faith Factor in American Politics*. Dallas, Texas: Word Publishing.

Reichley, A. James. 1985. *Religion in American Public Life*. Washington, D.C.: Brookings Institution.

Ribuffo, Leo. 1983. *The Old Christian Right: The Protestant Far Right from the Great Depression to the Cold War*. Philadelphia, Pa.: Temple University Press.

Rudnick, Milton L. 1966. *Fundamentalism and the Missouri Synod: A Historical Study of Their Interaction and Mutual Influence*. St. Louis, Mo.: Concordia Publishing House.

Russell, C. Allyn. 1976. *Voices of American Fundamentalism*. Philadelphia, Pa.: Westminster Press.

Sandeen, Ernest R. 1967. "Towards a Historical Interpretation of the Origins of Fundamentalism." *Church History* 36: 307–21.

———. 1970. *The Roots of Fundamentalism: British and American Millenarianism, 1800–1930*. Chicago: University of Chicago Press.

School and Church. 2 vols. 1918–1921. Minneapolis, Minn.: Northwestern Bible and Missionary Training School.

Shipley, Maynard. 1927. *The War on Modern Science*. New York: Alfred A. Knopf.

Szasz, Ferenc Morton. 1982. *The Divided Mind of Protestant America, 1880–1930*. Tuscaloosa: University of Alabama Press.

Tarrow, Sidney. 1994. *Power in Movement: Social Movements, Collective Action and Politics.* Cambridge: Cambridge University Press.

Wacker, Grant. 1984. "Uneasy in Zion: Evangelicals in Postmodern Society." In *Evangelicalism and Modern America*, edited by George Marsden, 17-28. Grand Rapids, Mich.: Eerdmans.

Wilcox, Clyde. 1993. *God's Warriors: The Christian Right in Twentieth-Century America.* Baltimore, Md.: Johns Hopkins University Press.

Wills, Gary. 1990. *Under God: Religion and American Politics.* New York: Simon and Schuster.

2

The Changing Nature of Christian Right Activism: 1970s–1990s

Matthew C. Moen

This chapter examines the development of the U.S. Christian Right over time, from an incipient social protest movement in the mid-1970s to an institutionalized political player in the 1990s. This examination is warranted for three reasons. First, scholars have often examined the Christian Right's activities and influence in politics, without giving commensurate attention to the equally important effects that political activism has had on the Christian Right over time. In a sense, we have disproportionately studied *only* one side of the causal relationship between the Christian Right and politics, while neglecting the other. Accordingly, we have produced accounts of the Christian Right's influence on Capitol Hill (Hertzke 1988; Moen 1989); in particular election cycles (Johnson and Tamney 1982; Himmelstein and McRae 1984; Brudney and Copeland 1988; Smidt 1987, 1989; Guth and Green 1991; Kellstedt, Green, Guth, and Smidt 1994; Penning 1995; Rozell and Wilcox 1995); and on public opinion and political parties (Buell and Sigelman 1985; Guth and Green 1986, 1987; Sigelman, Wilcox, and Buell 1987; Jelen 1987, 1991; Wilcox 1987; Hertzke 1993; Persinos 1994; Oldfield 1996).

In contrast, we have produced very few studies of political activism's effects on the organizations and leaders of the Christian Right. Those scholars who have addressed these effects, however, typically suggest that the Christian Right is too inflexible to survive its encounter with politics, and, therefore, is preordained to "rise and fall." In fact, they suggest it has already fallen (Bruce 1988, 1992, 1995; Kivisto 1995).

21

Elsewhere, I have criticized this "rise and fall" approach because it understates the extent of the Christian Right's adaptiveness and it halts as much as it advances understanding of the Christian Right by focusing attention on its viability rather than on its evolution over time. I have responded with an alternative framework for understanding the Christian Right's development which suggests that the Christian Right has been proceeding through expansion, transition, and institutionalization, into a period of devolution (Moen 1995; forthcoming). The strength of this framework is its ability to summarize major changes in a parsimonious fashion, though that is also its weakness. Categorization schemes such as this tend to oversimplify and lose relevance as time passes. This chapter adds a more enduring theoretical component to my descriptive work on the development of the Christian Right.

Second, this inquiry is justified on historical grounds. The Chief Counsel for the Separation of Powers Subcommittee of the U.S. Senate Judiciary Committee during the Reagan presidency, Tom Bovard, mentioned the need to examine the Christian Right in broad historical terms: "The goals of any major group take [at least] a generation to come to fruition, and it is my belief that if the Christian Right is patient . . . , the nation will be changed" (Bovard 1984). Ralph Reed, Executive Director of Christian Coalition, buttressed that view through his comparisons of a budding Christian Right to a transgenerational civil rights movement, and through his own framework for understanding the development of the Christian Right over time, which is centered around the 1988 presidential candidacy of his benefactor, Pat Robertson (Reed 1996; Kaufman 1994). The studies of the Christian Right's clout in particular elections, administrations, and congresses are intrinsically important and the cornerstone of any efforts to construct more comprehensive frameworks. By the same token, they are narrowly focused snapshots that must be accompanied by studies offering more panoramic views. While scholars have examined activism by religious conservatives in the context of previous religious revivals (Hammond 1983) and twentieth-century activities (Wilcox 1992), we have basically neglected that component of history involving the development and transformation of the contemporary Christian Right, which now spans two decades.

Third, this inquiry is justified on theory-building terms. Political scientists have long recognized the need to develop more sophisticated interest group theory through case studies (Arnold 1982; Walker 1983), while sociologists have recognized the need to test social movement theory through practical examples (Zald and Ash 1966). The Christian

Right has now existed long enough to serve as a case study for theory building in both of those disciplines, as well as across them. While some cross-fertilization exists, especially relative to the social status of those supporting the Christian Right (Conover 1983; Harper and Leicht 1984; Miller 1985; Bruce 1988; Smidt 1988; Moen 1988; Wald, Owen, and Hill 1989; Wilcox 1992; Wilcox, Jelen, and Linzey 1995), political scientists have generally stayed focused on the Christian Right's power, while sociologists have remained interested in its rise and raison d'etre. Theoretical bridges have not been built across the disciplines, except in rare cases (Lienesch 1982). This chapter connects the two academic disciplines and tests the explanatory power of the organizational strand of social movement theory by seeing how well it can account for numerous and varied political developments in the Christian Right over two decades. In so doing, I encourage scholars to examine certain interdisciplinary theoretical connections, which offer some potential rewards.

Social Movement Theory and the Christian Right

A voluminous and steadily expanding literature exists on social movements that is aptly and appropriately summarized in other places (Morris and Mueller 1992). The principal component of that literature is resource mobilization theory, a perspective adopted in about three-fourths of the relevant articles in sociology journals during the 1980s (Mueller 1992). It displaced earlier theories of social movements that emphasized the grievances and deprivations of followers, focusing instead on the mobilization of resources: money, labor, and materials (McCarthy and Zald 1977). Its intellectual origin is usually traced to Mancur Olson's (1965) challenging observation that it is actually irrational for people to incur personal costs in pursuit of collective benefits; the rational choice is to be a "free rider." Resource mobilization theory arose, in part, to explain the incentives and mechanics of collective action.

Within resource mobilization theory, several permutations exist (McCarthy and Zald 1977). Scholars variously focus upon the relationship of collective action to: (1) preexisting networks (such as churches in the case of the Christian Right); (2) significant changes in the political realm (such as the work of the feminist movement); (3) the attitude of the regime (such as government revocation of tax exemptions for private schools or regulation of home schools); and (4) the vitality of organizations (such as the Christian Coalition). In each case, the role of available resources remains a principal theme, although William Gamson (1987, 1) has observed that all the permutations of resource mobilization theory contribute "to different aspects of social movements."

Scholars have not systematically applied any of these permutations to the Christian Right. Only a few political scientists have ventured into resource mobilization theory, usually doing so as part of more ambitious tasks (Lienesch 1982; Wilcox 1992) or en route to introducing students to concepts in the study of religion and politics in the United States (Wald 1997; Fowler and Hertzke 1995). For their part, sociologists have mentioned resource mobilization theory in a book on the rise and character of the Christian Right (Liebman and Wuthnow 1983), but the pertinent chapters (Latus 1983; Wuthnow 1983; Liebman 1983; Himmelstein 1983) accomplish goals other than the systematic application of theory. Moreover, the chapters focus on the first variant of resource mobilization theory—the one that stresses preexisting networks, such as churches and electronic ministries. Steve Bruce (1988) offered a more extensive and elegant theoretical discussion in a "rise and fall" context, asserting the centrality of resource mobilization theory in explaining the rise of the Christian Right. Furthermore, he contributed to the theoretical framework, proposing the corollary that emerging social movements must anticipate a likelihood of future successes before they will fully mobilize. Here too, though, Bruce pursued a task other than application of resource mobilization theory, actually inviting readers to skip the opening chapter outlining his theoretical addition (Bruce 1988). In short, resource mobilization theory has been mentioned, but only partially and not very systematically applied to the Christian Right.

This is especially true of the fourth variant of resource mobilization theory, which focuses on organizational vitality. This is a particularly promising choice vis-à-vis the Christian Right, given its history of multiple organizations. Quite apart from that correlative reason, it is attractive for a methodological reason: organizations are tangible objects, not analytic phantoms. Finally, organizational survival is a prerequisite to a social movement attaining other goals, so it is an attractive focal point.

The organizational tributary of the resource mobilization stream, as Gamson (1987) has described it, arises from earlier work (Gerth and Mills 1946; Weber 1947; Selznick 1948; Michels 1949; Smelser 1962) but is actually highlighted in more recent work (Zald and Ash 1966; McCarthy and Zald 1977). This tributary argues that organizations embedded within social movements experience striking transformations as they interact with the social order. Specifically, *organizational goals* become transformed, *organizational maintenance* becomes the overriding concern, and *organizational leadership* becomes centralized and highly oligarchical. Those three major elements of the organizational tributary frame the rest of this chapter.

Organizational Goals

Resource mobilization theory argues that social movement organizations gradually adjust to the social consensus; they replace unattainable goals with more diffuse goals (Zald and Ash 1966). These related propositions certainly apply to the Christian Right. Its process of accommodation to the societal consensus, which is a rhetorical and tactical shift toward the political mainstream on the part of its elite leaders (Moen 1992, 1995), has been underway for a long time and is evidenced in many different ways.

First, the Christian Right has altered its rhetoric over time, replacing the language of moralism in the 1970s with the language of liberalism in the 1990s (Moen 1992, 1995). During the Christian Right's early years, its leaders spoke in highly moralistic terms, such as "putting God back in the government" (Jorstad 1981). They created organizations with strong moral overtones such as the Moral Majority and the Christian Voice, and they framed public policy issues in similar terms, demanding that Congress pass constitutional amendments "putting God back in the schools" and stopping "murder of the unborn." As leaders became aware of the problems of framing issues in moralistic, sectarian terms—it limited the appeal of the social issues and invited fierce opposition—they recast a range of issues in the liberal language of rights, freedom, and equality. One early observer of this trend quoted a Moral Majority official as saying that prayer in schools and abortion were now clearly viewed as civil rights issues, involving freedom for religious expression and equality for the unborn (Hertzke 1988). Those reformulations were supplemented with an emphasis on "parental rights" (over the curriculum of schools and the accessibility of illicit materials to children over the internet), on "student rights" (to form voluntary religious organizations in schools and to give prayers at graduation ceremonies), and on "religious equality" (as a counterweight to secular views in classrooms). More recently, Christian Right leaders have cast opposition to gay rights measures in terms of "no special rights" (Morken 1994). They have stressed the themes of equality and choice in their "Contract with the American Family" and when defending the Republicans' "Contract with America." In a different vein, leaders claim that they suffer discrimination on the basis of their religion (Wilcox 1996), demanding an end to "religious apartheid" and a place for religious expression. These formulations are consistent with sociological theory that predicts movement toward the societal consensus; leaders of the major Christian Right organizations now use more familiar and widely accepted language when they frame issues for the public. They may still use the earlier rhetoric when speaking only to supporters (Bruce 1988), so this shift toward the rhetorical mainstream is, of course, a work in progress.

Second, the Christian Right has vastly expanded its range of issues. In its early days, the Christian Right was pigeonholed by a subset of social issues such as prayer in schools, abortion, and gay rights. Its leaders staked out positions on other domestic and foreign policy matters for public consumption, but they committed resources to the social issues (Moen 1989). While social issues remain critical to its fundraising efforts (Godwin 1988), the Christian Right has taken measured steps beyond narrow issues, toward matters such as crime, term limits, welfare reform, tax cuts, and other items contained in the Republicans' "Contract with America" (Moen 1995). All of those initiatives are placed under the moniker of "pro-family" policies. Ralph Reed (1993) has led the effort to expand the Christian Right's political agenda in order to fill the vacuum left in the wake of the Reagan administration (Moen 1992) and to appeal to a broader cross-section of the population; accordingly, the Christian Coalition put considerable resources behind the "Contract with America" in the 104th Congress (Salant 1995). Although the efforts of the Christian Coalition do not symbolize the entire Christian Right, they demonstrate a leading organization's shift toward the political mainstream. Moreover, its efforts confirm the proposition that unattainable goals, such as constitutional amendments on social issues, are commonly jettisoned in favor of more diffuse goals.

Third, the Christian Right has given ground on social issues. Its leaders have dropped demands that homosexuals be banned from teaching and that AIDS patients be quarantined. They quit lobbying long ago on Capitol Hill for the "Family Protection Act," an omnibus bill packed with social remedies. Many religious conservatives practice home schooling, but they seem more willing to submit to state standards and accreditation now than in the early 1980s, when the fire storm over Faith Baptist School in Louisville, Nebraska, instigated civil disobedience. Demands for tuition tax credits exclusively for parents whose children attend private, religious schools have been replaced by proposals for education vouchers for all parents under the auspices of "school choice." Early efforts to pass a constitutional amendment permitting prayer in public schools have been largely abandoned in favor of "equal access" for student religious groups in schools (Hertzke 1988) and for student-led approaches, such as prayers at graduation exercises.

Even abortion, a "life-or-death" issue for many religious conservatives, shows some shift toward the societal consensus. While abortion was opposed without exceptions by Christian Right leaders in the 1970s, most now make room for the standard exceptions (rape, incest, or life of the mother), and such luminaries as Ralph Reed, Pat Robertson, and Phyllis Schlafly even broached the possibility of remanding the issue back to the states, a remarkable change of position from demanding a constitutional amendment banning the practice nationwide (Moen 1995). More recently, Reed even suggested discarding constitutional amendment language (a mainstay of Republican Party platforms) from the 1996 platform. Reed (1996, 29) stated that as a "tactical matter it is true that amending the Constitution may be the most remote weapon at our disposal at this time." However, he and other Christian Right leaders backtracked when their organizations revolted at such concessions in the midst of writing the Republican Party platform in San Diego. In fact, Reed even felt compelled to restate his pro-life credentials, and then to participate in victory proclamations after the constitutional amendment language was incorporated into the platform. Interestingly, though, social conservatives allowed dissenting opinions on abortion in the platform appendix, a tiny but nevertheless tangible concession by those dominating the platform committee. Still, at this point in time, abortion probably provides less supporting than contrary evidence of a shift toward the societal consensus by the Christian Right, but the current furor might not be a very reliable indicator. Elite leaders have been reassessing their positions for some time, and outside the limelight of a presidential campaign (and cognizant of the inevitability of RU-486), it is reasonable to anticipate other modest shifts toward the social consensus.

Fourth, the Christian Right has adopted the vehicles and tactics of the political mainstream. In the 1970s, it was not clearly affiliated with any political party; according to Bob Billings, the first Executive Director of Moral Majority, the Christian Right only shifted toward the Republican Party when the 1980 Reagan campaign reached out to it (Billings 1984). Subsequently, the Christian Right became an active, if not dominant, partner in the Republican Party (Oldfield 1996). Scholars have chronicled this relationship in many dimensions in too many places to cite; it is sufficient to note that this previously unaligned social protest

28 *Matthew C. Moen*

movement today operates within the confines of a major political party. The Federal Election Commission's complaint against the Christian Coalition for allegedly violating its nonpartisan, tax-exempt status bespeaks this shift toward the political mainstream.

Similarly, the Christian Right has adopted conventional political strategies, such as registering voters, recruiting candidates for office, organizing political action committees, stacking party caucuses, disseminating scorecards on officeholders, mobilizing voters through fax chains and telephone trees, and contributing labor to particular campaigns. On the flip side, it has mostly abandoned experiments with "stealth" campaigns (Morken 1993). Its tactics are now very similar to those of other groups in politics, yet another example of its steady move to the center.

Fifth, the Christian Right has replaced anti-intellectual conspiracies (such as "secular humanism") with more scientific approaches to public policy. The prototype for this shift has been the Family Research Council, headed by Gary Bauer, which gathers evidence to support public policies that encourage the traditional, two-parent family. Among other things, the Council's work helped pave the way for the family tax cuts proposed in the Contract with America, and then promoted by Republican presidential nominee Bob Dole. The Council's work has been supplemented by a range of efforts across different issues, including introduction of scientific evidence on early fetal viability, survey data on the unpopularity of same-sex marriage, commissioned polls on the sanctity of religious freedom issues, and logically argued editorials on the merits of devolving power from the federal government to the states. The Christian Right contains a wide variety of viewpoints within the broader confines of social conservatism, ranging from obtuse to well-reasoned claims at all levels of aggregation (Lienesch 1993); the important point is that Christian Right leaders approach the public arena today like other political players. Conspiracy theories and biblical pronouncements have been cast aside in favor of more rigorous approaches to public policy.

Taken together, these changes demonstrate the utility of the organizational strand of resource mobilization theory for understanding developments in the Christian Right. Its current rhetoric, issue selection and issue positions, positioning in the Republican Party, and approach to public policy all signal movement toward the societal consensus. Contrary evidence can be marshaled because it does exist, and public and private pronouncements may vary (Bruce 1988), but the evidence is overwhelming that the Christian Right has been heading toward the mainstream, just as the theory predicts.

Organizational Maintenance

Resource mobilization theory suggests that the leaders of a social movement become preoccupied with organizational maintenance (Zald and Ash 1966). Their concern is well-founded—a social movement cannot endure without an organizational infrastructure. While the maintenance argument is hardly unique—it has been used in areas such as bureaucracy (Allison 1971), organizational culture (Ott 1989), and budgeting (Wildavsky 1984)—it seems to explain a great deal about the Christian Right's organizational patterns.

For instance, it helps explain the multiplicity of organizations over the years. Paul Webber (1994) identified twenty-seven evangelical and fundamentalist Christian groups active in the 1990s; some other groups were active in the 1980s, such as the National Christian Action Coalition, Religious Roundtable, and Freedom Council. The sheer number of organizations in the Christian Right suggests something of a preoccupation with creating and maintaining them.

Then, too, the maintenance argument can help account for the persistent division-of-labor within the Christian Right. In the early 1980s, different organizations focused on mobilizing voters, recruiting ministers into politics, setting the policy agenda, and lobbying (Moen 1989). Different organizations still strive to fill separate niches in order to gain and retain a market share of the conservative Christian cohort. Accordingly, some organizations serve as brokers in Republican Party politics (Christian Coalition). Others seek to activate women (Concerned Women for America and the Eagle Forum). Some are solely focused on litigation (American Center for Law and Justice and the Home School Legal Defense Association). Some are strongly motivated by abortion (American Life League), while still others focus particularly on television programming (American Family Association), gay rights (Traditional Values Coalition), and school board elections (Citizens for Excellence in Education). In a different vein, some organizations pitch their message to evangelicals, others to fundamentalists, and still others to charismatics. The list of variations is naturally finite but nevertheless impressive. Two decades after the Christian Right arose, it consists of more than two-dozen groups with specialized missions pursuing common goals.

The maintenance argument also accounts for key mergers. Zald and Ash (1966) argued that merger constitutes a last effort to salvage an organization, a proposition evidenced by Jerry Falwell's attempt to combine a declining Moral Majority with a newly formed Liberty Federation, followed in turn by an unsuccessful effort to renew Moral Majority once the announced merger sputtered. Several organizations experiencing turbulent financial situations in the mid-1980s combined their resources under the umbrella of the American Coalition for Traditional Values. The coalition worked for the reelection of Ronald Reagan in 1984, and then announced an expansion of its mission just prior to shutting down amidst revelations of close ties to the Reverend Sun Myung Moon (Moen 1992). Its leader, the Reverend Tim LaHaye, ended the organization for reasons congruent with the maintenance theory. LaHaye realized that he could not keep the organization afloat once its ties to Moon were publicized, and that he risked the viability of Concerned Women for America (headed by his wife) by prolonging the matter. Pat Robertson folded the remnants of the Freedom Coalition—disbanded amidst an Internal Revenue Service investigation into its tax-exempt status—into his presidential candidacy, and then launched Christian Coalition out of that candidacy. Bob Billings collapsed Christian School Action, formed in the late-1970s to resist federal government intrusion into private religious schools, into a much broader National Christian Action Coalition, a move that kept it alive for seven more years. In short, the organizational maintenance argument provides a convincing framework for understanding key mergers.

The maintenance argument also plausibly explains rivalry. Some observers have focused on animosity between Pat Robertson and Jerry Falwell, often explaining the antipathy in terms of doctrinal disputes or personality conflicts. However, one can just as easily see their differences in the context of organizational maintenance—the need for Virginia-based television evangelists to maintain their political operations. Analyzing the conflict in those terms makes sense of Ralph Reed's (1996) indirect (but stinging) attack on Falwell for spreading gossip about President Bill Clinton. The same thought applies beyond the well-known personal rivalries, into much broader ideological conflicts. The "cottage industry" spawned by the Christian Right (embodied in groups such as People for the American Way and Fight the Right), can be understood in terms of symbiotic organizational maintenance. Each side in this ideological conflict is dependent upon making outrageous allegations about the other in order to successfully solicit the funds that prop up its organizations. For reasons of maintenance, they also offer a wide variety of purposive and material incentives—membership certificates, pins, and stickers.

Although causality cannot be assigned, the organizational maintenance argument provides a sensible framework for understanding discernible patterns already noted in the literature. The rise, retrenchment, and institutionalization of groups are comprehensible in the context of organizational maintenance—all of them tried to survive, but only those with the clearest missions, most able leaders, and most committed followers were able to outlast the topsy-turvy process of too many groups in pursuit of too few resources.

At this point, I wish to suggest a corollary to resource mobilization theory, namely that tactical shifts are likely to reflect the outcome of the intramural struggle for organizational maintenance. The Christian Right offers some evidence. With few exceptions, the victors in its intramural struggle for organizational survival have been those strongly oriented toward the grass roots: Concerned Women for America, Christian Coalition, and Focus on the Family. The vanquished have been the national, direct-mail lobbies launched in the late-1970s (Hertzke 1988). As a result, the Christian Right's strategic grassroots shift proceeds beyond simple expediency toward open advocacy for devolving political power to subnational units, such as states, towns, and even neighborhoods. Put another way, the Christian Right's current support for devolution can be partly explained by the outcome of its intramural struggle for organizational maintenance. The validity of this proposition can be tested by close examination of organizational struggles and strategic shifts, either in the future with the Christian Right or comparatively with other social movements.

Organizational Oligarchy

Resource mobilization theory posits that an oligarchy will eventually claim power within a social movement. Such centralization of authority, in turn, usually portends stagnation and factionalization, as disaffected members quit or form splinter groups outside the reach of an oligarchy (Zald and Ash 1966).

This theorem of resource mobilization theory is engaging, but very difficult to apply vis-à-vis the Christian Right. It may help explain the leadership of a small cadre of television evangelists in the late-1970s (Hadden and Swann 1981), whose electronic networks were easily converted into an identifiable social movement. It can also help explain the growing salience of more radical elements, such as Reconstructionists. Although their intellectual contribution to the movement has been considerable (Lienesch 1993), Reconstructionists have not shown up much on the national political scene until recently, when their positions were freely incorporated into the platform of the U.S. Taxpayers Party. That development is consistent with predicted factionalization, stemming from key leaders' efforts to nudge the Christian Right toward the political mainstream.

Yet, this theorem seems more erroneous than useful. It is directly contradicted by the broader patterns of leadership in the Christian Right over time. Instead of an oligarchy arising to claim power, as the theory predicts, a bevy of able leaders have surfaced at state and local levels to press the Christian Right's agenda (Shribman 1989). In fact, a central feature of the Christian Right since the mid-1980s has been a proliferation of leaders (Moen 1992). Likewise, the Christian Right is active and moving steadily toward the political mainstream, a development confirmed by the fact that one-third of all of the delegates to the 1996 Republican national convention claimed a link to religious conservatism (Elving and Benenson 1996). At least as we approach the new millenium, the Christian Right is hardly the oligarchical movement predicted by organizational theory.

Looking Back and Ahead

The organizational tributary of the resource mobilization stream in the social movement literature provides a reasonable framework for interpreting major developments in the Christian Right over time. Among other things, it can help account for the substitution of classical liberal for moralistic language, the development of a broader political agenda, the incremental retreat on key social issues, the gravitation toward the GOP, and the development of more sophisticated approaches to public policy. It can also account for the multiplicity of groups in the Christian Right, their tacit division of labor, the merger of key organizations, the persistence of personal and ideological rivalries, and more broadly, the rise, retrenchment, and institutionalization of organizations. In contrast, it cannot account (at least at this time) for the largely decentralized leadership structure of the Christian Right.

This equation seems unchanged by the 1996 election cycle. The Christian Right continues to operate with a decentralized (and sometimes competing) set of leaders, whose organizations pursue somewhat different missions (Wald 1997). Moreover, the Christian Right still acts within the confines of the Republican Party. Exit polls showed that 17 percent of white voters in 1996 self-identified with the Christian Right (Langer 1996). They supported Republican presidential candidate Bob Dole by a two-to-one margin over Democratic President Bill Clinton, and they voted for Republican House candidates over Democratic candidates by a 70 percent to 25 percent margin (Bennet 1996; Clymer 1996). In the words of Ralph Reed, religious conservatives provided a "fire wall that prevented a Bob Dole defeat from mushrooming into a meltdown all the way down the ballot." That view was seconded by pundit, Doug Bailey, who said "the Christian Coalition is one of the major reasons the Republican majority in Congress was retained" (Dorning and Warren 1996). Following the election, Pat Robertson expressed his determination to work within the Republican Party in the years ahead, pledging to bring about the nomination of a truly conservative candidate in the next presidential election cycle (Niebuhr 1996).

Religious conservatives are likely to retain their allegiance to the Republican Party, seeking a "voice" within it rather than an "exit" from it (Oldfield 1996). They currently wield influence within state party organizations, and many of their leaders have personal incentives to remain active in the party structure. Those who suggest religious conservatives will leave the GOP to form a religiously oriented third party (Lowi 1995) ignore the voting patterns of recent elections, overlook the political calculations of leaders to eschew that course of action (Moen 1992), and dismiss the broader pattern of gradual incorporation into the political mainstream. Rather than leave the GOP, religious conservatives are likely to stay aboard, moving further along toward the political mainstream, just as social movement theory predicts.

References

Allison, Graham T. 1971. *Essence of Decision*. Boston: Little, Brown & Co.

Arnold, R. Douglas. 1982. "Overtilled and Undertilled Fields in American Politics." *Political Science Quarterly* 97 (Spring): 91–103.

Bennet, James. 1996. "Most Delegates Conservative, Male, and White." *New York Times*, 12 August.

Billings, Bob. 1984. Interview by author. 26 July, Washington, D.C.

Bovard, Tom. 1984. Interview by author. 11 July, Washington, D.C.

Bruce, Steve. 1988. *The Rise and Fall of the New Christian Right*. New York: Oxford University Press.

———. 1992. "The Future of the New Christian Right." In *Fundamentalism in Comparative Perspective*, edited by Lawrence Kaplan, 38–73. Amherst: University of Massachusetts Press.

———. 1995. "The Inevitable Failure of the New Christian Right." In *The Rapture of Politics*, edited by Steve Bruce, Peter Kivisto, and William H. Swatos Jr., 7–20. New Brunswick, N.J.: Transaction Publishers.

Brudney, Jeffrey L., and Gary W. Copeland. 1988. Ronald Reagan and the Religious Vote. Paper presented at the annual meeting of the American Political Science Association, 1–4 September, Washington, D.C.

Buell, Emmett H., Jr., and Lee Sigelman. 1985. "An Army That Meets Every Sunday? Popular Support for the Moral Majority in 1980." *Social Science Quarterly* 66: 426–34.

Clymer, Adam. 1996. "Republicans Retain Control of the House." *New York Times,* 6 November.

Conover, Pamela. 1983. "The Mobilization of the New Right: A Test of Various Explanations." *Western Political Quarterly* 36: 632–49.

Dorning, Mike, and James Warren. 1996. "Labor Regains Relevance; Conservative Christians Flex Their Muscle." *Chicago Tribune,* 7 November.

Elving, Ronald D., and Bob Benenson. 1996. "Religious Conservatives' Visibility Will Be Large." *Washington Times,* 8 August 8, 11.

Fowler, Robert Booth, and Allen D. Hertzke. 1995. *Religion and Politics in America.* Boulder, Colo.: Westview Press.

Gamson, William. 1987. "Introduction." In *Social Movements in an Organizational Society,* edited by Mayer N. Zald and John D. McCarthy, 1–7. New Brunswick, N.J.: Transaction Publishers.

Gerth, Hans, and C. Wright Mills. 1946. *From Max Weber: Essays in Sociology.* New York: Oxford University Press.

Godwin, R. Kenneth. 1988. *One Billion Dollars of Influence.* Chatham, N.J.: Chatham House.

Guth, James L., and John C. Green. 1986. "Faith and Politics: Religion and Ideology among Political Contributors." *American Politics Quarterly* 14: 186–200.

———. 1987. "The Moralizing Minority: Christian Right Support among Political Contributors." *Social Science Quarterly* 68: 598–610.

———, eds. 1991. *The Bible and the Ballot Box.* San Francisco: Westview Press.

Hadden, Jeffrey K., and Charles E. Swann. 1981. *Prime Time Preachers.* Reading, Mass.: Addison-Wesley.

Hammond, Philip E. 1983. "Another Great Awakening?" In *The New Christian Right,* edited by Robert C. Liebman and Robert Wuthnow, 207–23. New York: Aldine.

Harper, Charles L., and Kevin Leicht. 1984. "Explaining the New Religious Right: Status Politics and Beyond," In *New Christian Politics,* edited by David Bromley and Anson Shupe, 101–11. Macon, Ga.: Mercer University Press.

Hertzke, Allen D. 1988. *Representing God in Washington.* Knoxville: University of Tennessee Press.

———. 1993. *Echoes of Discontent.* Washington, D.C.: CQ Press.

Himmelstein, Jerome H. 1983. "The New Right." In *The New Christian Right,* edited by Robert C. Liebman and Robert Wuthnow, 13–30. New York: Aldine.

Himmelstein, Jerome H., and James A. McRae Jr. 1984. "Social Conservatism, New Republicanism, and the 1980 Election." *Public Opinion Quarterly* 48: 592–605.

Jelen, Ted G. 1987. "The Effects of Religious Separatism on White Protestants in the 1984 Presidential Election." *Sociological Analysis* 48: 30–45.

————. 1991. *The Political Mobilization of Religious Beliefs.* New York: Praeger.

Johnson, Steven D., and Joseph B. Tamney. 1982. "The Christian Right and the 1980 Election." *Journal for the Scientific Study of Religion* 21: 123–31.

Jorstad, Erling. 1981. *The Politics of Moralism.* Minneapolis, Minn.: Augsburg.

Kaufman, Leslie. 1994. "Life Beyond God." *New York Times Magazine*, 16 October.

Kellstedt, Lyman A., John C. Green, James L. Guth, and Corwin E. Smidt. 1994. "It's the Culture, Stupid! 1992 and Our Political Future." *First Things* 42: 28–33.

Kivisto, Peter. 1995. "The Rise or Fall of the Christian Right? Conflicting Reports from the Frontline." In *The Rapture of Politics*, edited by Steve Bruce, Peter Kivisto, and William H. Swatos Jr., 1–5. New Brunswick, N.J.: Transaction Publishers.

Langer, Gary. 1996. 1996 Exit Poll: Crunching the Nuggets. Briefing paper, ABC News, Washington, D.C., 12 November.

Latus, Margaret Ann. 1983. "Ideological PACs and Political Action." In *The New Christian Right*, edited by Robert C. Liebman and Robert Wuthnow, 75–99. New York: Aldine.

Liebman, Robert C. 1983. "Mobilizing the Moral Majority." In *The New Christian Right*, edited by Robert C. Liebman and Robert Wuthnow, 49–73. New York: Aldine.

Liebman, Robert C., and Robert Wuthnow, eds. 1983. *The New Christian Right.* New York: Aldine.

Lienesch, Michael. 1982. "Right-Wing Religion: Christian Conservatism as a Political Movement." *Political Science Quarterly* 97: 403–25.

————. 1993. *Redeeming America: Piety & Politics in the New Christian Right.* Chapel Hill: University of North Carolina Press.

Lowi, Theodore J. 1995. *The End of the Republican Era.* Norman: University of Oklahoma Press.

McCarthy, John D., and Mayer N. Zald. 1977. "Resource Mobilization and Social Movements: A Partial Theory." *American Journal of Sociology* 82: 1212–41.

Michels, Robert. 1949. *Political Parties.* Glencoe, Ill.: Free Press.

Miller, W. E. 1985. "The New Christian Right and Fundamentalist Discontent." *Sociological Focus* 18: 325–26.

Moen, Matthew C. 1988. "Status Politics and the Political Agenda of the Christian Right." *Sociological Quarterly* 29: 23–31.

————. 1989. *The Christian Right and Congress.* Tuscaloosa: University of Alabama Press.

————. 1992. *The Transformation of the Christian Right.* Tuscaloosa: University of Alabama Press.

————. 1995. "The Fourth Wave of the Evangelical Tide: Religious Conservatives in the Aftermath of the 1994 Elections." *Contention: Debates in Society, Culture, and Science* 5 (Fall): 19–38.

————. Forthcoming. "The U.S. Christian Right in the 21st Century." In *Prophetic Religions, Mobilization, and Social Action in the Twenty-First Century,* edited by Anson Shupe and Bronislaw Misztal. Westport, Conn.: Greenwood.

Morken, Hubert. 1994. No Special Rights: The Thinking behind Colorado's Amendment #2 Strategy. Paper delivered at the annual meeting of the American Political Science Association, 1–4 September, New York.

Morris, Aldon D., and Carol McClurg Mueller, eds. 1992. *Frontiers in Social Movement Theory.* New Haven, Conn.: Yale University Press.

Mueller, Carol McClurg. 1992. "Building Social Movement Theory." In *Frontiers in Social Movement Theory,* edited by Aldon D. Morris and Carol McClurg Mueller, 3–25. New Haven, Conn.: Yale University Press.

Niebuhr, Gustav. 1996. "Christian Coalition Looks to 2000." *New York Times,* 7 November.

Oldfield, Duane M. 1996. *The Right and the Righteous: The Christian Right Confronts the Republican Party.* Lanham, Md.: Rowman & Littlefield.

Olson, Mancur. 1965. *The Logic of Collective Action.* Cambridge: Harvard University Press.

Ott, J. Stephen. 1989. *The Organizational Culture Perspective.* Pacific Grove, Calif.: Brooks/Cole.

Penning, James M. 1995. "Pat Robertson and the GOP: 1988 and Beyond." In *The Rapture of Politics,* edited by Steve Bruce, Peter Kivisto, and William H. Swatos Jr., 105–22. New Brunswick, N.J.: Transaction Publishers.

Persinos, John. 1994. "Has the Christian Right Taken over the Republican Party?" *Campaigns & Elections* 15 (September): 21–24.

Reed, Ralph. 1993. "Casting a Wider Net." *Policy Review* 59 (Summer): 31–35.

————. 1996. "We Stand at a Crossroads." *Newsweek,* 13 May, 28–29.

Rozell, Mark, and Clyde Wilcox, eds. 1995. *God at the Grass Roots.* Lanham, Md.: Rowman & Littlefield.

Salant, Jonathan D. 1995. "Alliance of Private Groups Pushes GOP Contract." *Congressional Quarterly Weekly Report,* 28 January.

Selznick, Philip. 1948. "Foundations of the Theory of Organization." *American Sociological Review* 13 (February): 25–35.

Shribman, David. 1989. "Going Mainstream: Religious Right Drops High-Profile Tactics, Works on Local Level." *Wall Street Journal,* 26 September, 18.

Sigelman, Lee, Clyde Wilcox, and Emmett H. Buell Jr. 1987. "An Unchanging Minority: Popular Support for the Moral Majority, 1980 and 1984." *Social Science Quarterly* 69: 876–84.

Smelser, Neil. 1962. *Theory of Collective Behavior*. New York: Free Press.

Smidt, Corwin. 1987. "Evangelicals and the 1984 Election." *American Politics Quarterly* 15: 419–44.

————. 1988. "The Mobilization of Evangelical Voters in 1980." *Southeastern Political Review* 16: 3–33.

————. 1989. "Change and Stability among Southern Evangelicals." In *Religion in American Politics*, edited by Charles W. Dunn, 147–59. Washington, D.C.: CQ Press.

Wald, Kenneth D. 1997. *Religion and Politics in the United States*. 3d ed. Washington, D.C.: CQ Press.

Wald, Kenneth D., Dennis Owen, and Samuel Hill. 1989. "Evangelical Politics and Status Issues." *Journal for the Scientific Study of Religion* 28: 1–16.

Walker, Jack L. 1983. "The Origins and Maintenance of Interest Groups in America." *American Political Science Review* 77: 390–406.

Webber, Paul J. 1994. Divided We Stand: Religious Pluralism in the United States. Paper presented at the annual meeting of the American Political Science Association, 1–4 September, New York.

Weber, Max. 1947. *The Theory of Social and Economic Organizations*. New York: Oxford University Press.

Wilcox, Clyde. 1987. "Popular Support for the Moral Majority in 1980: A Second Look." *Social Science Quarterly* 68: 157–66.

————. 1992. *God's Warriors: The Christian Right in Twentieth-Century America*. Baltimore, Md.: Johns Hopkins University Press.

————. 1996. *Onward Christian Soldiers?* Boulder, Colo.: Westview Press.

Wilcox, Clyde, Ted G. Jelen, and Sharon Linzey. 1995. "Rethinking the Reasonableness of the Christian Right." *Review of Religious Research* 36: 263–76.

Wildavsky, Aaron. 1984. *The Politics of the Budgetary Process*. 4th ed. Boston: Little, Brown & Co.

Wuthnow, Robert. 1983. "The Political Rebirth of American Evangelicals." In *The New Christian Right*, edited by Robert C. Liebman and Robert Wuthnow, 167–85. New York: Aldine.

Zald, Mayer N., and Roberta Ash. 1966. "Social Movement Organizations: Growth, Decay, and Change." *Social Forces* 44 (March): 327–40.

Part II

Organization and Strategy of the Christian Right

3

The Christian Right Old and New: A Comparison of the Moral Majority and the Christian Coalition

Mary E. Bendyna and Clyde Wilcox

In autumn 1988, the Christian Right appeared defeated, and fundamentalists seemed likely to make yet another retreat from American public life. The Moral Majority was bankrupt, and the Christian Voice had closed its Political Action Committee and was subsisting on a limited budget. Pat Robertson had spent a record amount seeking the presidential nomination but failed to win a single primary. Some scholars wrote of the inevitable failure of the Christian Right, and many journalists wrote the movement's obituary.

By autumn 1996, however, the Christian Right was clearly resurgent. The Christian Coalition, Focus on the Family, and Concerned Women for America were large, national organizations with real grassroots power. The Republican Party's presidential nominee, U.S. Senator Bob Dole, saw his language on tolerance of abortion rejected by the GOP platform committee, and Christian Right forces controlled or were important forces in state Republican party organizations across the country (Green, Guth, and Wilcox 1995). In a year when party moderates made a real push to roll back pro-life language in the platform, the Christian Right trounced them. At the GOP convention, the Christian Coalition unveiled a sophisticated, high-tech whip system which Ralph Reed announced as a "dry run for 2000."

The newfound political muscle of the Christian Right is real, and the movement's strength in the GOP represents the most successful foray

41

of a social movement into a political party since the labor movement's incursion into the Democratic Party early in the century. How can it be that a movement that appeared dead in 1988 has become a major political force just eight years later? Part of the answer lies in contrasts between the Moral Majority, the best known organization of the 1980s, and the Christian Coalition, the most publicized organization of the 1990s. The leadership of the Christian Coalition studied the mistakes of the Moral Majority and learned many important lessons.

The Moral Majority

In the late 1970s, a number of Christian Right organizations were formed with considerable fanfare. Three made a major effort to be political players: the Moral Majority, Christian Voice, and Concerned Women for America. Of these, the Moral Majority received the lion's share of publicity, primarily because Jerry Falwell welcomed media attention and fit many preconceived stereotypes of southern fundamentalist preachers. The Moral Majority claimed a membership of more than four million, with more than two million active donors (Johnson and Bullock 1986). The membership figures of the organization were almost certainly greatly exaggerated. In Ohio, for example, the statewide organization claimed a membership of 20,000, but had a mailing list of just 285 names (Wilcox 1992). Yet the group did generate considerable revenue in its early years from a mailing list developed from Falwell's "Old Time Gospel Hour."

The Moral Majority attempted to build state chapters in every state, and then to build chapters in every county, primarily through Falwell's denomination, the Baptist Bible Fellowship. Falwell was the great success story of the denomination, having built the Thomas Road Baptist Church from scratch into a mega-church with more than 15,000 members. So when he called other pastors within the denomination and asked for their help in building a political organization, he found a receptive audience. More than half of all state chairmen were from the Baptist Bible Fellowship, and the rest were mostly from independent Baptist churches (Liebman 1983). Within states, county chairmen were also drawn disproportionately from the Baptist Bible Fellowship.

The Baptist Bible Fellowship is even more decentralized than most Baptist denominations, with a strong emphasis on the role of the individual pastor. Falwell followed this model in the Moral Majority as well, and allowed the local chapters considerable autonomy. This decentralization had, at best, mixed results: among active state chapters, one attracted national attention for its protests against anatomically correct cookies, while others became embroiled in controversy because of extreme policy pronouncements.

Yet, most state chapters were generally inactive (Hadden, Shupe, Hawdon, and Martin 1987; Wilcox 1992). Indeed, only a few states, such as Indiana and Washington, made much of an effort to build active county chapters. In many ways, the very resources that allowed the Moral Majority to quickly assemble an organization on paper prevented it from building a strong grassroots presence. The preachers in the Baptist Bible Fellowship are religious entrepreneurs, often starting churches in their living rooms with a congregation of their neighbors, hoping eventually to expand their following and build a church. Those who succeed generally immediately proceed to plan construction of church schools. For most of these men, religious construction was more important than building a political organization, and so although they lent their names and church space to the Moral Majority, they did not give it much time.

The Baptist Bible Fellowship clergy exhibited one other characteristic that limited their ability to build active organizations. They were an especially particularistic lot, anxious to distinguish their doctrine from the faulty beliefs of other Baptist churches, and, of course, from pentecostal, evangelical, and mainline Protestant churches as well as Catholics. Their antipathy toward Catholics was strong, and they were also highly critical of pentecostals and charismatics. In fact, one county chairman in Ohio preached that pentecostals spoke with the tongues of Satan.

Small wonder, then, that studies of state chapters in Ohio and Indiana revealed a membership dominated by independent Baptists, primarily from the Baptist Bible Fellowship. In Indiana, Georgianna (1989) found that 75 percent of members belonged to independent Baptist churches, and in Ohio the figure was slightly over half. A significant portion of the remaining members in both states were Southern Baptists. The leadership in Ohio seemed genuinely surprised that Catholics had not joined their movement, although their statewide meetings were held after the Bible Baptist Fellowship meetings, which occasionally even featured particularistic sermons highly critical of Catholics.

Thus, the optimistic plans for the Moral Majority to evolve into a grassroots organization never materialized, and instead the organization was primarily limited to a small national organization funded by direct mail. The yields of conservative direct mail plummeted in 1984 after

Ronald Reagan's commercials reassured the electorate that it was already "morning in America," and after increasing numbers of conservative groups seeking dollars flooded mailboxes with solicitations. Soon after the 1984 election, the Moral Majority faced financial difficulties, and eventually Falwell disbanded the group.

In its approach to government, the Moral Majority was also largely ineffective. It put pressure on its allies to make difficult votes, succeeding only in alienating the group from its friends (Moen 1989). It buried Congress in misinformed messages about the Civil Rights Restoration Act, and the naive language in some of its letters and telegrams provided an opportunity for the media to ridicule the group.

Although Jerry Falwell claimed that he was disbanding the Moral Majority in 1989 because it had achieved its aims, the organization, in reality, had accomplished little. Abortion remained legal, mothers continued to enter the workplace in increasing numbers, and cities and private companies accorded gays and lesbians increasing benefits and protections. Moreover, there was no evidence that the Moral Majority succeeded in shaping public opinion: data from the General Social Survey showed that between 1978 and 1989, the public became slightly more pro-choice, substantially more supportive of gender equality, and slightly more supportive of gay rights.

Although the Moral Majority ultimately failed, it did differ from previous generations of Christian Right organizations in important ways that helped pave the way for the Christian Coalition. First, the Moral Majority was unabashedly partisan. Falwell had endorsed Republican candidates in Virginia since the 1970s, and quickly became an enthusiastic cheerleader for the national party and a fixture at party conventions in the 1980s.

Second, the Moral Majority took positions on a wide range of issues, ranging from the gold standard and ending welfare to support for South African apartheid and aid to Nicaraguan contras to opposition to abortion and gay rights. Unlike Christian Voice, the Moral Majority made no attempt to link these policy positions to biblical passages, but they did aggressively inform the membership on new issues through *The Moral Majority Report*. The Moral Majority even staked conservative positions on economic issues including subminimum wage, welfare spending, and a balanced budget.

Finally, the national leadership of the Moral Majority announced the goal of building a truly interfaith coalition on morals. The group did not incorporate the words "Christian" or even "Religious" in its name, and Falwell appealed to Catholics and Jews to join fundamentalists, evangelicals, and pentecostals in a crusade to restore the United States. The attempt to attract broad religious support was at best incompetent; one speaker at a Moral Majority function claimed that "God does not hear the prayer of the Jew," and Falwell's book (1981), *The Fundamentalist Phenomenon*, attacked evangelicals as moderates and "violently rejected" the pentecostal claims of the gifts of the Spirit. Yet, Falwell sounded first the audacious goal of building a coalition of morally conservative Americans which inspired the Christian Coalition to turn it into reality.

It is worth noting that several of the organizational decisions of the Moral Majority were controversial within the evangelical community. Many Democrats objected to Falwell's exclusive relationship with the GOP, and that decision doubtlessly limited the appeal of the group to Catholics and blacks. By staking conservative positions on economic issues including welfare, labor and environmental issues, the Moral Majority alienated many evangelicals who were social conservatives but economic moderates. And, by staking a position on issues such as apartheid and the subminimum wage, Falwell angered many evangelicals who thought that these were exclusively political, not moral or religious issues.

The Transition: The Robertson Campaign

In September 1986, the Rev. Marion (Pat) Robertson announced that he would run for U.S. president if he received at least three million signatures on petitions urging him to do so. Allen Hertzke (1993) has argued that these signatures served a symbolic purpose in convincing closet supporters that he was a viable candidate, and a substantive one in demonstrating that Robertson could win in a low-turnout, three-candidate contest. It served a legal purpose as well, for Robertson could not legally solicit those who had given to his tax-exempt television ministry to give to his presidential campaign, but those who chose to sign the petitions could legally be asked to give to the campaign.

The campaign got off to a good start. Robertson's first campaign finance filing was delivered to the Federal Election Commission on a sixteen-foot truck, and contained the names of more than seventy thousand contributors. He arguably came in first in the initial balloting in the multistage Michigan caucus-convention, and surprised GOP strategists by finishing second, ahead of George Bush in the Iowa caucuses.

After Iowa, however, the Robertson campaign endured some very negative publicity. Robertson stated that he knew where the hostages were being held in Lebanon (although he had yet to share this information with the Reagan administration), and that there were Soviet missiles in the caves of Cuba. When fellow charismatic televangelist Jimmy Swaggart was caught in a sex scandal, Robertson blamed the Bush campaign. Media coverage of an old story that Robertson had married his wife after she was far along in her pregnancy, and of a new story about his settling a lawsuit concerning allegations that his father had kept him out of the Korea conflict, served to undermine Robertson's claim to the moral high ground. Robertson did not win a single primary in 1988, although he did win several caucuses, where the advantages of a strong network of pentecostal and charismatic churches were evident.

Robertson's support in pentecostal and charismatic churches came from his clear identification with the gifts of the Spirit on the "700 Club." Most of Robertson's contributors were regular donors to his "700 Club," but the campaign maintained that they never solicited the "700 Club" list. Yet, he sought to appeal beyond that base: he spoke positively of other religious traditions and frequently had Catholics, mainline Protestants, evangelicals, and even Jews as guests on his show, which was cohosted by an African American. Robertson had frequently argued that religious Americans of all types should join together to save the United States from its slide into a secular society, and he emphasized this appeal in the early days of his campaign.

Robertson's campaign overtly appealed to blacks, Catholics, and conservative Protestants across the theological spectrum. Yet, Robertson's base was pentecostal and charismatic Christians, and research shows that he attracted few votes and little money beyond this base (Green and Guth 1988; Wilcox 1992). Falwell endorsed George Bush, not Robertson, and fundamentalists were even less likely to vote for Robertson on Super-Tuesday than were other whites. This suggests that Robertson's campaign suffered the limitations of religious particularism, despite his personal attempts to create an ecumenical base. While charismatic Robertson welcomed fundamentalists to join his crusade, the fundamentalists politely refused.

Although Robertson spent more money than any previous presidential candidate in history to win just thirty-five pledged delegates, his campaign continued to work behind the scenes to influence the national convention, and to gain a foothold in state Republican parties. In many states, the votes of GOP presidential delegates were bound by state law to go to the winner of the primary, but the actual selection of delegates took place through a series of caucuses and conventions. The Robertson campaign encouraged its supporters to work in these caucuses to send Christian conservatives to the convention.

In the process, Robertson's supporters gained influence in state and local party organizations. Christian conservatives were surprised by both the ease with which they were able to dominate local party organizations and the success they enjoyed at the state level. Even as Robertson endured a crushing defeat in his personal quest for the presidency, the seeds for a new Christian Right were sown.

The Christian Coalition

In 1989, as the Moral Majority folded its tent, Robertson announced the formation of the Christian Coalition. The goal was to maintain the enthusiasm of the insurgents who had packed party caucuses across the country, and to build an infrastructure to enable conservative Christians to continue their efforts to influence the GOP. Robertson hired Ralph Reed, a young Republican activist, to manage the organization. While Robertson continues to sign fund-raising letters and to speak at conventions, Reed presents a smoother, more reassuring face to television cameras.

The Christian Coalition has made a real attempt to build at the grass roots. They claim to have state, county, and precinct organizations active in all fifty states, although they generally refuse to provide the necessary information to confirm these claims. The organization also boasts a membership of some 1.9 million members, although this figure is almost certainly an exaggeration. In 1994 and 1995, the organization was mailing only slightly over 350,000 copies of its magazine, *Christian American*, which it sent to anyone who made even a small contribution (Oldfield 1996). Even accounting for multiple memberships in a single household, this would suggest that the organization's membership is substantially less than a million.

Yet, the actual membership figures doubtlessly understate the influence of the Christian Coalition, in that a single member in a congregation of conservative Christians can distribute voter guides, enlist volunteers for a political campaign, or in other ways influence an election. The Christian Coalition and other groups of the contemporary Christian Right frequently seek not a majority in a given congregation, but just a small group of members who can influence the politics of others in the pews.

Moreover, there is no denying that the Christian Coalition has built an active grassroots organization that has substantial numbers of activists. Across the country, the Christian Coalition has distributed millions of voters guides in churches, and in other ways demonstrated its organizational strength. In Virginia, the organization has forty county chapters, and many more district and precinct committees. In South Carolina the organization claims a chapter in every county. The group's *Leadership Manual* states:

> A decade from now, the organizations that mobilize voters and activists in the counties and precincts of America will control the political agenda. . . . The most effective way to influence public policy in the United States is to organize a strong grassroots company of committed Christians who know and understand how public policy affects them and the world in which they live and work. Mobilizing a trained force of Christian activists at the local level of government will make it possible for Christians to accomplish results that will astound those who are on the sidelines watching. (Fisher, Reed, and Weinhold 1990, 2, 4)

It is one thing, of course, to attempt to build a grassroots organization, but it is another entirely to succeed. Reed wants to have identified some ten million pro-family voters, and to have a neighborhood coordinator in place in each of the nation's 175,000 precincts by the millennium. If the organization achieves only part of this goal, it will be the most comprehensive grassroots organization in history. The organization claims to have more than seventeen hundred local chapters in place across the fifty states already, with more forming every week.

How has the Christian Coalition succeeded in building strong local chapters where the Moral Majority failed? First, the Christian Coalition has not built its organization around preachers, but around small business leaders and other political activists. Although all of the county chairs of the Moral Majority in 1982 were pastors, Laura Berkowitz and John Green (1996) of the University of Akron found that this was true for only 15 percent of Christian Coalition county chairs in Ohio. Nearly half were housewives—an important talent pool for conservative religious groups. Others were middle managers, retired businessmen, and blue-collar workers.

This is important because particularistic preachers may turn away those whose doctrine does not accord with their own, but political activists want to build an organization with enough volunteers to distribute materials and perhaps be influential in local GOP politics. Thus, the Christian Coalition has built a political, not a religious, organization.

Although the Christian Coalition is decidedly more political in its orientation and more pragmatic in its strategies than the Moral Majority was, it has not abandoned the reliance on churches in building its grassroots networks. However, it has built these links largely through lay church liaisons.

Moreover, the Christian Coalition has attended carefully to building the morale of its followers and to inspiring them to do what is often tedious political work. The annual "Road to Victory" conference, coupled with events held in different states, helps build group identity among members. In contrast, the Moral Majority used rallies to launch its organizational efforts, but then failed thereafter to hold such rallies periodically.

Second, to build a large organization, it is important to put religious prejudice on the backburner. Christian Coalition training materials instruct leaders in how to defuse religious tension, and to get Catholics and Baptists and members of the local Assemblies of God congregation to work together stuffing envelopes. Reed wrote: "People of faith have a right to be heard, and their religion should not disqualify them from serving in public office or participating in the party of their choice. . . . This is not a vision exclusively for those who are evangelical or Roman Catholic or Greek Orthodox or Jewish. This vision makes room for people of all faiths—and those with no faith at all" (1994, 11).

Thus far, this ecumenical appeal appears to be working. The limited evidence available suggests that the Christian Coalition has attracted members from across denominational lines. Ralph Reed revealed that an internal poll of Christian Coalition members indicated that 25 percent belonged to mainline Protestant churches, 10 to 15 percent attended Pentecostal services, half were Baptists, and 5 to 10 percent attended "other" churches, including the Catholic church (Rozell and Wilcox 1995). More recently, the Christian Coalition has reported that Catholics comprise 16 percent of its total membership. However, since the Christian Coalition refuses to release membership lists or the results of these internal surveys, it is impossible to verify these claims (Bendyna 1996).

A survey of GOP state convention delegates in Minnesota, Texas, Virginia, and Washington revealed that supporters of the Christian Coalition came from a wide variety of religious denominations. In Texas, Christian Coalition supporters are primarily Baptists, but in Virginia they include many mainline Protestants and a spattering of Catholics as well. In Minnesota, approximately one in four supporters of the Christian Coalition in the state GOP is Catholic. Indeed, in Fairfax County,

Virginia, more than 40 percent of Christian Coalition supporters in the county GOP committee are Catholics.

What appears to bring together this religious coalition is a sense of shared purpose in support of candidates and issues. One Catholic activist in the Christian Right told the authors about stuffing envelopes for Oliver North along with Baptist and mainline Protestant women and talking about their religious differences. Another Catholic activist in Virginia wrote in a letter accompanying the survey that he was now socializing with fundamentalists and evangelicals—an activity that would have seemed impossible a decade ago.

In Virginia, issues, not religious divisions, most strongly predict support among GOP activists for such Christian Right candidates as Oliver North and Michael Farris. Moreover, issues and ideology predict support for the Christian Coalition far better than religious divisions. This does not mean that the Christian Right is homogenous; North drew disproportionately from Catholics but Farris did not, and the Christian Coalition is significantly more popular among pentecostals and evangelicals than among mainline Protestants or fundamentalists. But it is clear that the old religious divisions are fading, and religious conservatives of the Christian Right have learned to work (and sometimes to play) well with others.

Beyond the Evangelical Core: The Christian Right Reaches Out

If the Christian Coalition is to continue to grow, it must broaden its appeal to Catholics, mainline Protestants, and other groups. The organization is already far more popular among evangelicals and pentecostals than was the Moral Majority. Although there is some room to expand support among fundamentalists, the organization is already nearing its potential limits in the broad evangelical community, for not all evangelicals are conservative or likely to support the Christian Right. Surveys show that slightly more than half of evangelicals rate the Christian Coalition favorably—a figure that almost exactly matches the percentage of evangelicals who hold packages of issue positions consistent with the Christian Coalition platform (Wilcox 1996).

The Christian Coalition's outreach efforts to Catholics are especially noteworthy, particularly since studies of the Moral Majority found few Catholics in its membership and little support among Catholics for its agenda. Like Jerry Falwell before them, Pat Robertson and Ralph Reed have long made overtures to Catholics and have welcomed Catholic cooperation. One of the more obvious examples of Catholic-Christian Coalition collaboration has been in the distribution of Christian Coalition voter guides. Perhaps the most prominent example of this was when the Archdiocese of New York joined forces with the Christian Coalition during the New York City school board elections in 1993 and allowed the distribution of Christian Coalition voter guides in Catholic parishes.

The Christian Coalition has recently undertaken a much more concerted effort to attract Catholic membership and support. For the last several years, the Christian Coalition has had a Catholic liaison to facilitate contact between the Christian Coalition and various Catholic diocesan and parish authorities and to build links with other Catholic organizations. The Christian Coalition has also made efforts to increase Catholic participation in its annual "Road to Victory" conferences by featuring Catholic speakers, including displays by Catholic organizations, and holding sessions on forging Catholic-Evangelical alliances. Moreover, unlike the Moral Majority, the Christian Coalition has included Catholics in leadership and staff positions in the national, state, and local organizations (Bendyna 1996).

The most ambitious effort to increase Catholic involvement in and cooperation with the Christian Coalition was the creation of the Catholic Alliance in 1995. This division of the Christian Coalition is intended both to expand Catholic membership in the Christian Coalition and to create a distinctively Catholic variant within the Coalition that might be more appealing to Catholics and assuage whatever fears or misgivings they might have about joining a predominantly evangelical organization (Bendyna 1996).

Whether these efforts to enlist Catholic participation and support will be successful remains to be seen. Although some Catholics support the issue positions of the Christian Coalition, most Catholics do not share its views on most issues. Moreover, although the Christian Coalition and the Catholic Alliance claim that they have met with some success, they have also met with a great deal of opposition from the Catholic community. Some of the harshest criticism has come from some of the U.S. Catholic bishops who have roundly criticized the Christian Coalition and the Catholic Alliance for their positions on welfare reform, health care reform, and capital punishment, as well as for their failure to promote policies that protect poor children and immigrants. In addition, many Catholic Church authorities have explicitly prohibited the distribution of Christian Coalition and Catholic Alliance materials on church property because of their partisan nature. The morally traditional Catholics to whom the Christian Coalition is most likely to appeal are also the Catholics who are most likely to be attentive to the pronouncements of their bishops. It is not yet clear whether the Christian Coalition will be able to overcome these obstacles and make significant inroads among Catholics.

Although Ralph Reed frequently includes Jews and even occasionally Muslims in his language about "people of faith," there is little evidence that the Christian Coalition has made serious inroads into these religious communities. Here the organization's choice of name—*Christian Coalition*—is instructive perhaps of its sincerity. Although the Christian Coalition did for a time employ a prominent Jewish lobbyist as head of its legislative affairs office and always has at least one Jewish rabbi speak at its annual conventions, the 1996 convention was scheduled on Rosh Hashanah. When asked about this timing, one spokesperson for the organization retorted that there are usually more Jews outside protesting the Christian Coalition than inside participating in the convention.

In addition to its attempts to broaden its base beyond denominational boundaries, the Christian Coalition has recently stepped up its efforts to build alliances across racial lines. To this end, the Christian Coalition appointed a national liaison for community development to facilitate connections with the African American community. In the wake of the rash of firebombings in African American churches, leaders of the Christian Coalition also met with black church leaders to discuss the burnings and other racial issues. The Christian Coalition also established a "Save Our Churches Fund" and has begun to distribute these funds to help rebuild the affected churches.

Although blacks share a spirit-filled, evangelical religion with many white members of the Christian Coalition, few have joined the organization thus far. Here there are two limiting factors. First is the obvious Republican partisanship of the Christian Coalition. Until recently, Reed has made little effort to hide the Republican tilt of the organization, which the Federal Election Commission has sued for undisclosed partisan spending in federal elections. Reed and Robertson are frequent delegates to GOP state and national conventions, and have chosen to participate solely in the Republican Party. Black Democrats will not flock to such an organization, regardless of their social views. Perhaps more importantly, the Christian Coalition has recently staked conservative positions on welfare and other social service programs—positions that put them at odds with most black evangelicals.

A less partisan Christian Coalition might have made a genuine effort to influence both parties—through evangelicals in the GOP and blacks and Catholics in the Democratic Party. The involvement of the Congress On Racial Equality in distributing Coalition voters guides in the nonpartisan New York school board races points to the possible success of that kind of movement.

Organizational Learning in the Christian Right

Publicly, Ralph Reed (1994, 192) wrote that Jerry Falwell "accomplished his objective of reawakening the slumbering giant of the church-going vote. He had passed the torch to a new generation of leadership who launched new organizations and redirected the pro-family impulse in a more permanent, grassroots direction."

However, Reed made it clear that the Christian Coalition learned from the mistakes of the Moral Majority. He wrote that "chastened by the movement's earlier shortcomings, these pro-family leaders were determined to learn from the past." He then sagely quoted Cal Thomas, a former Moral Majority leader, as noting that the opportunity "to transform the culture was quickly squandered when it was decided to emphasize fund raising instead of building the political machinery to exercise real power" (Reed 1994, 194). Reed thanked Falwell for being the pioneer, but it is clear from his writings and from his private comments that Christian Coalition elites studied the failures of the Moral Majority and attempted to build a movement that avoided that group's mistakes.

Central to this strategy has been the careful attention to building political organizations at the local level. When a Georgetown University graduate student called the Christian Coalition to see if there was a local chapter in his southern district of Fairfax County, the response was "no, do you want to start one?" Yet, not just anyone can head a Christian Coalition chapter—Reed and his staff have been careful to identify the most extreme activists and keep them from leadership positions. And the organization strongly encourages lay leaders.

What makes this kind of grassroots organization possible is the spirit of ecumenism of the organization. By building outside of specific churches and by repeating the mantra of the power of a coalition of "people of faith," the Christian Coalition appears to have begun to erode at least some of the religious particularism that plagued the Moral Majority. The victory is not yet complete, for fundamentalists remain somewhat less likely to join the group than other evangelicals. Yet this may not matter, for fundamentalists do appear to pay attention to Christian Coalition voter guides. One particularistic fundamentalist in Fairfax County noted that he could never support Pat Robertson nor join the Christian Coalition because of its association with Robertson. Yet, he said that he and everyone in his church looked forward to the Coalition's voter guides, and could certainly back candidates favored by the Coalition.

Nevertheless, for all of its successes, the Christian Coalition may have made a major tactical mistake in allying itself so openly with the Republican Party. First, this decision limits its potential support among blacks and Catholics, and makes the organization appear to be more partisan than religious. Second, the logic of party coalitions dictates that the Christian Coalition must support candidates and policies that are not fully consistent with the group's platform. Indeed, the "Contract with the American Family," announced with some fanfare in 1995, has as many "mainstream" Republican planks (support for a flat tax and ending welfare) as "Christian Right" Republican planks (banning certain abortion procedures). By getting in bed with the GOP, the Christian Coalition has in many ways forfeited its prophetic role, and may have alienated some of its own members as well.

It is also not clear whether the decision to build within a single party has accomplished much for the Christian Coalition, although the jury is still out on this point. Certainly the contemporary Christian Right, more than any other social movement in this century, has succeeded in influencing the GOP—to the point that it could rebuff a presidential candidate's call for platform language, and control state and local party organizations across the country. Yet, even within the party, its success has been mixed. Although the Christian Coalition won on the language of the 1996 GOP platform, Bob Dole immediately announced that he had not read the document, and party chair, Haley Barbour, made a similar statement. Dole did not mention abortion during the campaign, and in one presidential debate announced that he had never personally discriminated against gays in hiring in his Senate office.

The 1996 elections were a mixed bag for the Christian Coalition. The organization claimed to have distributed 46 million voters guides to some 125,000 churches on the Sunday before the election, yet some of its strongest supporters were defeated—Steve Stockman, Dave Funderburk, Fred Heiniman, and others. Overall, however, the new GOP freshmen associated with the Christian Right did about as well as all new Republican members. Moreover, the Christian Right clearly picked up seats in the Senate, making that body even more conservative than in 1994. Yet, it is unclear whether this will matter. After nearly a decade of active involvement in elections, it is still difficult to point to concrete policy accomplishments of the organization.

Although the Christian Coalition has hired a first-rate lobbying staff and joined in eclectic coalitions to increase its muscle on Capitol Hill (in marked contrast to the Moral Majority), the GOP Congress appears to have given the organization only symbolic gratification during its two years of control. The principal accomplishments for the Christian Right in the 104th Congress were a ban on one procedure for late-term abortions, which was overridden (and would have left in place other procedures for these same cases), a ban on pornography on the Internet, which is unlikely to survive a Court challenge, and a bill that maintains many current limits on gay marriage. The vote on a school prayer amendment that U.S. House Speaker Newt Gingrich promised at the Christian Coalition convention in 1994 never took place.

Paradoxically, the Christian Coalition and the contemporary Christian Right have more influence on political party organizations than any social movement of the twentieth century, but they have had far less influence on society than the labor, civil rights, or feminist movements, and appear to be fighting a rearguard battle against an insurgent gay and lesbian rights movement. These other social movements all asked Americans to end their discriminatory behavior toward movement members. The Christian Coalition routinely charges that society discriminates against Christians, and, in those rare documented cases, the organization has often succeeded in remedying the problem.

Yet, to succeed at the larger agenda of banning abortions, rolling back gay rights, and taking control of the education system, the Christian Right would have to persuade Americans of the validity of their vision. Here the Christian Coalition has been no more successful than the Moral Majority. Americans are more supportive of legal abortion and gay rights in 1996 than they were in 1989. And it remains true that the generation most supportive of the Christian Coalition agenda is one that is slowly passing from the scene, inevitably leaving behind a more tolerant America.

No matter how many local chapters the Christian Coalition builds, and no matter how sophisticated its computerized whip system at party conventions, the battle for moral legislation must be fought in the hearts and minds of voters. The 1996 GOP convention showcased pro-choice women for a reason—polling data showed that the party was hurt by its visible association with the Christian Right. Ultimately, the new, improved Christian Right will fail like its earlier incarnations unless it can do a better job of convincing Americans of the truth of its moral vision.

References

Bendyna, Mary E. 1996. Catholics and the Christian Right: Resonance or Dissonance? Presented at the annual meeting of the American Political Science Association, 30 August, San Francisco.

Berkowitz, Laura, and John Green. 1996. Personal communication with authors. 15 November.

Falwell, Jerry. 1981. *The Fundamentalist Phenomenon: The Resurgence of Conservative Christianity*, with Ed Dobson and Ed Hindson. Garden City, N.Y.: Doubleday.

Fisher, William L., Ralph Reed Jr., and Richard L. Weinhold. 1990. *Christian Coalition Leadership Manual*. Chesapeake, Va.: The Christian Coalition.

Georgianna, Sharon Linzey. 1989. *The Moral Majority and Fundamentalism: Plausibility and Dissonance*. Lewiston, N.Y.: Edwin Mellon Press.

Green, John C., and James L. Guth. 1988. "The Christian Right in the Republican Party: The Case of Pat Robertson's Supporters." *Journal of Politics* 50: 150–65.

Green, John C., James L. Guth, and Clyde Wilcox. 1995. The Christian Right in State Republican Parties. Presented at the annual meeting of the Midwest Political Science Association, 12–14 April, Chicago.

Hadden, Jeffrey K., Anson Shupe, James Hawdon, and Kenneth Martin. 1987. "Why Jerry Falwell Killed the Moral Majority." In *The God Pumpers: Religion in the Electronic Age,* edited by M. Fishwick and R. Browne, 101–15. Bowling Green, Ohio: Popular Press.

Hertzke, Allen D. 1993. *Echoes of Discontent: Jesse Jackson, Pat Robertson, and the Resurgence of Populism*. Washington, D.C.: CQ Press.

Johnson, Loch, and Charles Bullock III. 1986. "The New Religious Right and the 1980 Congressional Elections." In *Do Elections Matter?* edited by B. Ginsburg and A. Stone, 148–63. New York: M. E. Sharpe.

Liebman, Robert C. 1983. "Mobilizing the Moral Majority." In *The New Christian Right: Mobilization and Legitimation*, edited by R. Liebman and R. Wuthnow, 50–73. New York: Aldine.

Moen, Matthew. 1989. *The Christian Right and Congress*. Tuscaloosa: University of Alabama Press.

Oldfield, Duane. 1996. *The Right and the Righteous: The Christian Right Confronts the Republican Party*. Lanham, Md.: Rowman & Littlefield.

Reed, Ralph. 1994. *Politically Incorrect: The Emerging Faith Factor in American Politics*. Dallas, Texas: Word Publishing.

Rozell, Mark, and Clyde Wilcox. 1995. *God at the Grass Roots: The Christian Right in the 1994 Elections*. Lanham, Md.: Rowman & Littlefield.

Wilcox, Clyde. 1992. *God's Warriors: The Christian Right in Twentieth-Century America*. Baltimore, Md.: Johns Hopkins University Press.

———. 1996. *Onward Christian Soldiers: The Religious Right in American Politics*. Boulder, Colo.: Westview Press.

4

Charting the Coalition:
The Local Chapters of the
Ohio Christian Coalition

Laura Berkowitz and John C. Green

By fall 1996 most observers would have agreed that the Christian Coalition had "arrived" politically, becoming the centerpiece of the Christian Right and a symbol of the movement's clout. The Coalition had attained one of its primary goals: "a place at the table" for conservative Christians in national politics. This new place was a result in large measure from its grassroots organization and its ability to mobilize voters.

Nevertheless, while much discussed, relatively little is actually known about the Christian Coalition's grassroots structure. This chapter addresses this void by describing the organization's local chapters in the state of Ohio, which, overall, displayed a great deal of diversity. Roughly one-quarter of the Ohio chapters are strong and effective, an equal proportion hardly exist at all, with the remaining displaying modest levels of strength. As with other expressions of the Christian Right, such chapters are strongest at the confluence of grievances, resources, and opportunities for political action. Thus, the Christian Coalition has considerable muscle at the grass roots, but less than friends may assume or foes fear.

The Christian Right at the Grass Roots

When the "new" Christian Right appeared in 1980, it was widely assumed to have a strong grassroots presence. Indeed, the movement's flagship organization, Jerry Falwell's Moral Majority, was seen as a "disciplined, charging army" (Fitzgerald 1981). Scholars quickly discovered, however, that the local elements of the Moral Majority and other movement organizations were weak and ineffective (Hadden, Shupe, Hawdon, and Martin 1987; Jorstad 1990). In fact, the initial Christian Right organizations were largely "top down" affairs, using modern communications technologies to both express and incite discontent among conservative Christians.

Indeed, the grassroots weakness of the Christian Right helps account for its initial failures (Bruce 1988). This weakness prompted further attempts at local organizing, notably the American Coalition for Traditional Values in 1984 (Jorstad 1990, 62) and Pat Robertson's presidential nomination bid in 1988 (Hertzke 1993). These efforts showed promise and, by the late 1980s, many movement activists endorsed a more determined "return to the grassroots" (Moen 1992). No group stressed this strategy more than the newly formed Christian Coalition.

Under the direction of Executive Director Ralph Reed, the Coalition set out to build a grassroots organization in conscious imitation of the local structures of parties and interest groups (Reed 1996). The goal was to develop at least one local chapter in every county and eventually recruit at least one activist per precinct nationwide. Once in place, this local structure could be employed to get out the "Christian" vote as well as conduct other political activities. These plans were part of a broader plan that included a reformulated "pro-family" agenda, more inclusive membership, and a pragmatic approach to electoral politics (Reed 1996).

Of course, building strong local organizations is difficult. Witness, for example, the problems the major political parties and interest groups have in building their local organizations (Wilson 1973). Strong local units of any sort are likely to be the exception rather than the rule. Nevertheless, the literature on social movements offers some clues as to where the Christian Coalition is likely to have had the most success in this regard. These can be distilled under the rubric of grievances, resources, and opportunities (Green, Guth, and Hill 1993).

Like other social movements, the Christian Right is primarily motivated by grievances to which established political institutions are perceived to be unresponsive (Tarrow 1994). Specifically, conservative Christians are disturbed by what they perceive as the moral decay in American society, exemplified by matters such as abortion and gay rights, but extending to such other issues as education, religious liberty, and size of government. In recent times, the movement has sought to redress its grievances by focusing on achievable legislative goals and by broadening its agenda to include economic issues (Wilcox 1992).

If grievances alone created grassroots organizations, then strong local groups would be more common. However, resources must be mobilized to build and operate local units. Typically such resources are found among preexisting nonpolitical organizations associated with the aggrieved populations (Zald and McCarthy 1987). In the case of the Christian Right, sectarian churches among evangelical Protestants and related parachurch organizations are the crucial sources of resources. In recent times, the movement has attempted to reach out to conservatives in other religious communities, including other evangelicals, mainline and black Protestants, and Roman Catholics (Green, Guth, Smidt, and Kellstedt 1996).

Grievances and resources are most potent when they can be used effectively in situations with the greatest likelihood of success (McAdam 1982). For the Christian Right, such pragmatism has increasingly meant supporting viable conservative Republican candidates in politically competitive areas, places where even modest numbers of voters can affect the outcomes. In recent times, the movement has expanded its range of activities to the recruitment of candidates and involvement in party politics (Rozell and Wilcox 1995; Green 1993).

Movement leaders are critical to the impact of these factors. After all, it is leaders who define grievances and then focus them on achievable goals, find resources and then organize them effectively, and identify opportunities and then marshall followers to take advantage of them. The strategy of the Christian Coalition is directed precisely at molding these elements to support strong local units. Thus, we would expect to find the strongest chapters where the movement's grievances are strong and well developed, resources are plentiful and well organized, and opportunities are good and acted upon. By the same token, the weakest chapters should occur in the absence of these factors, and modest strength should appear where only some factors were present.

The Study

This study is based on in-depth interviews with twenty-six chairs of local Christian Coalition chapters in Ohio, chosen from a list provided by the state office. The interviewees were selected so as to capture the range of chapter strength and activity. First, the leaders of the four strongest chapters (as identified by the state chair) were included, and three of the four were interviewed. Second, the remaining chairs were divided by region and size of county, and twenty-six names were chosen at random from among these divisions. Twenty-three interviews were completed. Three persons so selected claimed to be just a "contact" person in their county and refused an interview on the grounds that there was no local chapter. Semistructured telephone interviews were conducted in summer 1995, and averaged an hour in length.

Ohio provides a good context in which to study the local structure of the Christian Coalition. A diverse and politically competitive state, it stands between the Christian Right's strongholds in the South and the hostile turf in the Northeast. Conservative Christians make up a small minority of the population, who, if mobilized, can make a critical difference in elections but by themselves cannot dominate politics even at the local level. Ohio is famous for its organizational politics, and viable grassroots party organizations are still common (Mayhew 1986). The Christian Right has been active in the state since the days of the Moral Majority (Wilcox 1992), and it was counted as moderately influential in state Republican politics in the mid-1990s (Persinos 1994). Thus, Ohio represents a strong test of the Christian Coalition's "return to the grass roots."

The Ohio Christian Coalition

In 1995 the Christian Coalition had one or more chapters in sixty-nine of eighty-eight counties in Ohio. However, these local units varied dramatically in strength, falling into five categories: Core Chapters, Going Concerns, Just Getting Started, Limited Operations, and Chairs without Chapters. Associated with the latter is a sixth category, "counties without chairs": a small number of counties with a "contact person" but with no chapter. After a brief summary of these categories, we will discuss their characteristics in more detail.

1. Core Chapters. These chapters were by far the strongest and most effective, accounting for about 5 percent of the local units. Led by skilled pragmatists, these multifaceted organizations were resource-rich and well-integrated with other elements of the Coalition. They espoused the Coalition's pro-family agenda, recruited broadly among religious conservatives, and were closely linked to other pro-family organizations. The Core Chapters best embody the philosophy of the Christian Coalition. Located in highly competitive areas, they reflect a potent confluence of grievances, resources, and opportunities.

2. Going Concerns. These chapters were smaller, less active, and less well-endowed than the Core Chapters, but were nonetheless effective organizations. They accounted for about 20 percent of the local units and resembled the Core Chapters in terms of leadership skills, religious diversity, integration with the Coalition, and links to the pro-family movement. However, these chapters prized their autonomy and had a broader range of grievances. Many Going Concerns chairs interpreted the Coalition's "place at the table" as an opening to deploy their own menu of issues. These chapters also tended to be located in politically competitive areas, and while resources and opportunities contributed to their strength, their diffuse grievances tended to undermine it.

3. Just Getting Started. As the name implies, these chapters were of recent origin, founded during and after the 1994 election. This category made up about 30 percent of the local units. Because of their newness, these chapters were less well developed and less effective than the previous categories. Some showed signs of becoming Going Concerns or even Core Chapters in the future, while others may become Limited Operations (see below). Compared to the Core Chapters, their grievances were more campaign oriented, religious resources more exclusive, approach more instrumental, and leadership skills untried. Also located in politically competitive areas, their distinguishing mark was a focus on candidates and campaigns. Here the confluence of grievances, resources, and opportunities is still in flux.

4. Limited Operations. These chapters were, in many respects, less successful versions of the Going Concerns, and they also made up about 20 percent of the local units. Compared to the Core Chapters, these groups were less religiously diverse, poorly integrated with the Coalition, and weakly linked to other pro-family groups. Fiercely independent, they partook even less of the philosophy of the Christian Coalition, focusing on a narrow social issue agenda. Compared to the Going Concerns, the chairs were far less skillful and pragmatic. These chapters had neither focused their grievances nor developed adequate resources. Consequently, they failed to exploit available political opportunities, which were somewhat less common than in the previous categories.

5. Chairs without Chapters. This category is made up of one- or two-person operations with no real organization. It accounted for 20 percent of the local units; the related group of "counties without chairs" made up another 5 percent. These chairs were classic purists, and several fit the common, negative stereotype of Christian Rightists: ultraconservative, narrowminded, and intolerant. They, thus, represented the antithesis of the Christian Coalition's philosophy. Because of their narrow grievances, religious particularism, and uncooperative attitudes, it is doubtful that viable chapters will ever develop from these efforts. Still, these leaders have little to work with: they have few skills, very limited resources, and few political opportunities.

Table 4.1 summarizes these patterns and sets the stage for a more detailed examination of the organizational strength, grievances, resources, and opportunities of these chapter types.

Organizational Strength

The chapter types differed dramatically in size, integration with other elements of the Coalition, and in level and type of activity. The Core Chapters were the largest, having between 40 and 100 regular volunteers, and many more occasional participants. Their mailing lists contained between 275 and 589 names; one chapter had combined its list with other local pro-family organizations for a total of 2,000. The Going Concerns chapters were smaller, with 10 to 15 regular volunteers, perhaps as many occasional participants, and mailing lists from 100 to 350. Just Getting Started and Limited Operations chapters were usually smaller, between 3 and 25 volunteers, some occasional participants, and mailing lists ranging from 5 to 100 names. Chairs without Chapters had no members other than the chairs and their immediate

TABLE 4.1
Ohio Christian Coalition Chapters: Types and Characteristics

	Core	Going Concerns	Just Getting Started	Limited Operations	Chairs without Chapters
Percent of Chapters	5%	20%	30%	20%	25%*
Strength					
Size	largest	large	mixed	small	minuscule
Integration	strong	strong	weak	weak	nonexistent
Activity	comprehensive	extensive	developing	limited	minimal
Grievances	pro-family agenda	broad social issues	mixed; political issue	narrow social issue	right-way
Resources					
Membership	highly diverse	diverse	diverse	diverse	none
Networking	very strong	very strong	embryonic	weak	nonexistent
Opportunities					
Local Context	highly competitive	competitive	competitive	somewhat competitive	uncompetitive
Leadership	self-starters; highly skilled, pragmatic	recruited via movement; skilled pragmatic instrumental	recruited via election; untried, instrumental	recruited by Coalition; unskilled, instrumental	recruited by Coalition; inept purist

* Includes counties without chairs

families. The first two types of chapters scheduled regular meetings, while the next two had meetings on an irregular basis.

The chapters also varied in their integration with the Christian Coalition's state and national offices. The Core Chapters were in frequent contact with the state and national organizations, and valued the information, training, and materials provided. Chairs of these chapters were also regular and enthusiastic participants at Coalition conferences and workshops at the national, state, and regional levels, and some had sponsored these events.

The Going Concerns and Just Getting Started chapter chairs also valued the state and national headquarters as sources of information, training, and materials. Most were in regular contact with both offices and over one-half had participated in national, state, or regional Coalition conferences. However, these chairs were defenders of local autonomy, believing, for example, that while the national headquarters set boundaries, local chapters should have great latitude within those bounds, particularly in terms of the issues emphasized. One chair likened the Christian Coalition to the Southern Baptist Convention—the chapters share the same basic tenets but each governs itself. Solidarity incentives were very important for the Core Chapters and to a lesser extent, the Going Concerns, but less so for the Just Getting Started group, perhaps because of their newness.

The Limited Operations chairs had much less appreciation for and contact with the state and national offices, and only one chair was in regular contact with both. While they agreed that the higher level offices provide useful information and assistance, they also believed that such advice often did not fit their local situation. One chair commented that it was hard to implement training according to national guidelines, and others voiced concern that the national organization tried to dictate local priorities. Instead, the leaders believed that the agenda should originate with the local chapters: "The Coalition should be run by the grass roots, not by the suits." One chair argued that the Coalition should not attempt to usurp the functions or role of already established pro-family organizations. The Christian Coalition is not necessarily a coalition, but a "coalition of coalitions," whose function is to coordinate electoral activities among conservative Christians. Not surprisingly, Chairs without Chapters have very limited contact with the state and national offices, and many complained about the volume of communications received from them.

One indicator of integration was the chairs' perception of the most important Christian Right leaders. The Core Chapters chairs uniformly volunteered Pat Robertson and Ralph Reed as the key leaders, while the Going Concerns chairs had a broader list, adding James Dobson, Billy Graham, Chuck Colson, Jerry Falwell, and James Kennedy. Dobson, Kennedy, and Alan Keyes joined Robertson for Just Getting Started chairs, while the Limited Operations chairs named Dobson, Rush Limbaugh, Pope John Paul as well as Robertson. The Chairs without Chapters considered Falwell, Tim LaHaye, and Robertson equally important.

The distribution of voter guides during campaigns was the central activity of all these chapters. National guides were distributed mainly in churches, but also via local businesses, bookstores, Bible clubs, mail, and, in one case, at the precincts on election day. The numbers of guides distributed ranged from a high of 100,000 to a low of 20. Several chapters also distributed independently produced guides for state and local candidates.

The Core Chapters were the most successful distributors and central to their efforts was the development of church liaisons (lay activists in targeted congregations) and contacts with local pastors. These chairs stressed the need for one-on-one contact because a "personal touch" makes distribution progressively easier. About one-half of the Going Concerns chapters used church liaisons, with one chapter having a liaison network with eight regional coordinators, while others simply contacted pastors. In contrast, a majority of the Just Getting Started and Limited Operations chapters relied on contacts with pastors and lists of churches provided by national headquarters. The Chairs without Chapters distributed guides in churches on a very limited basis at the behest of the state and national offices.

These chapters are also engaged in a wide variety of other political activities, including promoting voter registration, holding get-out-the-vote drives, polling and canvassing, distributing candidate questionnaires, organizing forums, circulating petitions, recruiting candidates and party officials, writing newsletters, sponsoring booths at county fairs and commercial establishments, holding conferences, and disseminating literature of other pro-family groups. The level and type of activity was in large measure a function of chapters' organizational strength.

Core Chapters participated in all the above-mentioned activities on a large scale and on a regular basis. One chapter, however, also developed a "speaker bureau," which listed "experts" willing to speak to churches or other local organizations. Another hosted a weekly call-in show on a Christian radio station to discuss pro-family issues. All distributed various kinds of pro-family literature, and one chair even developed a videotape and audiotape resource library for chapter members. Yet another chair established an extensive fax and telephone network that could contact members and other conservative activists on short notice; in fact, she once mobilized some eighty people within hours to demonstrate at a congressman's local office. This chapter also regularly updated a recorded telephone message about issues and upcoming activities.

Going Concerns chapters also registered voters and distributed literature from other pro-family groups. One chapter cosponsored a local seminar with Focus on the Family, which was attended by two thousand people. Another publishes its own newsletter, which serves as a clearinghouse for local pro-family organizations, and a third wrote a weekly article for the local newspaper about Coalition activities. Another chapter is one of the ten newly created distribution points in Ohio for *Christian American* (the Coalition's national magazine); two others distribute it in bulk.

The activities of the other three types of chapters were much more restricted. Just Getting Started chapters did some voter registration and distributed some literature, but mainly focused on recruiting candidates for public and party office, in addition to voter guide distribution. Limited Operations chapters concentrated almost exclusively on distributing voter guides, while Chairs without Chapters engaged in very little conventional political activity, but did research the local presence of Communists or members of other threatening groups.

Grievances

All the chairs were primarily motivated by purposive incentives, stressing conservative social issues. Abortion was top priority, followed by a host of other related topics, including public education, gay rights, and perceived threats to religious life. These issues were clearly seen as symptoms of the larger problem of moral decay, and accordingly, the improvement of the nation's moral climate was understood as the Coalition's most important goal. However, there was considerable variation on this theme across the chapter types.

The Core Chapters fully endorsed the Coalition's pro-family agenda and strongly approved of the "Contract with the American Family," the Christian Coalition's pragmatic congressional agenda, modeled after Newt Gingrich's "Contract with America." As such, they adopted achievable stances on social issues, such as restricting rather than outlawing abortion in the short run, and endorsed many Republican policy proposals, such as a $500 per child tax credit. Their views on economic issues were in accord with the Coalition's broad agenda. All agreed, for instance, that fiscal issues are related to moral concerns in that "because immorality is funded by government, we must de-fund government." A specific example given was the termination of the legal services program because "[President Bill] Clinton removed oversight," allowing the program to become overly intrusive in private life.

Chairs of the Going Concerns chapters expressed a broader range of grievances than did chairs of the Core Chapters. A very important topic was a perceived threat to organized religion. Nearly all of these chairs believed that their religion is under attack from many quarters, including the media, universities, schools, and "liberals." However, most of them see economic questions to be just as important as social issues. But, they are deeply frustrated with the direction of government, both with the compromises of President George Bush and the policies of President Bill Clinton. The Just Getting Started chairs also strongly favored adding economic issues to the Coalition's social issues agenda, though they were most concerned with how issues might be linked to candidates and campaigns.

Heads of the Limited Operations chapters gave the purest expression to the underlying grievance of the Christian Right: the nation has abandoned the "old time" religion, and, as a result, is suffering from moral decline. A frequent grievance was the prohibition of prayer in public schools. Standard social issues appeared to be more intense and personal to this group. For example, the daughter of one chair was censured by her elementary school principal for silently saying grace at lunch, and another chair was upset when the Christmas program in her local public school was replaced by a secular "winter" program. As a result, these chairs were far less interested in expanding the agenda to economic issues.

The grievances of the Chairs without Chapters were the stereotypical fears of the "radical right." Social issues took second place to the specter of communism and related threats, including the United Nations, military weakness, and an imminent economic collapse. Most feared that fundamental personal rights were on "shaky ground" or already lost.

Resources

All chapters were dominated by religious people, most of whom were regular church attenders. However, the chapter types have quite different sources of membership. In keeping with the model of a "Christian coalition," the Core Chapters were the most diverse, containing charismatics and pentecostals, other evangelicals, mainline Protestants, and Roman Catholics. In fact, Catholics account for as much as one-half of the membership of some Core Chapters. One chair is herself a Catholic, and two used Catholic members to help recruit and organize coparishioners because "Catholics are better suited to reaching other Catholics." One likened the Coalition to a "big tent" where neither religious doctrine nor practice was a disqualification for participation. Another chair claimed she would even welcome atheists if they supported traditional values.

The Going Concerns chapters were also quite diverse, but drew more from evangelical and mainline Protestants. One chapter has members from fourteen different denominations, and holds its regular meetings in three different churches on a rotating basis. Several chapters had substantial Catholic membership, and one even had a few non-Christian members. One of these chairs argued that the word "Christian" should be deleted from the organization's name to encourage participation of people from other religious traditions. An opposite pattern occurred as well: some chapters had a much narrower membership, with no mainline Protestants or Catholics. Chairs of these chapters voiced concern about Christian "liberals," revealing the type of religious particularism that bedeviled the Moral Majority.

The Just Getting Started and Limited Operations clusters largely contained evangelical Protestants, with charismatics and Baptists most frequently mentioned. These clusters have very few Catholic members, although the chairs all claim that they would welcome them. All the Chairs without Chapters had themselves come from sectarian evangelical backgrounds and had little interest in religious diversity. One was quite opposed to cooperating with other kinds of religious people; he cited as an example the Methodist Federation for Social Action, which he claimed has been a communist front since the 1950s. Another cautioned against broader affiliations because "we are in the end times." Yet another worships in her home because she has found no church compatible with her beliefs.

All chapters are primarily composed of lay people, although most contain some clergy and several chairs were pastors. One of the Core Chapters had a substantial number of pastors as members, and over one-half of the Going Concerns, Limited Operations, and Just Getting Started chapters had at least one. Just one Chair without Chapter was a minister, and he indicated that it is extremely difficult to get church people involved in politics.

The chapters were primarily composed of white, middle-aged, middle-class, married people with children. Many members were housewives, and many others were in small business or managerial occupations. Limited Operations had the greatest diversity of age and socioeconomic status, and Chairs without Chapters were of very modest means. Some chapters reported a sizeable contingent of active older members, and one Core chapter had a large youth contingent. Several chairs reported overtures to racial minorities, though without success. Women are very well represented, accounting for more than one-third of the chairs, including many of the most skillful leaders.

Many chapters regularly cooperated with other pro-family groups, sharing projects, information, volunteers, mailing lists, fax machines, and in some cases, local chairs. By far the most important ally was Ohio Right to Life, followed by Focus on the Family. Other pro-family groups included the Ohio Roundtable, Concerned Women of America, the American Family Association, Citizens for Excellence in Education, the Eagle Forum, and the Rutherford Institute. Some chapters also networked with secular conservatives, such as the Heritage Foundation, the National Coalition for Protection of Children and the Family, and the Ohio True Blue Patriots.

The Core Chapters stressed the value of networking with other local organizations, and their connections were quite diverse. One chair endorsed joint work "to avoid burnout of the grass roots." Going Concerns chapters also worked extensively with other groups. However, few of the Just Getting Started or Limited Operations chapters networked regularly, and these contacts were limited to informal information-sharing. The Limited Operations chairs often missed obvious connections. For example, one chair was a home-schooler and active in a local group, and yet there was no cooperation between home-schoolers and the Coalition. The Chairs without Chapters have very few contacts with other organizations, though two chairs devoted time to various anticommunist organizations, such as the Christian Anti-Communist Crusade, and Citizens United, a group devoted to the impeachment of President Bill Clinton.

Opportunities

The distribution of political opportunities also varied by chapter type. All Core Chapters were located in suburban areas surrounding major metropolitan areas. While largely Republican, these areas are quite competitive politically at the local level and contain large numbers of swing voters in primary and general election contests. These communities are also quite culturally diverse, places where conservative Christians are a significant minority and routinely encounter people with very different values. These places are thus ideal sites for local efforts to make a difference in elections (Green, Guth, and Hill 1993).

About three-quarters of the other chapters were also located in these highly competitive areas, but the proportion declined from the Going Concerns and Just Getting Started chapters to the Limited Operations chapters and Chairs without Chapters. In fact, a large proportion of the last two categories were located either in rural GOP strongholds or urban Democratic bastions. Interestingly, the better the local political opportunities, the more likely the local chair was to be a skilled and pragmatic leader—which, in turn, contributed to chapter strength. This connection between good opportunities and good leaders reveals an important point: the Christian Coalition itself represents an important opportunity for local activists to participate in politics.

All Ohio chairs were relative newcomers to politics, but they were recruited in different ways. The Core chairs were classic "self-starters." Only one had any prior political experience: she was a Ronald Reagan national convention delegate in 1984 and paid staffer for the 1988 Pat Robertson presidential campaign. A more typical chair had been politically inactive until 1992, when the election of President Bill Clinton so agitated her that she sent letters about Clinton instead of her usual Christmas cards. These self-starters were intensely pragmatic, deeply concerned with achieving political results, and the most skillful and efficacious leaders.

The Going Concerns chairs had long-standing interests in politics prior to joining the Coalition. Many were members of other pro-family organizations, such as Concerned Women for America and the Ohio Roundtable, and most were recruited by friends and associates already active in the movement. The Just Getting Started and the Limited Operations chairs were characterized by a newly acquired interest in politics in addition to recent activity. Just Getting Started chairs were largely recruited by the Coalition in the context of the 1994 campaign, while the Limited Operations chairs were recruited earlier via contact with the Coalition or the "700 Club" and Pat Robertson.

There is more than a hint of instrumental incentives among these three categories. In each case, several chairs have either run or plan on running for public or party office, and at least one hopes for a paid position with the Coalition at the state level. The instrumental interests of these chairs appear to increase their incentives to work for the chapter and may enhance their effectiveness as chairs.

On the other hand, the Chairs without Chapters tended to be classic purists, unwilling to compromise or cooperate, and characterized by low levels of skill and efficacy. These chairs had very little conventional political experience, although several had spent years identifying local Communists and other threatening groups, and one had been peripherally involved with the Moral Majority. This group was recruited by either Coalition or "700 Club" mailings.

While all chapters are politically conservative and most chairs are active Republicans (one Core chair served on her county Republican executive committee), many chapters also included conservative Democrats and Independents. However, support for the GOP was based on ideological congruence. Indeed, all chairs indicated they would abandon the Republicans if they compromised too much on social issues, particularly on abortion. In this context, there was some support for a Christian "third party," especially among chairs of the Limited Operations chapters and Chairs without Chapters.

Charting the Coalition

What can we conclude, then, from our charting of the Ohio Christian Coalition's local chapters? To begin with, the local units vary considerably in organizational strength and activity. The Core Chapters are the sort of grassroots organizations any political group would want, and when combined with the Going Concerns, represent a potent source of influence in elections. In fact, the major party organizations in these counties have trouble mustering many more activists on a regular basis (although they are often more successful at election time). But, at the other extreme, the Chairs without Chapters and counties without chairs are numerous, largely ineffective, and unlikely to improve. The real test of the Coalition, however, lies with the Just Getting Started and Limited Operations chapters. It is here that improvement is possible and perhaps likely.

Thus, in Ohio at least, the Christian Coalition has much room for future expansion. In a relatively short time span, it has built some effective local units, but it will take great effort to maintain and expand its grassroots presence. The strategy of the Christian Coalition has clearly been an asset in this effort: chapter strength is associated with its reformulated agenda, broad-based recruitment, and pragmatic approach. However, this point of view is hardly universal among the Ohio chairs. Rival issue priorities, religious particularism, and purist style are found throughout the organization, and perhaps more so among the rank-and-file volunteers. As noted earlier, there are strikingly different ideas of what the Coalition should be about which, when combined with demand for local autonomy and the instrumental interests of many chairs, may undermine local chapters.

From a broader theoretical point of view, our findings highlight the multiple causes of organizational strength in social movements. As with other manifestations of the Christian Right, the strongest Coalition chapters occur where grievances, resources, and opportunities are common and combined in a productive fashion. Or, put another way, the Coalition is best organized where the motivations, means, and methods for political action are present and reinforce each other. Conversely, the Coalition is weakest where none of these factors are present. Although our findings must be interpreted with great caution, it is likely that these factors of strength are most common in the southern and western strongholds of the Christian Right, while few are evident in much of the Northeast. For the moment, however, we can conclude that the much-discussed grassroots power of the Christian Coalition does have some basis in fact.

References

Bruce, Steve. 1988. *The Rise and Fall of the Christian Right.* New York: Oxford University Press.

Fitzgerald, Francis. 1981. "A Disciplined Charging Army." *New Yorker* 57: 53–97.

Green, John C. 1993. "Pat Robertson and the Latest Crusade: Religious Resources and the 1988 Presidential Campaign." *Social Science Quarterly* 74: 157–68.

Green, John C., James L. Guth, and Kevin Hill. 1993. "Faith and Election: The Christian Right in Congressional Campaigns, 1978–1988." *Journal of Politics* 55: 80–91.

Green, John C., James L. Guth, Corwin E. Smidt, and Lyman A. Kellstedt, eds. 1996. *Religion and the Culture Wars: Dispatches from the Front.* Lanham, Md.: Rowman & Littlefield.

Hadden, Jeffrey K., Anson Shupe, James Hawdon, and Kenneth Martin. 1987. "Why Jerry Falwell Killed the Moral Majority." In *The God Pumpers*, edited by Marshall Fishwick and Ray B. Browne, 101–15. Bowling Green, Ohio: Bowling Green State University Press.

Hertzke, Allen D. 1993. *Echoes of Discontent.* Washington, D.C.: CQ Press.

Jorstad, Erling. 1990. *Holding Fast/Pressing On.* New York: Praeger.

McAdam, Douglas. 1982. *Political Process and the Development of Black Insurgency.* Chicago: University of Chicago.

Mayhew, David R. 1986. *The Place of Parties in American Politics.* Princeton, N.J.: Princeton University Press.

Moen, Matthew C. 1992. *The Transformation of the Christian Right.* Tuscaloosa: University of Alabama Press.

Persinos, John F. 1994. "Has the Christian Right Taken over the Republican Party?" *Campaigns & Elections* 15: 21–24.

Reed, Ralph. 1996. *Active Faith.* New York: The Free Press.

Rozell, Mark J., and Clyde Wilcox. 1995. *God at the Grass Roots: The Christian Right in the 1994 Elections.* Lanham, Md.: Rowman & Littlefield.

Tarrow, Sidney. 1994. *Power in Movement.* New York and Cambridge: Cambridge University Press.

Wilcox, Clyde. 1992. *God's Warriors: The Christian Right in Twentieth-Century America.* Baltimore, Md.: Johns Hopkins University Press.

Wilson, James Q. 1973. *Political Organizations.* New York: Basic Books.

Zald, Mayer N., and John D. McCarthy. 1987. "Religious Groups as Crucibles of Social Movements." In *Social Movements in an Organizational Society,* edited by Mayer N. Zald and John D. McCarthy, 67–95. New Brunswick, N.J.: Transaction Publishers.

Part III

The Christian Right across Religious Communities

5

Bringing in the Sheaves: The Christian Right and White Protestants, 1976–1996

John C. Green, Corwin E. Smidt, Lyman A. Kellstedt, and James L. Guth

"The conservatism of white evangelical Protestants," concluded a 1996 study of religion and politics, "is clearly the most powerful religious force in politics today" (Pew Research Center 1996, 21). This situation is of recent vintage. In 1896 a similar analysis surely would have identified the predecessors of today's mainline Protestants as "the most powerful religious force in politics" (Marsden 1990), and as late as the 1960s, the Protestant mainline was seen as a major voting bloc and the core of the Republican coalition (Kellstedt, Green, Guth, and Smidt 1994). In contrast, evangelicals were barely recognized as a separate religious tradition, let alone an electoral constituency, until quite recently. It took the 1976 election of a Southern Baptist Democrat, Jimmy Carter, to call attention to evangelicals. Since then, they have become a mainstay of the Republican Party, usurping the historic position of mainline Protestants (Kellstedt et al. 1994).

How did these changes come about? Any electoral shift of this magnitude has many causes, of course, but one key factor is the Christian Right. This social movement is regularly given credit for bringing evangelicals into the GOP, but also blamed for driving away other voters, including mainline Protestants (Wilcox 1994). This chapter assesses the impact of the Christian Right on the voting behavior of the two major white Protestant traditions between 1976 and 1996 and reveals, in the words of a venerable Protestant hymn, that the Christian Right has been "bringing in the sheaves," moving conservative evangelicals into the more conservative party. This harvest of votes has also sowed some seeds of discontent among mainline Protestants. Thus far, however, the GOP has more reason for rejoicing than for weeping.

Assessing the Impact of the Christian Right

Scholars have long struggled to understand the influence of social movements in democracies. Most have followed Gamson (1990) in identifying two kinds of impact: producing changes in public policy and establishing the movement as a legitimate participant in the policy process. Demonstrating policy change has been difficult because of the many influences affecting outcomes beyond movement activity (Huberts 1989). However, most observers agree that movement participation in the political process is a prerequisite for changing policy.

Accordingly, considerable attention has been paid to the political activities of social movements, including the scope of their demands, the strength and scale of their operations, and the development of a mass constituency (DeNardo 1985). The last of these is often the most enduring impact of a movement. After all, mobilizing a new constituency to challenge established institutions is the essence of movement politics, and few things alter democratic institutions more than a new set of regular participants (Tarrow 1994). Central to the development of a new constituency are changes in the attitudes of the targeted citizenry, including new identities, ideology, and/or partisanship (Klandermans 1984).

The contemporary Christian Right is a textbook example of this aspect of social movements. Beginning in the late 1970s, the movement sought to arouse conservative Christians to restore "traditional values" in public policy. From the beginning, movement leaders believed this goal could best be achieved by developing a Christian conservative voting bloc, and despite early talk of ecumenical appeal and bipartisanship, the Christian Right quickly targeted evangelical Protestant voters and the Republican Party. Although the movement has tried many tactics, all stressed religious ties as the basis for electoral mobilization. The best known tactic is the distribution of "voter guides" in churches and parachurch groups (Green, Guth, Smidt, and Kellstedt 1996).

The Christian Right's attempts to develop such a constituency encountered intense opposition. To begin with, the movement's prime targets among evangelicals resisted mobilization and conservatives in other religious traditions were even more recalcitrant. In addition, many Republican regulars feared that the Christian Right's involvement in the GOP would alienate other voters. And the movement's many opponents engaged in fierce countermobilization both within and outside of the Republican Party (Wilcox 1996).

Chief among the Christian Right's antagonists were liberal reformers in mainline Protestant churches, who disagreed with the religious premises of the movement, opposed the introduction of traditional values into the Republican agenda, and were strongly committed to policies the Christian Right condemned. When these reformers could not stop movement mobilization or inroads into the GOP, they threatened defection to the Democratic Party. However, in these struggles the reformers did not enjoy the full support of their mainline coreligionists, many of whom were sympathetic to or even at times members of the Christian Right (Jorstad 1990).

This complex confrontation was hardly surprising, since both Christian Rightists and liberal reformers were products of complex religious disputes. Since the late nineteenth century, two theological tendencies have contended in American Protestantism. One advocated "separation from the world," with a commitment to purity of religious belief and practice; the other urged "accommodation with the world," with a focus on the social acceptability of religious belief and practice. This disagreement appeared repeatedly within and among Protestant churches, producing, on the one hand, the evangelical tradition, an embodiment of the otherworldly emphasis, and on the other, the mainline tradition, which embraced worldly tendencies (Kellstedt, Green, Smidt, and Guth 1996b).

Although evangelicals and mainliners have often cooperated in politics, their religious differences more often put them at odds with each other. For example, evangelical beliefs have tended to produce social issue conservatism, emphasizing the regulation of individual behavior, while mainline beliefs have tended to generate social issue moderation or liberalism, stressing the reform of social structure. Just the opposite pattern often occurred on economic questions, with evangelicals being moderate to liberal on such matters and mainliners conservative. When combined with other factors, such as income and region, these attitudes produced differences in partisanship, so that, by the turn of the century, evangelicals tended to be Democrats and mainliners Republicans. And, when combined with broader ideological clashes, these attitudes generated support for rival social movements throughout the century: evangelicals repeatedly spearheaded right-wing movements—from the antievolution and anticommunist crusades to the contemporary Christian Right—and mainliners routinely led left-wing movements—from the Progressive to the civil, women's and gay rights movements.

It was in this variegated political context that the Christian Right sought to mobilize a new electoral constituency by moving socially conservative evangelicals from the increasingly liberal Democratic ranks to the more conservative Republican camp—much as liberal reformers have threatened to direct socially liberal mainliners in the opposite direction. These efforts prompt two related questions. First, did the Christian Right help create a new Republican constituency among evangelicals? Second, did the movement contribute to losses from the old Republican constituency among mainline Protestants?

Data and Methods

To answer these questions, this chapter compares the political attitudes and behaviors of white evangelical and mainline Protestants in 1976 and 1996, using the 1976 National Election Study and the 1996 National Survey of Religion and Politics.[1] These two presidential elections constitute appropriate points for this inquiry: 1976 was just prior to the advent of the "new" Christian Right, while by 1996 the movement had achieved a "place at the table" among Republican elites. These elections were also very similar: relatively close contests in which moderate Republicans lost to moderate Democrats, both of whom, ironically, happened to be members of evangelical denominations. Yet another similarity is the presence of Dole, the GOP vice-presidential nominee in 1976 and the presidential nominee in 1996.

We will follow a simple path in our analysis. First, we will compare white Protestants in both years on four political attitudes (abortion, self-identified ideology, affect toward the Christian Right, and self-identified partisanship) and GOP presidential vote. There is a rough logic to our choice of these variables and their ordering. Following the "funnel of causality" (Miller and Shanks 1996), we would expect religious affiliation to be linked to voting behavior by means of intermediate political attitudes. Attitudes on "traditional values," here represented by abortion, are an initial link and one that flows most directly from religion. A next, broader linkage is ideology, followed by partisanship, the attitude most directly tied to presidential vote choice.

Here we assume that positive affect toward the Christian Right can also serve as a link between religion and political behavior. This assumption is reasonable given that one of the movement's primary goals has been to mobilize conservative Protestants on behalf of Republican candidates. Although far from perfect, it is a simple measure of the movement's impact on individual voters. After discussing each of these variables and their bivariate relationship with presidential vote choice, we will consider their combined association with the vote.

We have defined evangelical and mainline Protestants by means of denominational affiliation (Kellstedt and Green 1993), and then divided the members of each tradition by high and low levels of religious commitment, using church attendance (high as monthly or greater attendance; low as less than monthly). Religious commitment is relevant here because of its association with politically relevant cues (Kellstedt, Green, Guth, and Smidt 1996a), and because of the religious focus of the Christian Right's efforts to mobilize votes (Kellstedt, Smidt, Green, and Guth 1996c).

There are, unfortunately, measurement problems that complicate this analysis. Religious affiliation is not measured particularly well in the 1976 study. Indeed, it was the rise of the Christian Right that highlighted these problems and produced major improvements in the measurement of religious variables (Leege and Kellstedt 1993), changes that were incorporated in the 1996 survey. Thus, the earlier data must be used with some caution. For example, the percentage of mainline Protestants declines substantially over the period, from 25 percent of the electorate in 1976 to 18 percent in 1996. While much of this decline may reflect the continuing shrinkage in mainline membership, some may be the result of better measurement of denominational affiliation in 1996. Over the same time period, evangelical affiliation remained about the same—24 percent in 1976 and 27 percent in 1996.

Measuring affect toward the Christian Right is more problematic. Because the contemporary movement had not yet appeared, the 1976 survey had no direct measure of movement affect. However, religion was prominent in the 1976 campaign and respondents were asked to judge whether Ford or Carter would "bring moral and religious standards to government." We combined these two items to produce a measure of "proto-support" for the movement. First, we summed the agree responses to the Carter and Ford items (ratings of "3" or better on the seven-point scale, where a "1" was "strongly agree"; other responses were coded as zero). Next, this sum was recoded into a five-point scale based on the strength of agreement (at one end respondents who strongly agreed that both candidates would support such standards, and at the other end, those who felt neither candidate would do so).

While there are obvious limitations to this variable, the logic is straightforward: bringing moral and religious standards to government was the chief goal of the Christian Right and belief that one or both of the major candidates would do so represents a minimal measure of potential support for the movement. In addition, our measure of proto-support has a similar distribution to a direct measure of movement affect in the 1980 National Election Study.[2]

We were more fortunate with other measures. The 1996 survey contains a five-point Likert scale item assessing proximity to the Christian Right. With the exception of minor differences on the abortion item, the other variables used were very similar in both surveys; all the variables were trichotomized for purposes of presentation.[3] Although a full discussion is beyond the scope of this essay, statistical controls for sociodemographic factors do not alter the findings reported below.[4]

The Politics of White Protestants, 1976 and 1996

Our analysis begins with an overview of the political attitudes of evangelicals and mainline Protestants during the period under study, presented in table 5.1. Evangelicals were strongly pro-life on abortion, exceeding both the mainline and the country as a whole in both years.

TABLE 5.1
The Politics of White Protestants, 1976 and 1996

| | White Protestants | | | | Entire Country | |
| | Evangelical | | Mainline | | | |
	1976	1996	1976	1996	1976	1996
No. of Cases	(528)	(1087)	(571)	(727)	(2248)	(4037)
Abortion						
% Pro-Life	66	59	51	39	57	45
Ideology						
% Conservative	50	63	47	52	39	50
Christian Right						
% Support	46	55	39	30	41	35
Partisanship						
% Republican	35	52	52	49	34	43
Presidential Vote						
% Republican	53	59	64	51	49	42

Source: 1976 National Election Study, Center of Political Studies, University of Michigan; 1996 Survey of Religion and Politics, Survey Research Center, University of Akron (Ohio).

However, the pro-life position declined for all groups over the period. This change may reflect slight differences in question wording.[5] Although evangelicals show the least change on abortion, these data modestly contradict the trends on ideology, which show a rightward trend for all groups. In 1976 about one-half of both Protestant traditions were conservative, more so than the country as a whole, but by 1996 evangelicals had become markedly more conservative than mainliners, who, in turn, now matched the nation. In contrast, support for the Christian Right diverged sharply over time. Among evangelicals, movement affect increased from less than one-half to majority backing. For the mainline, movement affect declined, from about two-fifths to less than one-third, as it did for the entire country.

Larger changes occurred in partisanship. In 1976 just over one-third of evangelicals considered themselves Republicans, about the same as the country as a whole, while a majority of mainliners identified with the GOP. By 1996 about one-half of evangelicals were Republican, actually exceeding the mainline, which experienced a slight decline in GOP identification. These changes were reflected in presidential vote choice. Just over one-half of evangelicals supported Gerald Ford over Jimmy Carter in 1976, but almost three-fifths backed Bob Dole over Bill Clinton and Ross Perot twenty years later.[6] Mainline Protestants show an opposite pattern, with almost two-thirds backing Ford but then just one-half voting for Dole.

These patterns are even clearer when religious commitment is taken into account, as shown in table 5.2. In both years, high commitment evangelicals were uniformly more pro-life, conservative, and supportive of the Christian Right than their low commitment coreligionists. The same patterns hold for the mainline, although these groups are always less conservative than their evangelical counterparts. Partisanship and vote choice present a sharp contrast. Among evangelicals, there were only modest differences between the high and low commitment groups in 1976, but major gaps in 1996, with the highly committed producing the strongest Republican vote. Mainliners had a more varied pattern. Among mainliners, GOP identification declined slightly overall, but the highly committed remained more Republican than the less committed. A similar difference between the high and low commitment groups appeared for GOP vote choice in 1976, but by 1996 the two mainline categories matched each other, with just over one-half voting Republican.

What does this overview reveal? Over the past twenty years, evangelicals have, on balance, become even more conservative, and brought

TABLE 5.2
The Politics of White Protestants, 1976 and 1996
Controlling for Religious Commitment

	Evangelical				Mainline			
	1976		1996		1976		1996	
Level of Commitment	Hi	Lo	Hi	Lo	Hi	Lo	Hi	Lo
No. of Cases	(307)	(218)	(767)	(320)	(342)	(229)	(447)	(229)
Abortion								
% Pro Life	76	56	68	40	58	39	40	24
Ideology								
% Conservative	60	34	69	47	49	41	53	50
Christian Right								
% Support	51	40	60	40	40	37	36	22
Partisanship								
% Republican	36	33	56	40	56	44	51	45
Presidential Vote								
% Republican	53	50	66	36	67	60	51	52

Source: 1976 National Election Study, Center of Political Studies, University of Michigan; 1996 Survey of Religion and Politics, Survey Research Center, University of Akron (Ohio)

their support for the Christian Right, partisanship, and voting for president in line with their conservatism. These changes have been particularly strong among the highly committed. During the same period, Protestant mainliners have become less pro-life on abortion, much less supportive of the Christian Right, and less supportive of Republican presidential candidates, but, in contrast, their self-identified conservatism has increased. Here the impact of religious commitment is less clear: the low commitment group changed the most on social issues and movement affect, but the highly committed changed most on vote choice.

The Impact of the Christian Right, 1976 and 1996

What are the combined effects of these political attitudes, and especially, affect toward the Christian Right? To answer this question, we sorted the four attitudinal variables into ten categories that summarized underlying patterns; they are listed in table 5.3. The major division is between respondents who supported the Christian Right (the top half of the table) and those who were either neutral toward or opposed to the Christian Right (the bottom half of the table). The Christian Right division contains four categories, respondents who identified themselves as:

TABLE 5.3
White Protestants and National Politics, 1976 and 1996
The Relative Size of Attitudinal Categories

| | Evangelical | | | | Mainline | | | |
| | 1976 | | 1996 | | 1976 | | 1996 | |
Level of Commitment	Hi	Lo	Hi	Lo	Hi	Lo	Hi	Lo
Christian Right								
Republican								
Conservative, Pro-Life	9	4	28	9	12	8	15	6
Pro-Life Only	6	6	2	5	5	5	2	1
Non-Republican								
Conservative, Pro-Life	7	4	10	9	5	2	6	4
Pro-Life Only	16	11	6	5	6	8	5	1
Non-Christian Right								
Republican								
Conservative, Pro-Life	10	4	18	15	16	16	23	27
Pro-Life Only	3	5	4	5	6	5	1	1
Moderates	8	13	4	0	14	14	9	10
Non-Republican								
Conservative, Pro-Life	9	6	10	12	4	6	8	11
Pro-Life Only	12	18	5	8	11	7	7	3
Moderates	20	29	13	27	21	29	24	36

Source: 1976 National Election Study, Center of Political Studies, University of Michigan; 1996 Survey of Religion and Politics, Survey Research Center, University of Akron (Ohio)

(1) Republican, conservative, and/or pro-life; (2) Republican and pro-life, but not conservative; (3) non-Republican (including independents and Democrats), conservatives, and/or pro-life; and (4) non-Republican and pro-life, but not conservative. Identical categories are found under the non-Christian Right division, with the addition of two "moderate" categories (including moderates and liberals).[7]

Table 5.3 shows the relative size of these categories for all four religious groups in both elections. First, note that the largest change occurred among high commitment evangelicals (in the first row): the proportion of Christian Right Republican conservatives increased fourfold (9 to 28 percent). Also, the Christian Right non-Republican pro-life category declined by more than one-half over the period (16 to 6 percent in the fourth row). Presumably, this shift resulted from the transformation of pro-life independents and Democrats into conservative Republicans, due, in part, to movement activities.

Note, however, that parallel but smaller changes also occurred in the non-Christian Right categories: the proportion of Republican conservatives increased (10 to 18 percent) and the non-Republican pro-life category declined (12 to 5 percent). These shifts may reflect the indirect influence of the movement, but may also result from other attractions to the GOP. In addition, the number of Republican and non-Republican moderates fell over the twenty-year period. The remaining categories changed less dramatically. For example, low-commitment evangelicals show smaller, but similar shifts toward the Republican conservative and the pro-life categories.

The mainliners show less dramatic changes, as evident in table 5.3. The proportion of Republican conservatives among high-commitment mainliners increased in both the Christian Right and non-Christian Right categories, but at lower levels than among their evangelical counterparts. The highly committed mainliners also had modest increases in the non-Republican moderate category. Meanwhile, low-commitment mainliners showed increases in the non-Christian Right categories, particularly non-Republican moderates, but also declines in the Christian Right categories. These shifts in the mainline may represent a modest backlash against the Christian Right.

Thus, movement affect is associated with shifts in political attitudes among white Protestants over the period under study. The movement apparently helped convert social issue conservatives into Republican conservatives, particularly among highly committed evangelicals, the key targets of the movement. At the same time, there was a much more modest shift away from conservatism and the GOP among low-commitment evangelicals and both sets of mainliners. These figures suggest the Christian Right has on balance helped the Republicans, but these gains have not been without cost.

What about the presidential vote? In table 5.4 these same ten categories are used to look at the presidential vote in 1976 and 1996; the entries represent the percentage of each category voting Republican for president, including minor party ballots and nonvoters in the GOP category not shown in the table. We present vote choice in this fashion to control for differences between the 1976 and 1996 elections that might distort comparisons, such as minor party candidates and turnout.[8]

A strong and intuitively satisfying *vertical* pattern appears in table 5.4: the GOP presidential vote in both years declines as we move from Republican conservatives to non-Republican moderates. Note, however, that the Christian Right categories differ little from their non-Christian Right counterparts. This suggests that the most important sources of the vote in causal sequence are: partisanship, ideology, abortion, and affect toward the Christian Right. Thus, the impact of the Christian Right on the vote appears to have been indirect, by changing the political attitudes of its targets.

There are also several important *horizontal* patterns in table 5.4. The

TABLE 5.4

White Protestants and National Politics, 1976 and 1996
Republican Presidential Vote

	Evangelical				Mainline			
	1976		1996		1976		1996	
Level of Commitment	Hi	Lo	Hi	Lo	Hi	Lo	Hi	Lo
Christian Right								
Republican								
Conservative, Pro-Life	79*	75	83	61	80	79	80	65
Pro-Life Only	61	54	50	0	59	55	50	0
Non-Republican								
Conservative, Pro-Life	43	22	20	7	31	25	25	6
Pro-Life Only	20	14	22	0	19	0	21	0
Non-Christian Right								
Republican								
Conservative, Pro-Life	78	70	83	46	80	69	81	69
Pro-Life Only	90	50	67	47	71	36	80	100
Moderates	28	38	43	0	55	42	38	33
Non-Republican								
Conservative, Pro-Life	20	39	31	25	27	36	18	33
Pro-Life Only	12	18	5	8	11	7	7	3
Moderates	9	11	5	3	20	15	5	5

* Entries are percentage of each category that voted Republican for president
Source: 1976 National Election Study, Center of Political Studies, University of Michigan; 1996 Survey of Religion and Politics, Survey Research Center, University of Akron (Ohio)

first is simple: in both elections, comparable groups of evangelicals and mainliners voted similarly. For example, some four-fifths of Christian Right Republican conservatives among high-commitment evangelicals and mainliners voted for Ford in 1976 and Dole in 1996. Another horizontal pattern of interest involves comparing the high- and low-commitment groups in each tradition, with the former voting Republican more often. Hence, it appears that once the attitudes that link white Protestants to vote choice are taken into account, the differences between religious traditions are minimized, while the differences based on commitment persist.

Another interesting horizontal pattern in table 5.4 is the change in Republican vote between 1976 and 1996. Despite the greater weakness of the GOP in 1996, Republican conservatives among high-commitment evangelicals and mainliners supported the party at about the same high rate as in 1976 (some four-fifths), which differed little from the support of their non-Christian Right counterparts in both elections. Thus, the supporters of the Christian Right voted for the Republican ticket at the same rate as other core Republican constituencies. However, the Republicans lost ground in other places. Low-commitment mainliners, and to a slightly lesser extent, low-commitment evangelicals were less supportive of the GOP in 1996. And, although the patterns are idiosyncratic, the losses were most dramatic among the less Republican and less conservative categories.

Table 5.5 concludes our analysis by reporting the relative contribution of each category to the total Republican vote cast in 1976 and 1996. The first row shows the total proportion of the GOP vote provided by each religious group and the results are quite revealing. For example, high-commitment evangelicals became almost twice as important to the Republican presidential coalition over the period, rising from 16.5 percent to 32.9 percent. And, although the relative importance of low-commitment evangelicals declined (9.0 to 6.2 percent), evangelicals as a group accounted for almost two-fifths of all Republican votes in 1996, up from one-quarter in 1976.

The largest contribution to this reversal came from a single category: Christian Right Republican conservatives among high-commitment evangelicals. In 1976 this group accounted for 3.4 percent of Ford's votes, but by 1996 it made up 15.6 percent of Dole supporters—more than a fourfold increase. Indeed, this group alone almost equaled *all* the votes Republicans received among high-commitment evangelicals in 1976 (15.6 to 16.5 percent). However, as before, impressive gains were

TABLE 5.5
White Protestants and National Politics, 1976 and 1996
Percentage of Total Presidential Vote

	1976 GOP Vote Evangelical				1996 GOP Vote Mainline			
	1976		1996		1976		1996	
Level of Commitment	Hi	Lo	Hi	Lo	Hi	Lo	Hi	Lo
%Total GOP Vote	16.5	9.0	24.7	9.7	32.9	6.2	17.4	7.3
Christian Right								
Republican								
Conservative, Pro-Life	3.4*	1.1	4.9	2.3	15.6	1.8	6.3	.1
Pro-Life Only	1.7	1.1	1.5	.9	1.4	.2	.2	0.0
Non-Republican								
Conservative, Pro-Life	1.4	.3	.8	.2	1.4	.2	.5	.5
Pro-Life Only	1.4	.5	.6	0.0	.8	0.0	.4	0.0
Non-Christian Right								
Republican								
Conservative, Pro-Life	3.8	1.1	6.7	3.8	9.6	2.2	7.8	4.6
Pro-Life Only	1.2	.8	2.6	.5	.9	.7	.6	.3
Moderates	1.1	1.7	4.1	2.1	.5	0.0	1.4	.6
Non-Republican								
Conservative, Pro-Life	.9	.8	.6	.8	2.0	.8	.5	.9
Pro-Life Only	.8	.5	1.5	.3	.3	.1	.1	0.0
Moderates	.8	1.1	2.0	1.5	.4	.2	.6	.3

*Entries are percent of Republican presidential vote.
Source: 1976 National Election Study, Center of Political Studies, University of Michigan; 1996 Survey of Religion and Politics, Survey Research Center, University of Akron (Ohio)

also posted among non-Christian Right Republican conservatives (3.8 percent to 9.6 percent) and non-Republican conservatives (0.9 to 2.0 percent). However, the GOP lost ground in most of the other categories, even among high-commitment evangelicals.

In contrast, the relative importance of high-commitment mainline Protestants to the Republican coalition declined considerably, from 24.7 to 15.4 percent of the votes received, and support from the low-commitment group fell as well (9.7 to 7.3 percent). Overall, the mainliners decreased from about one-third of the GOP presidential votes to one-quarter. These figures are one place where the measurement differences between the two surveys may matter: much of this change could be due to the more accurate assignment of denominations to religious traditions in 1996 given its more in-depth coding scheme for denominations or by the actual decline in mainline affiliation between 1976 and 1996.

In any event, the relative decline in mainline Republican support masks complex patterns. For example, Christian Right Republican conservatives among high-commitment mainliners actually increased their contribution to the Republican ticket (4.9 to 6.3 percent) as did their non-Christian Right counterparts (6.7 to 7.8 percent). Significant losses occurred among non-Christian Right moderates (4.1 to 1.4 percent). Similar declines occurred among most categories of low-commitment mainliners in 1996 as well. Non-Christian Right Republican conservatives constitute the conspicuous exception, as they modestly increased their contribution to the GOP (3.8 to 4.6 percent).

Bringing in the Sheaves

We can now offer some answers to the questions posed at the outset of our analysis. First, the Christian Right appears to have been an important factor in the development of a new constituency for the Republican Party. The movement has been "bringing in the sheaves," harvesting conservative Protestant votes for the GOP. High-commitment evangelicals contribute the bulk of this harvest, although it includes some low-commitment evangelicals and high-commitment mainliners as well. Thus, the Christian Right has contributed directly to the ascendancy of evangelicals in the Republican coalition.

Our findings suggest the outlines of the causal mechanism behind the Christian Right's influence: the conversion of social issue conservatives into political conservatives and Republicans. The movement dramatically expanded the number of Republican conservatives among evangelicals, and once converted, they cast ballots very much like other Republican conservatives, though perhaps with somewhat different policy agendas (Green, Guth, Kellstedt, and Smidt 1994). Such conversions give the movement a double boost—on the one hand, producing voters predisposed to support Republican candidates and, on the other, creating a constituency that is responsive to the movement's mobilizing efforts (Kellstedt et al. 1996c).

Second, the Christian Right is also linked to losses among the old Republican mainline constituency. Some low-commitment mainliners not supportive of the movement did indeed move away from the GOP and conservatism, much as liberal reformers threatened. Interestingly, very similar losses occurred among high-commitment mainliners less firmly connected to the GOP or conservatism and also among low-commitment evangelicals. Although some of these losses may reflect continued decline in the membership of mainline Protestants, the Christian Right appears to have also sowed seeds of discontent.[9] Thus far, however, the impact of the Christian Right has been on balance positive for the Republican Party.

Notes

1. We wish to acknowledge the Inter-University Consortium for Political and Social Research for making available the 1976 National Election Study. These data were originally collected by the Center of Political Studies at the University of Michigan. The second National Survey of Religion and Politics was conducted by the Survey Research Center at the University of Akron with a grant from the Pew Charitable Trusts. A pre-election survey was run in spring 1996 with a postelection follow-up done beginning the day after the election on November 5. All interpretations presented here are solely the responsibility of the authors.

2. The 1980 National Election Study survey measure asked if the respondent felt "warm" or "cold" toward "evangelical groups in politics such as the Moral Majority." When this measure is recoded into quintiles, 51 percent of high-commitment evangelicals fall into the top two categories, exactly the same percentage as for our "proto-support" measure in 1976. There is also a close fit for high-commitment mainliners—39 percent in 1980 and 40 percent in 1976. As one might expect, the measures diverge more for low-commitment evangelicals (34 percent to 40 percent) and low-commitment mainliners (27 percent to 37 percent).

3. The variables were trichotomized as follows: abortion (1-no restrictions; 2-some restrictions, 3-life of mother or prohibit all abortions); ideology (1-extremely liberal, liberal, slightly liberal; 2-moderate; 3-slightly conservative,

conservative, extremely conservative); partisanship (1-strong Democrat, Democrat, lean Democratic; 2-independent; 3-lean Republican, Republican, strongly Republican); Christian Right affect (1-top two categories; 2-middle category; 3-bottom two categories).

4. Statistical controls for the effects of income, education, age, gender, and region on the attitudinal variables and presidential vote choice produced very similar patterns for the data in tables 5.1 to 5.5.

5. The abortion question had the same basic structure in both surveys, but the 1976 item mentioned "children" in the most pro-choice response categories, and thus may have produced a more pro-life response.

6. The resultant percentages presented here differ from some of our other published work due to the need here to create more comparable measures of religious commitment across the 1976 and 1996 surveys. See Kellstedt, Green, Guth, and Smidt 1997.

7. To simplify presentation, we combined several categories that produced very similar results. For instance, all other things considered, respondents who were conservative and pro-life and those who were conservative and not pro-life showed very similar results on presidential vote choice in 1976 and 1996. In a parallel fashion, respondents who were opposed to the Christian Right and those who were neutral generated similar results, as did independents and Democrats, and moderates and liberals.

8. Consistent with previous work on minor-party voting (Gilbert, Johnson, and Peterson 1995), the high-commitment categories were the least supportive of Ross Perot in 1996. Likewise, high-commitment respondents were the most likely to vote (Kellstedt et al. 1996b). Although turnout is very difficult to assess accurately with survey data, the high-commitment group showed the smaller decline in turnout between 1976 and 1996 (59 to 55 percent for evangelicals, 67 to 62 percent for mainliners) than their low-commitment counterparts (47 to 34 percent for evangelicals, 56 to 50 percent for mainliners).

9. It is not clear, however, how many of these defections were directly due to the Christian Right's agenda. As in 1992 (Green, Guth, Kellstedt, and Smidt 1994), evidence suggests that most of the defectors in 1996 were motivated by economic issues. So, here too, the impact of the movement may be largely indirect, by shifting the focus of the GOP away from economic concerns rather than alienating voters with social issue conservatism. In recent times, the Republicans have had at least as much trouble on the economic front as with social issues.

References

DeNardo, James. 1985. *Power in Numbers: The Political Strategy of Protest and Rebellion.* Princeton, N.J.: Princeton University Press.

Gamson, William A. 1990. *The Strategy of Social Protest.* 2d ed. Belmont, Calif.: Wadsworth.

Gilbert, Christopher, Timothy Johnson, and David Peterson. 1995. "The Religious Roots of Third Candidate Voting." *Journal for the Scientific Study of Religion* 34: 470–84.

Green, John C., James L. Guth, Lyman A. Kellstedt, and Corwin E. Smidt. 1994. "Murphy Brown Revisited: The Social Issues in the 1992 Election." In *Disciples and Democracy*, edited by Michael Cromartie, 43–67. Grand Rapids, Mich.: Eerdmans.

Green, John C., James L. Guth, Corwin E. Smidt, and Lyman A. Kellstedt. 1996. *Religion and the Culture Wars: Dispatches from the Front.* Lanham, Md.: Rowman & Littlefield.

Huberts, Leo W. 1989. "The Influence of Social Movements on Government Policy." In *Organizing for Change: Social Movement Organization in Europe and the United States,* International Social Movement Research, Vol. 2, edited by Bert Kandermans, 395–426. Greenwich, Conn.: JAI Press.

Jorstad, Erling. 1990. *Holding Fast/Pressing On.* New York: Praeger.

Kellstedt, Lyman A., and John C. Green. 1993. "Knowing God's Many People: Denominational Preference and Political Behavior." In *Rediscovering the Religious Factor in American Politics,* edited by David C. Leege and Lyman A. Kellstedt, 53–71. Armonk, N.Y.: M. E. Sharpe.

Kellstedt, Lyman A., John C. Green, James L. Guth, and Corwin E. Smidt. 1994. "Religious Voting Blocs in the 1992 Election: The Year of the Evangelical?" *Sociology of Religion* 55: 307–26.

———. 1996a. "Grasping the Essentials: The Social Embodiment of Religion and Political Behavior." In *Religion and the Culture Wars: Dispatches from the Front,* edited by John C. Green, James L. Guth, Corwin E. Smidt, and Lyman A. Kellstedt, 174–92. Lanham, Md.: Rowman & Littlefield.

———. 1996b. "The Puzzle of Evangelical Protestantism: Core, Periphery, and Political Behavior." In *Religion and the Culture Wars: Dispatches from the Front,* edited by John C. Green, James L. Guth, Corwin E. Smidt, and Lyman A. Kellstedt, 240–66. Lanham, Md.: Rowman & Littlefield.

———. 1996c. Explaining the Republican Takeover of Congress: The Role of Religion. Paper prepared for the annual meeting of the American Political Science Association, August 31, San Francisco.

———. 1997. "The 49% Solution." *Books & Culture* (March/April): 24–25.

Klandermans, Bert. 1984. "Mobilization and Participation: Social Psychological Expansions of Resource Mobilization Theory." *American Sociological Review* 49: 583–600.

Leege, David C., and Lyman A. Kellstedt, eds. 1993. *Rediscovering the Religious Factor in American Politics.* Armonk, N.Y.: M. E. Sharpe.

Marsden, George M. 1990. *Religion and American Culture.* New York: Harcourt Brace Jovanovich.

Miller, Warren E., and J. Merrill Shanks. 1996. *The New American Voter.* Cambridge: Harvard University Press.

Pew Research Center. 1996. "The Diminishing Divide: American Churches, American Politics." Washington, D.C.: The Pew Center for the People and the Press.

Tarrow, Sidney G. 1994. *Power in Movement.* Cambridge: Cambridge University Press.

Wilcox, Clyde. 1994. "Premillennialists at the Millennium: Some Reflections on the Christian Right in the Twenty-First Century." *Sociology of Religion* 55: 243–61.

————. 1996. *Onward Christian Soldiers?* Boulder, Colo.: Westview Press.

6

Catholics and the Christian Right: An Uneasy Alliance

R. Scott Appleby

The Republican Party in 1996 pinned no small measure of its electoral hopes on the support of American Catholics.[1] The recent history of national voting patterns gave rise to such hopes, as the shifting Catholic vote has, since 1976, correlated with victory at the polls. In the 1980s Catholics made up the core of "Reagan Democrats." In fact, prior to the '96 election, the majority of Catholics had not voted for a Democratic presidential candidate in twenty years, since they supported Carter in '76.[2] Deepening what seemed to be a trend toward the GOP, 52 percent of Catholics voted Republican in the 1994 congressional elections, the first time the majority of Catholics had done so in a midterm election.

The expectation that "the Catholic vote" might prove decisive in the 1996 election, repeated so frequently as to become part of the conventional wisdom, encouraged GOP politicians and worried Democrats, especially after President Bill Clinton aggravated pro-life Catholics with his veto of a proposed ban on partial-birth abortions. The shift in Catholic voting patterns was the subject of a pre-election issue of *Rising Tide,* a magazine published by the Republican National Committee. Ed Gillespie, the author of the lead article, boasted that "we Catholics provided the margin of victory needed to create the first Republican Congress in 40 years," and claimed that the Democratic Party's abandonment of "the values many of us hold dear" prompted the defection from the Democrat-Catholic coalition built during the New Deal era. Contemporary Democrats, he charged, are gutting defense to pay for social spending, opposing tax cuts for working Americans, and mandating discrimination in the form of quotas. Just as high taxes, stifling business regulations, and forced busing drove Catholic families from the cities to the suburbs, so "the national Democrat Party grew so liberal it drove ethnic Catholics from our once natural political home." Unlike southern conservatives, however, Catholics may vote Republican, but most have yet to acknowledge that they *are* Republicans. Thus, the '96 election offered the opportunity to make the Catholic vote "a permanent part of the Republican majority" (Gillespie 1996, 18).

If such an opportunity did exist, it was not realized in the election, which saw a majority of Catholics voting for Clinton over his Republican rival, Bob Dole. Christian Right activists, who tended overwhelmingly to support GOP presidential and congressional candidates, were among the most vigorous recruiters of Catholics to the conservative political cause. This chapter examines their efforts and explains the limited nature of their attractiveness to Catholic voters.

The Christian Coalition and the Catholic Alliance

Ralph Reed, the "wunderkind" of the mostly evangelical Christian Coalition, crafted the initial strategy to increase Catholic participation in the Christian Right. Unlike many of his predecessors in the Christian Right leadership, the thirty-four-year-old Ph.D. in American history (Emory University, 1988) eschewed narrowly confessional or sectarian rhetoric, preferring to describe his allies generically as "religious conservatives" and his political program as "the pro-family movement." A seasoned political operative, Reed recognized that the first wave of the movement, in the 1980s, had suffered from exclusivist tendencies, an appearance of indifference or even hostility toward nonevangelicals, and a flawed political strategy centered on politicians and judges in Washington, D.C., rather than on ecumenical, grassroots work in local communities. In a calculated attempt to broaden the Christian Right's base and to overcome negative stereotypes (which reached a new low following Patrick Buchanan's inflammatory "culture war" address to the 1992 Republican convention), Reed specialized in crafting compelling statements of compassion for the poor and oppressed, declarations of respect for political opponents, homilies on the virtues of gradualism and the limited capacity of politics to achieve true social reform, and promises of "a higher standard in truth and civility" in the future than has been evident in the movement's past (Reed 1996; Appleby 1996).

Although Reed was fond of claiming the political support of 30 million religious conservatives, he knew that Protestant evangelicals and fundamentalists could not be mobilized in such numbers; were the Christian Coalition to realize anything approaching its self-advertised political clout, the organization would need to attract a significant portion of the conservative Catholic population. Thus, as early as 1992, he began to play to that audience, especially on abortion, the most obvious and significant issue on which Christian Coalitioners and conservative Catholics were of one mind.

In 1995 Reed delighted Gillespie and other Republican political operatives by announcing plans to establish a "Catholic Alliance," putatively the Roman Catholic affiliate of the Christian Coalition. When a liberal Catholic political activist responded to the announcement by complaining that Catholics already have a political home ("It's called the Catholic Church"), Reed had an answer ready at hand. While Catholic social teaching encourages Catholic laity to greater political activism, he commented, the Church lacks a suitable vehicle to mobilize and organize the politically aroused faithful. The Catholic Alliance would become that vehicle, Reed promised, with the goal of increasing Catholic participation in the pro-family movement by 250,000 by Election Day 1996 and by more than 2 million by the end of the decade (Reed 1996, 219). In 1996, with the potential Catholic constituency clearly in mind, Reed drafted a pro-life plank for the GOP platform that quoted Mother Teresa and Pope John Paul II and echoed Catholic proposals for reform of foster care and adoption systems designed to support compassionate and humane alternatives to abortion such as making transracial adoptions easier.

By the time the 1996 campaign was officially launched on Labor Day, however, the new Catholic "vehicle" still had quite a long road to travel. According to its first executive director, Maureen Roselli, the Catholic Alliance numbered only 30,000 members as of September 1, 1996—a figure obtained by counting everyone on the mailing list, that is, everyone receiving a free subscription to the organization's newsletter. Presumably far lower was the number of members who had invested any amount of money or time in the Alliance (Roselli 1996; Steinfels 1996).

The Alliance got off to a shaky start, Roselli admitted, when Reed failed to consult with Catholic advisors before issuing the original announcement, the wording of which alienated many Catholics. Reed had a way of sounding condescending even when trying to build bridges; although he assured "sympathetic members of the American bishops' conference" that "we do not wish to speak for the Roman Catholic church or to usurp the authority of the bishops, which we respect" (Appleby 1996, 24), several bishops immediately denounced the Catholic Alliance.

In fact, the relationship between the Catholic Church and the Christian Right has been characterized by the Church's attitude of ambivalence toward the Christian Right. On the one hand, the U.S. bishops take the word "Catholic" to be their institutional trademark and have consistently resisted any attempts by outsiders to infringe upon the copyright. In the run-up to the 1996 election, they were particularly concerned about the diffusion of the Catholic voice when movements and groups claiming the name "Catholic" issued political statements at odds with their own positions.

On the other hand, many Catholic bishops feel that religious faith and practice is particularly vulnerable in contemporary American society, and they welcome allies in the struggle for religious freedom and viability. According to their 1995 Statement of Political Responsibility, for example, the bishops advocated many of the same positions taken by the Catholic Alliance/Christian Coalition, including strong opposition to abortion, the return of power to state and local governments (which is compatible with the Catholic principle of subsidiarity), and a stand against what they saw as creeping secularism in the tendency to interpret the U.S. Constitution's guarantee of religious freedom as freedom *from* religion's influence (*Origins*, 1995). Furthermore, much of the criticism of the Christian Right has taken the form of an attack on any religiously inspired participation in the political debate. "We should be watchful," as one Catholic official put it, "for the rhetoric and arguments aimed at marginalizing the religious right might one day be turned against us" (Dowling 1996, 11).

Despite this ambivalence, the majority of Catholic bishops in the mid-1990s feared that any decentering of the Catholic voice would contribute to a *de facto* democratization—and splintering—of the Church. "Just as Catholics for a Free Choice and other such groups suggest to the general public that not all Catholics agree with positions adopted by their bishops on birth control, abortion, and in-vitro fertilization, so will the religious right serve to suggest that not all Catholics accept the positions of Church leaders in social justice matters," wrote Richard J. Dowling, executive director of the Maryland Catholic Conference. "The Christian Coalition gives Catholic dissenters on the right a place, politically, to go" (Dowling 1996, 12).

The opposition of the bishops was not the only obstacle faced by the Christian Coalition in its attempt to make inroads into the Catholic voting bloc. The fledgling Catholic Alliance, in order to be even marginally successful in meeting its ambitious goals, must find a way to overcome the checkered history of Catholic-Protestant political relations in the United States, the profound theological and ecclesiological differences between evangelical Protestants and conservative Catholics, and the plurality and diversity of Catholic religious and political cultures in the United States.

Historical Patterns

In order to appreciate the difficulties faced by the Catholic Alliance and other elements of the Christian Right who would build a political coalition with American Catholics, one must understand the historical patterns of Catholic affiliation, ethnicity and assimilation; the political birth, aging and death of twentieth-century generational cohorts; and the fragmentation of Catholic religious culture following the Second Vatican Council (1962–65). The experience of the immigrant church shaped a dual political legacy for the twentieth century. On the one hand, nineteenth-century Irish-American Catholics, in reaction to the nativist policies formulated by the Know-Nothing Party on the eve of the Civil War, gave their allegiance to the Democrats. The allegiance grew stronger a generation later, when Catholics generally associated the Republicans and evangelical Protestants of the Progressive era with a new wave of anti-Catholicism promoted by the American Protective Association, whose members took an oath not to hire Catholic workers and to oppose Catholic candidates for political office (Ellis 1956). On the other hand, the influx of southern and eastern European Catholic immigrants in the 1880s and 1890s began to tip the Catholic vote toward the GOP.

This political divide among ethnic Catholics set the stage, David Leege (1996) observed, for the volatility of partisan affiliation and presidential vote choices that characterized Catholic politics in the twentieth century. Ethnic history and assimilation patterns determined Catholic partisanship. General patterns over the course of the century indicate that English, Scandinavian, and German Catholics have been solidly Republican; eastern European, Polish, Irish, Italian Catholics have been evenly split, especially in the most recent period; while French, Hispanic, and African American Catholics have remained solidly Democratic.

Trends within and across these various ethnic blocs have developed at different times and under various circumstances. With the 1928 presidential campaign of Al Smith, the rise of the Ku Klux Klan, and a new wave of nativism associated with the GOP, Catholics began moving en masse to the Democratic Party, and swelled its ranks during the presidency of Franklin Roosevelt. The New Deal coalition endured throughout the first two postwar decades and coincided with the assimilation of European Catholic ethnics into the American mainstream, the ascendancy of large numbers of Catholics into the middle class, and the suburbanization of the Catholic population.

In many ways this was the golden age of U.S. Catholicism. Catholic institutions, such as the parish and the parochial school, provided a strong sense of identity and solidarity for generations of immigrants, and served as way stations on the road to Americanization. Under the theological-philosophical canopy of neo-Thomism a revival in spirituality and associational life led to a parallel renewal of Catholic literature, art, and history (Halsey 1980; Gleason 1987). The 1940s and 1950s saw the popular culture's celebration of Catholic "innocence," patriotism, sports, and even religious life (with movies about attractive priests and nuns who would break out into song on a moment's notice). One historian, citing U.S. writer Flannery O'Connor, described the corresponding attitude of "Catholic smugness" (Dolan 1985, 352).

Neo-Thomism, versions of which informed the curricula of the parochial school system and Catholic colleges and universities, inculcated subtle and not-so-subtle political lessons. Ideologically, Catholic voters came closest in this period to forming a viable bloc. Fervid patriotism, virulent anticommunism, and strong identification with the working class and labor unions were the staples of the Catholic political identity. In the 1940s and 1950s, a majority of Catholics tended to vote Democratic with the exception of the presidential races of the 1950s, when they backed Eisenhower. In 1960, with an overwhelming confidence that they had arrived fully and permanently on the American political and cultural scene, 83 percent of Catholic voters helped to ensure the election of the first Catholic president, John F. Kennedy.

The 1960 election definitively removed the political stigma marking Catholics. Ironically, the election of a Catholic Democrat thereby also made it possible for the Republican Party to court the Catholic vote and promote Catholic politicians within its ranks. Social forces during the 1960s further contributed mightily to the unraveling of the New Deal Catholic coalition. The breakup of ethnic neighborhoods, the consolidation of suburbia, the divisive crisis of the Vietnam war, the violent controversy over civil rights and race relations in general and busing in particular, and the capture of the Democratic party by limousine liberals alienated Catholics from one another and from the Democratic Party.

When the Catholic baby boomers of the post–World War II era began to move into the economy in the 1970s, they ended any hope of reconstituting the old Catholic vote, for they formed a new generational cohort of voters with tendencies quite different from the New Dealers. For all their disgruntlement with the Democrats, no more than 35 percent of New Deal Catholics ever joined the Republican Party. Yet, boomers have always been less Democratic than their New Deal-era parents; the youngest part of this generation, which entered the electorate in 1980, was 20 percent less Democratic than their parents. Among this youngest cohort, Republican Catholics outnumber Democratic Catholics, and they are more loyal to their party. The Catholic boomers are disproportionately southern, and as fully Republican as are southern evangelical Protestants. The youngest boomers provided the Catholic margin for Ronald Reagan and George Bush, and they are part of the core of the Republican Party of the future (Leege 1996, 5–6).

When Catholics drifted to the GOP in the 1980s, on the surface they were repeating the patterns of the 1920s and the presidential elections of the 1950s. In a deeper sense, however, the current situation is unprecedented. The Catholic electorate is different in the 1990s in large part because the Catholic Church is radically different from that it was before the recent voting shift began approximately twenty years ago. If one admits even a degree of correlation between religious culture and political affiliation, it is clear that the changes brought by the Second Vatican Council to American Catholic religious culture stand behind the shifts in the Catholic electorate. Understanding the resulting new configurations of Catholic identity helps to explain why the potential candidates for membership in the Catholic Alliance form a very small pool indeed.

The Consequences of Internal Pluralism

By the time of Kennedy's election to the presidency, Catholic smugness was already giving way to Catholic conformity with the norms of the mainstream culture. Vanishing were the triumphant, massive public rituals that had been common in the presuburban world of American Catholicism. Such rituals were a powerful expression of the American Catholic devotional ethos, and withdrawal from them by the church laity signaled a dramatic shift in Catholic sensibility—away from formal ritual, sin, authority, and the supernatural (Dolan 1985, 221). The meanings and relationships symbolized in these rituals, originally developed in the context of a hierarchically controlled, deferential and devotional insular church, no longer expressed the values of Catholics yearning for the suburbs. The suburbs fostered family-centered activities and "pushed people away from commitments to participation in larger social networks." In short, the 1950s was "a key decade of change in the devotional ethos that had dominated the Catholic world view since the nineteenth century" (Kelly 1994, 317–18).

The waning of the comprehensive authority of the parish priest over his once-immigrant flock was also well advanced. By establishing his political independence from the pope and the bishops without losing his Catholic identity, Kennedy became an icon for the new postwar generation of upwardly mobile Catholics. These university-educated Catholic scientists, lawyers, politicans, and business executives—the parents of the baby boomers—were more likely than their immigrant grandparents to compartmentalize their religious identity and take their political and economic signals from the secular order rather than from their priests and bishops. Vatican II's emphasis on lay autonomy and leadership, coupled with its ringing endorsement of religious freedom, the priority of conscience, and the separation of church and state (enunciated in *Dignitatis Humanae,* the Declaration on Religious Liberty, which was crafted in large part by the American Jesuit John Courtney Murray), inadvertently reinforced the new sense of political independence and contributed to the fragmentation of the Catholic vote.

Among the most far-reaching consequences of Vatican II was the rise of theological pluralism within Roman Catholicism. Almost overnight, it seemed, biblical theology, versions of liberation theology, and other experiential theologies displaced neo-Thomism at the center of the Catholic intellectual world. The new theologies mirrored a new paradigm for the relationship between church and world, as Vatican II popularized the image of the church as a pilgrim on earth, a sinner on the road to salvation, in marked contrast to the preconciliar, Tridentine notion of the church as the spotless Bride of Christ, the "perfect, eternal society."

The awareness of options within Roman Catholicism inspired bold ventures (and misadventures) in religious education. Parochial school curricula, Confraternity of Christian Doctrine (CCD) textbooks, and adult education programs were overhauled. Influential Catholic educators questioned the compatibility of "education" and "formation," two concepts that preconciliar Catholics had understood to be intimately related. Reformers criticized Catholic educators for concentrating on content and failing to form free thinkers, while others attacked the very concept of formation, preferring to support an educational method supposedly more in keeping with secular progressive models of learning and with the new Catholic emphasis on ecumenism.

The model of Christian formation proposed by such critics adopted the progressive school's emphasis on the learner rather than the material to be learned. When conservatives complained that focusing on the learner would distract Catholic educators from teaching "objective" Church doctrine and cultivating obedience to the commandments and adherence to devotional practices, liberals dismissed those goals as inappropriate for a Church "no longer living in the climate of the last few hundred years—the climate of a Church intent on self-preservation, spending its efforts to hold its own, to preserve, to fight off attacks, to centralize authority, and to maintain order within the ranks" (Ryan 1964, 166–67).

"Reform" of parochial school and catechetical instruction and curriculum proceeded in somewhat haphazard fashion and failed to address the concern for the continuing education and formation of young adults and older Catholics. The institution seemed at a loss, so much so that Catholic priest and theologian Richard McBrien devoted a book (1969) to the fundamental question, *Do We Need the Church?* Five years later, in 1974, he found little reassurance when he surveyed postconciliar educational practice, and was moved to ask, *Has the Church Surrendered?* Theologians, McBrien reported, were challenging assumptions much more basic than the necessity of Catholic schools, including the nature and mission of the Church, the development of doctrine, the content of Christian ethics, and the authority of the papacy (McBrien 1974, 34). Each religious educator must work his or her way "through this difficult time of reconceptualization and reformulation" (McBrien 1977, 62).

Unfortunately, the crisis in American Catholic education and formation occurred at a moment when most Catholic laity needed more, not less, direction and explanation from the clergy regarding the changes introduced by the Council. Just when American Catholic educators were emphasizing process over content, the universal church was offering a great deal of "new" content to master.

The most politically charged development of Vatican II was the church's strong, renewed emphasis on the tenets of Catholic social teaching, an unfolding tradition inaugurated by Pope Leo XIII in 1891 with the promulgation of his encyclical *Rerum Novarum* (The Condition of Labor). Based on natural law, *Rerum Novarum* defended the right of workers to organize, asserted the inviolable and sacred right of the individual to own private property, and condemned atheistic socialism as well as the excesses of laissez-faire capitalism. From the time of Leo XIII, Catholic social teaching has been a specifiable body of doctrines and principles governing Catholic participation in the social order. As such, it forms the foundation of American Catholic political philosophy; it constitutes, in other words, the official frame of reference for every Catholic exercising his or her civic rights in the political order.

Certain documents of Vatican II—especially *Gaudium et Spes,* the Pastoral Constitution on the Church in the Modern World—can be read as positioning this body of social teaching in the very center of Roman Catholic self-understanding, doctrinal teaching, and pastoral practice. Vatican II's rejection of the theological dualism that had sometimes justified Catholic withdrawal from public policy debates, and its vigorous embrace of "the work of justice in the service of peace," shifted the church's attention from the heavenly reward to the mundane political and economic work to be done. In 1971 a synod of Catholic bishops meeting in Rome to reflect on this legacy of Vatican II issued the document *Justice in the World,* which proclaimed a principle held dear by a generation of Catholic social activists and educators: "Action on behalf of justice and participation in the transformation of the world fully appear to us as a constitutive dimension of the proclamation of the Gospel, or, in other words, of the Church's mission for the redemption of the human race and its liberation from every oppressive situation." (O'Brien and Shannon 1992, 289).

In several social encyclicals, Pope John Paul II has contributed key insights, developments, and applications to this growing body of social teaching. Its basic principles include: (1) the *common good,* the notion that Catholics ought to pursue policies and programs that serve the best interests of the public at large rather than a particular subgroup within society; (2) *solidarity,* the affirmation that all people at every level of society should participate together in building a just society; (3) *subsidiarity,* the dictum that greater and higher associations or governing bodies ought not to do what lesser and lower (more local) associations can do themselves (a sort of Catholic federalism); (4) a *preferential option for the poor,* a principle with concrete implications for a host of social programs, beginning with welfare; (5) the *priority and inviolability of human rights,* especially the cornerstone right to life, but also the economic rights to own private property, to work for a just wage, and so on; and (6) a *preferential option for the family* as the basic social unit.

However, a monumental case of bad timing hurt Catholics in the postconciliar years. Just when these principles were being articulated and discussed at the highest levels, most American Catholics—clergy, laity, and women religious alike—had neither the necessary preparation nor the specialized knowledge necessary to disseminate Catholic social teaching at every educational level. For over a decade prior to Vatican II, a small elite company of diocesan and religious order priests had been preparing for the changes, in effect, by studying the new theology from Europe and the growing tradition of Catholic social doctrine. In the 1960s they crafted their own programs of social action in urban and rural areas. When Vatican II seemed to give an official blessing to these efforts, these pioneers began to promote the teaching of the Catholic social tradition in the parishes as well as the Catholic colleges and universities. Their impact was limited, however, by other crises such as the growing number of defections from the priesthood and sisterhood, which diverted pastoral attention and energies elsewhere.

In short, the new pluralism had its dizzying downside. The debate about the proper relation of education and formation led to a general confusion in catechetical circles, exacerbated by the tendency of the new generation of directors of religious education to adopt what amounted to a pastiche approach to curricular reform—a dash of scripture here, a touch of pop psychology there. A stultifying randomness characterized methods of instruction and textbook content in the late 1960s and throughout the 1970s. In most cases, the coherent principles and teachings of Catholic social teaching regrettably did not form the foundation of the new catechetical approach.

Sociologist William Dinges has aptly characterized the period as a time of "severe disorientation, dysfunction, and institutional declension" (Dinges 1991, 80). The majority of American Catholic priests and women religious continued to work within the structures of parish and diocese, but they were serving an increasingly sophisticated American Catholic laity at home in the professional and business worlds—a laity that was increasingly qualified to participate in church governance. In the decade following the council, significant numbers of priests and women religious left the ministry, while others deserted traditional religious forms and abandoned preconciliar devotions, distinctive garb, and prescribed behavioral patterns and lifestyles. By the early 1970s, the Catholic Church in the United States had become paralyzed by dissent, by the variety of seemingly conflicting teachings attributed to Vatican

II, and by searching questions about the appropriate roles of clergy, laity, and women religious. Disarray and confusion in Catholic education was perhaps the strongest symptom of the identity crisis (Appleby 1989).

As a result, boomer Catholics, especially the younger members of the generation, either were not sufficiently exposed to the "new" body of Catholic social doctrine, or rejected it, along with other forms of authoritative teaching. In either case, it is clear that many boomers did not understand, much less experience, the intimate relationship between the new vernacular Mass and Vatican II's call to greater engagement in the works of social justice. The liturgical reforms, properly practiced and interpreted, were intended to reinforce the church's turn to the world; often, however, they served merely to confuse or bore untutored Catholics.

Thus, what could have been a stable and comprehensive foundation for a new Catholic solidarity on public and political issues became, instead, the province of a minority of "social justice Catholics," the subgroup of aging New Dealers and fresh-faced boomers who did accept and internalize Catholic social doctrine. These college-educated Catholics tend to be consistent participants in the sacramental life of the church, avid readers of the Bible, and leaders in voluntary and charitable organizations dedicated to the improvement of the social and economic conditions of the poor.

The explosion of pluralism in theology and moral teaching also contributed to the vague sense that much of Catholic teaching was offered on a consumerist model— take what you want and ignore the rest. Ironically, the U.S. bishops, who railed against "pick-and-choose Catholicism" in the 1970s and 1980s, may have contributed inadvertently to the ethos informing it. In their widely publicized pastoral letters on the economy and the arms race, the bishops acknowledged that people of good will, including Catholics who shared their basic theological assumptions and moral principles, have a right to disagree on the prudential application of those principles in formulating specific public policies. American Catholic neoconservatives took full advantage of this admission in rejecting the specific recommendations of the bishops' pastoral letter on the U.S. economy (*Economic Justice for All,* 1986). And, in the 1980s, other high-profile Catholic laymen (including cabinet members of Presidents Richard Nixon and Ronald Reagan) also offered spirited opposition to the efforts of U.S. bishops to disseminate Catholic social teaching through their pastoral letters.

In short, like most major historical events, Vatican II had unintended consequences. The postconciliar theological and religious pluralism, coupled with the failure of Catholic catechesis in general and the teaching of Catholic social doctrine in particular, helped to put an end to "the Catholic bloc" as a political entity. Plural Catholic religious cultures led to the contemporary situation of plural Catholic political cultures in the United States.

By the 1990s, the three generations of laypeople in the Church included pre-Vatican II Catholics, born before 1940; Vatican II Catholics, born in the 1940s and 1950s; and post-Vatican II Catholics, born in the 1960s and 1970s (D'Antonio, Davidson, Hoge, and Wallace 1996, 65). The Catholics whom Leege calls "New Deal Catholics" include the preconciliar generation as well as the older Catholics who came of age during Vatican II. The older boomers are also Vatican II Catholics, but those younger came of age in the postconciliar period.

On any number of religious and sociomoral issues, from a yearning for democracy in the Church to a belief in the supremacy of the individual in moral decisions, each succeeding generation has been increasingly liberal. On economic questions, however, lay Catholics have become increasingly conservative, with the younger boomers constituting by far the most conservative cohort.

According to a team of sociologists who published their findings in 1996, more than 50 percent of post-Vatican II Catholic laity (Leege's younger boomers) believe that the individual rather than the magisterium is the supreme moral judge in matters of birth control, abortion, homosexuality, and sex outside of marriage. At the same time, this research demonstrates that levels of religious commitment have declined over the generations: whereas 59 percent of pre-Vatican II Catholics think that "the Church is important," only 29 percent of the postconciliar Catholics agree with the statement (D'Antonio et al. 1996, 75). Mass attendance and daily prayer have fallen off in the same proportions, as have general levels of familiarity with Church teaching. Whereas 26 percent of the pre-Vatican II Catholics and 24 percent of the Vatican II Catholics are aware of the U.S. bishops' 1986 pastoral letter on the economy, only 11 percent of the post-Vatican II Catholics know of its existence (D'Antonio et al. 1996, 75–76).

Post–Vatican II Catholic boomers place a higher priority on being a good "Christian" than on being a good "Catholic." They have a deinstitutionalized and democratic view of the Church, reserving the right to make up their own minds on religious and moral as well as political and economic issues. They believe they have direct access to the Creator's love apart from the institutional Church and are more likely to disagree with the Church's teachings. They are almost entirely uninformed about Church teachings and lack a vocabulary that would help them to form a Catholic identity or interpret their Catholic experiences. Finally, they are situational in their ethical thinking (D'Antonio et al. 1996, 83–89). "Let's face it; we've lost" is the way one Vatican II Catholic sizes up the battle to pass on a distinctive Catholic identity to the next generation (Carlin 1996, 8).

One team of Catholic sociologists is more sanguine. They argue that catechesis and Catholic education have not failed, and point to data indicating that the postconciliar Catholics with the most Catholic schooling are more committed, if less traditional, than Catholics with less Catholic schooling. On abortion, however, those with high levels of Catholic schooling *are* more traditional than their peers (D'Antonio et al. 1996, 99–100).

Young Catholic boomers, natural political conservatives, would seem to be natural candidates for membership in new Christian Right organizations like the Catholic Alliance, but they are not. Those who are Republican say they are attracted to the party on economic rather than sociomoral grounds. Survey data indicate that the more deeply religious Catholics—those who pray and attend Mass regularly—are less likely to be Republican, despite the party's antiabortion platform. Indeed, among both New Deal and baby boom Catholics, "those for whom religion is *less* salient in both groups are more likely to vote Republican." New Deal Catholics, the data indicate, are more religiously involved and socially compassionate on welfare issues.

In short, the younger Catholic boomers are already Republicans—indeed, they form a significant part of the base of the so-called Gingrich revolution—but they are not engaged by the sociomoral issues (abortion, school prayer, and so on) upon which organizations like the Catholic Alliance presumably stand or fall. Their parents, on the other hand, are attracted to these social issues and the moral agenda of the Christian Right, but they remain within the Democratic fold because they are closer to the Democratic Party on all but a couple of the "consistent life ethic" issues. "Research has shown the catechesis of the parents to be far more communitarian, while for the children to be heavily individualistic" (Leege 1996, 6).

Prominent in this profile is the weakness—the relatively limited impact—of Catholic social teaching as it has been interpreted and taught by the U.S. bishops and the "social justice Catholics" working in the parishes and educational institutions. Young Catholic boomers have been notably reluctant to support legislation and other policy initiatives designed to translate the "common good" and the "preferential option for the poor" into taxpayer-supported public welfare programs. The future seems to be with them, given the aging and death of preconciliar, New Deal Catholics. Strikingly, 30 percent of those who describe themselves as Catholic in surveys never attend Mass and are not religious; they are also disproportionately under forty-five years of age. When economic issues predominate, these younger boomers vote Republican; when social issues are paramount, they vote Democratic. At the other end of the spectrum are the (far less numerous) social justice Catholics: when economic issues are paramount, they vote Democratic; when social issues are front-burner, they vote Republican (Leege 1996, 7).

Locating a Catholic Constituency for the Christian Right

A new Christian Right–inspired organization like the Catholic Alliance appeals to neither of these cohorts; indeed, it appeals to few, if any, of the contemporary Catholic cultures. First, white Catholic liberals, including the social justice Catholics described above, tend to decry the influence of the Christian Right, which they see as captive of the upper class and hostile to the poor. Although the Catholic bishops as a body are conservative on sociomoral issues like abortion, they tend to be left-of-center on social and economic issues and opposed to many of the positions taken by the Christian Coalition. As we have seen, the bishops as a body failed to endorse the Catholic Alliance, and many individual bishops publicly denounced it.

Second, survey data on Hispanic Catholics, Asian Catholics, and African American Catholics indicate that Christian Right–style organizations like the Catholic Alliance face an uphill battle with all three voting blocs. Catholic leaders from each of these groups have voiced their opposition to the Republican Party due to its policies on immigration and affirmative action—and they tend to identify the Christian Right with the Republican Party. The Christian Coalition has had limited success in its efforts to establish a nonpartisan identity and to recruit Hispanic Americans and African Americans to its own local branches. On the other hand, opposition to abortion runs high among these Catholics, complicating their political allegiances and providing a potential opening for the Alliance.

Third, as noted above, many white Catholic middle- and upper-middle-class boomers, especially the younger cohort, are already Republican, or tend to vote Republican. But most of these Catholics are motivated primarily by economic rather than sociomoral issues, and are unlikely to join a Christian Coalition–style Catholic organization.

That leaves, as the natural constituency for the Catholic Alliance, the Catholic subculture of religiously conservative and traditionalist or "orthodox" Catholics. These two groups have a similar religious orientation in that they reject many of the postconciliar developments in the American Catholic community, but they differ on the evaluation of the Council itself, the diagnosis of the present situation of the church, and the type of remedies, political or otherwise, to be sought. Thus I shall treat them separately.

In current political discourse, the term "conservative Catholics" (Roman Catholics who are religiously orthodox) is used interchangeably with "Catholic conservatives" (Catholics who are politically conservative). This is misleading, however, for it is the highly motivated cadre of conservative Catholic activists and polemicists, rather than the politically and economically conservative boomer Catholics, who are the Catholic counterpart to the Christian Right. These activist conservative Catholics are relatively few in number, however, and do not represent—and are not able to mobilize—a Catholic version of the hundreds of thousands of evangelical Protesant precinct workers nationwide who turn out the vote for the Christian Coalition.

Some of these conservative Catholics are found on the membership rolls of Chrisitan Right organizations, including those headed by Catholics like Phyllis Schlafly of the Eagle Forum, which seek to counter feminist influence and economic agendas. Neoconservative Catholics, such as George Weigel, Richard John Neuhaus, and Michael Novak, collaborate with conservative evangelicals, but they are intellectuals and think-tank denizens rather than political organizers. There are, it is true, New Right Catholic political operatives such as Paul Weyrich, founder of the Free Congress Foundation and the Heritage Foundation, who have made common cause with the Christian Right in the past. Weyrich, in fact, coined the phrase "moral majority" and helped to establish the Rev. Jerry Falwell's organization of that name (Kissling and Shannon 1994, 5). Unfortunately for the Catholic Alliance, however, conservative Catholics already have their own religiopolitical organizations, and are unlikely to join evangelical Protestants in a political coalition.

Among the most prominent of these organizations is the Catholic Campaign for America (CCA), founded in 1991 by Christian Right activist and Republican campaign official Marlene Ewell as a (supposedly nonpartisan) coalition of conservative Catholic leaders rather than a mass membership organization. Prominent Catholics such as William Bennett, Patrick Buchanan, former Treasury Secretary William Simon, and former Pennsylvania governor Robert Casey—all but the last are Republicans—make up the leadership of the organization. CCA convenes representatives of other conservative Catholic organizations such as Neuhaus's Institute on Religion and Public Life (publisher of the neoconservative journal *First Things*) and Legatus, Domino Pizza owner Thomas S. Monaghan's club for corporate executives. Opposition to abortion, homosexuality, and feminism are its political hallmarks. Like the Christian Coalition, CCA seeks to mobilize and train leaders at the local level, but thus far it has been most active among established national and state leaders, and is known more for its press conference and "gala" dinners than for its grassroots activism. At times CCA has cosponsored events with the Christian Coalition, such as a press conference excoriating media coverage of Pope John Paul II's 1993 visit to the United States. Significantly, CCA pronouncements refer only occasionally to American Catholic social teaching on economic justice and international peace, while adopting the Republican Party's general pro-family agenda (Askin 1994).

Other conservative Catholic organizations, such as the Opus Dei movement and the lay catechetical organization, Catholics United for the Faith, devote the lion's share of their energies to the internal pastoral and ecclesial affairs of the Roman Catholic Church, rather than to the campaigns of a secular political party. Unlike the CCA, they do not aspire to significant gains from grassroots political activism; like the CCA, they do not achieve such gains.

On the far-right end of the spectrum of conservative Catholics are the "orthodox" Catholics, also known as Catholic traditionalists. They are "fundamentalist" Catholics who take their religion dogmatically and find any form of collaboration with Protestants unpalatable. Unhappy or even furious with the way the reforms of Vatican II have been interpreted and implemented, they tend to be separatists. More apocalyptic than the vast majority of mainstream or conservative Catholics, traditionalists believe that the Church has fallen into apostasy—with the exception of the saved remnant, to which they belong. This conviction prevents traditionalist Catholics from turning their opposition to postconciliar Catholic liberalism into membership in a conservative Catholic organization. Unlike Protestant fundamentalists, however, traditionalist Catholics find it difficult, ideologically and organizationally, to reject the church and form a new one. A central dogma of Roman Catholicism is the divine source and nature of the Church itself;

would-be Protestant dissenters are unencumbered by such a teaching. As a result, most Catholic traditionalist organizations exist on the margins, unable or unwilling to mobilize significant numbers of followers for political action. Even if this were to change, however, such Catholics would not necessarily join the Catholic Alliance. Passionate opposition to abortion is indeed a notable characteristic of the traditionalist Catholics, but it is situated in a religious world far different from that of other conservative Christians (Dinges 1995, 241–55).

Conservative Catholics in general, with the exception of the elites of the CCA, are much more likely to take their political and social cues from the social encyclicals of Pope John Paul II than from the Republican Party platform. Keenly aware of what they see as the connection between the greed of pro-market conservatives and the selfishness of pro-choicers and the abortion industry, conservative Catholics disdain the GOP strategy of steering to the middle on social issues while going to the right on economic issues. That is exactly the opposite course from the one that would appeal to their deepest concerns. In the 1996 pre-election debate, orthodox Catholics referred darkly to "the New Age Republican agenda of more abortion and contraception, euthanasia, homosexual marriages, slashes in Medicare and Social Security, enforced work, school-to-work training programs, and, in international affairs, the role of 'global peacekeeper' " (Likoudis 1996, 8).

Uneasy Alliance Ahead

The two most important changes within the Catholic community in the last thirty years in the United States—a shift in voting patterns that has increased the Republican Party's share of the Catholic vote, and the community's increasingly lax adherence to Catholic teaching on everything from artificial birth control to social and economic teachings (particularly among the young and affluent)—are related. The social justice Catholics who emerged in the 1960s and 1970s were among those liberal Catholics who introduced pedagogical innovations into the educational system and supported dissent from official teaching (often with the intention of promoting a more liberal, social justice–oriented style of Catholicism to the detriment of traditional devotional practices). Ironically, this had the effect of undermining the authority of all Catholic teaching, including the social justice prescriptions, and therefore contributed inadvertently to the Catholic swing to the right in the 1980s.

Meanwhile, rank-and-file conservative Catholics pay more attention to the papal encyclicals than they do to their tax rates when voting. In the 1980s the GOP benefitted from the windfall of these voters into their camp by virtue of their opposition to abortion. But these Catholics witnessed twelve years of tepid action on this issue from Republican presidents. Furthermore, the absence of Catholic-concern issues from the Contract with America, and the blatantly political compromises of the '96 GOP convention, drove home the conclusion that the Republican Party is no friend of religiously conservative Catholics. These Catholics were uneasy about Dole and Gingrich and uncomfortable about cozying up to born-again Protestant evangelicals. They took as a matter of faith the connection between the consumer culture promoted by free-market capitalism and what Pope John Paul II called "the culture of death." Indeed, many traditionalist Catholics spoke quite harshly about capitalism—to the point of calling it an "evil system."

All this bodes ill for new Christian Right organizations such as the Catholic Alliance. Perhaps it will achieve supernova status, flaring vividly in a moment of novelty, never to be seen in the political heavens again. If it is to be more than that, the Alliance will have to negotiate the twisting path between Catholic religious culture and Catholic political affiliation—and do so amid the further complication that there are now a dizzying number of Catholic religious cultures in the United States.

Notes

I am indebted to John H. Haas, a Notre Dame Ph.D. candidate, for his assistance in researching the material for this chapter and collaborating with me in shaping some of its themes.

1. The importance of the U.S. Catholic vote is a matter of public record: while the 60 million Catholics constitute approximately one-fourth of the U.S. population, the 30 million voters among them account for 30 percent of the actual electorate. Furthermore, the Catholic population is concentrated in the ten largest electoral college states, including California, New York, Texas, and Florida (all of which contain sizeable populations of Hispanic Catholics, who continued in the 1990s to vote overwhelmingly Democratic, except for the Cuban Americans in Florida). In battleground states such as Michigan, Ohio, Illinois, Wisconsin, Pennsylvania, New Jersey, and Connecticut, Catholics account for up to 41 percent of the voters.

2. In 1992 Bush and Perot together attracted more Catholic voters than did Clinton.

References

Appleby, R. Scott. 1989. "Present to the People of God: The Transformation of the Roman Catholic Parish Priesthood." In *Transforming Parish Ministry: The Changing Roles of Catholic Clergy, Laity, and Women Religious*, edited by Jay Dolan, R. Scott Appleby, Patricia Bryne, and Debra Cambell, 3–127. New York: Crossroad.

———. 1996. Review of *Active Faith* by Ralph Reed. *Commonweal* 123 (27 September): 23–24.

Askin, Steve. 1994. *A New Rite: Conservative Catholic Organizations and Their Allies*. Catholics for a Free Choice.

Carlin, David R., Jr. 1996. "Let's Face It, We've lost." *Commonweal* 123 (17 May): 8–9.

D'Antonio, William V., James D. Davidson, Dean R. Hoge, and Ruth A. Wallace. 1996. *Laity American and Catholic: Transforming the Church*. Kansas City, Mo.: Sheed & Ward.

Dinges, William D. 1991. "Roman Catholic Traditionalism." In *Fundamentalisms Observed*, edited by Martin E. Marty and R. Scott Appleby, 66–101. Chicago: University of Chicago Press.

———. 1995. " 'We Are What You Were': Roman Catholic Traditionalism in the United States." In *Being Right: Conservative Catholics in America*, edited by Mary Jo Weaver and R. Scott Appleby, 241–69. Bloomington, Ind.: Indiana University Press.

Dolan, Jay P. 1985. *The American Catholic Experience*. Notre Dame, Ind.: University of Notre Dame Press.

Dowling, Richard J. 1996. The Catholic Alliance. Unpublished paper.

Ellis, John Tracy, ed. 1956. *Documents of American Catholic History*. Milwaukee, Wis.: Bruce Publishing Co.

Gillespie, Ed. 1996. "The Catholic Vote." *Rising Tide* (May/June): 1–5.

Gleason, Philip. 1987. *Keeping the Faith: American Catholicism, Past and Present*. Notre Dame, Ind.: University of Notre Dame Press.

Halsey, William M. 1980. *The Survival of American Innocence: Catholicism in an Era of Disillusionment, 1920–1940*. Notre Dame, Ind.: University of Notre Dame Press.

Kelly, Timothy. 1994. "Suburbanization and the Decline of Catholic Ritual in Pittsburgh." *Journal of Social History* 28 (Winter): 311–30.

Kissling, Frances, and Denise Shannon. 1994. "Who's Right? Catholics and the Culture War." In *A New Rite: Conservative Catholic Organizations and Their Allies*. New York: Catholics for a Free Choice.

Leege, David. 1996. The Catholic Vote in the 1996 Presidential Election. Unpublished lecture, 2 May 1996 at University of Notre Dame, South Bend, Indiana.

Likoudis, Paul. 1996. "Dole's 'Civility' Signals End of Party's Principles." *The Wanderer* 129 (June 20): 1, 8.

McBrien, Richard P. 1969. *Do We Need the Church?* New York: Harper & Row.
————. 1974. *Has the Church Surrendered?* Denville, N.J.: Dimension Books.
————. 1977. *Basic Questions for Christian Educators.* Winona, Minn.: St. Mary's College Press.
O'Brien, David J., and Thomas A. Shannon, eds. 1992. *Catholic Social Thought: The Documentary Heritage.* Maryknoll, N.Y.: Orbis Press.
Origins. 1995. Vol 25 (22): 369–83.
Reed, Ralph. 1996. *Active Faith: How Christians Are Changing the Soul of American Politics.* New York: The Free Press.
Roselli, Maureen. 1996. Interview by R. Scott Appleby. 31 August.
Ryan, Mary Perkins. 1964. *Are Parochial Schools the Answer? Catholic Education in Light of the Council.* New York: Holt, Rinehart and Winston.
Steinfels, Peter. 1996. "Beliefs." *New York Times*, 7 September.

7

Still Seeing in Black and White: Racial Challenges for the Christian Right

Allison Calhoun-Brown

Religion in the United States has always been fraught with racial tension. It is impossible to understand the challenge of racial diversity in the Christian Right without recognizing this fact. From the beginning of the Atlantic slave trade through the civil rights movement, the evangelical traditions of blacks and whites have been separate, distinct, and most often opposed to one another.

Blacks are overwhelmingly evangelical in orientation. They are substantially more likely than whites to say that they believe in the inerrancy of scripture, the divinity of Christ, his physical resurrection from the dead, and the necessity of a "born-again" experience in order to receive salvation (Wilcox 1992). However, they do not worship with white evangelicals who subscribe to exactly the same beliefs. In fact, the founding of many of the major black denominations was a direct response to racism (Lincoln and Mamiya 1990). The establishment of these organizations was not the result of doctrinal disagreement, but in response to unequal and restrictive treatment—in protest of the alarming inconsistencies between teachings and expressions of faith.

For whites, doctrinal orthodoxy supported slavery, segregation, and inequality; for blacks, this same orthodoxy became the basis for the struggle against these injustices. Black churches played a very important role not only in the teaching of the doctrine but in the struggle as well. Gayraud Wilmore captured the spirit of the relationship with the observation that "the NAACP met in many churches immediately after the benediction was pronounced. It used to be a truism that the black church was the NAACP on its knees" (Wilmore 1983, 142). The fact that Wilmore could assert that the black church and the leading social action organization were only minimally differentiated speaks to the impact that religion had on the ideology of African American people. The fact that Ralph Reed (1996), the head of the Christian Coalition, acknowledged that "there was a time in our nation's history when the white evangelical church was not only on the sidelines, but on the wrong side of the most central struggle for social justice in this century" speaks to the degree of divergence in the two evangelical traditions.

However, since late 1994 the theme of racial reconciliation has been sounded repeatedly in the evangelical community. Since then, the National Association of Evangelicals began discussing the possibility of closer relations with the Interdenominational National Black Evangelicals Alliance (*Christianity Today*, 6 Feb. 1995, 48); the nation's leading black and white Pentecostal groups used a foot washing ceremony to close years of racial separation (*Christianity Today*, 12 Dec. 1994, 58); the Southern Baptist Convention apologized for condoning racism (*Christianity Today*, 14 Aug. 1995, 53); and early in 1996, the evangelical men's movement, Promise Keepers, gathered almost 40,000 clergymen in Atlanta for an event called "Breaking Down the Walls" in which they pledged to reach beyond racial and denominational barriers (*Christianity Today*, 8 April 1996, 88; *Christian Century*, 6 March 1996: 254–55). While none of these organizations has an overtly political agenda, and none of these overtures will erase hundreds of years of history, the hope among some members of the Christian Right is that these acts can begin to create a climate that could foster greater racial inclusiveness not only in the evangelical religious community but in the political coalition called the Christian Right as well. "If millions of new recruits—churchgoing blacks and conservative Catholics—could be welded together in a great pro-family, Christian coalition, these frustrated Americans could control the national political agenda and lead the country back toward a more spiritual way of life" (*Wall Street Journal*, 19 July 1994, A1).

The logic is that for blacks, conservative doctrinal beliefs might well lead to conservative political attitudes and behaviors. However, this has not happened. Electorally, black evangelicals have not rallied with the Christian Right. This chapter examines the theoretical bases for this lack of mobilization and identifies opportunities and challenges to efforts to integrate the electoral constituency of the Christian Right, defined as those who adopt conservative political attitudes toward electoral objects because of their conservative religious values or beliefs. The emphasis upon electoral political objects is important because the desire of the Christian Right is not only for black evangelicals to hold conservative religious and social values, but to translate these preferences into the electoral arena. Of course, this definition encompasses a much larger number than those who actually belong to an organization of the Christian Right or even who "support" them or what they are doing. Most people never join political groups, and it is possible to hold conservative religious and political values and not be very favorable to particular Christian Right organizations (Sigelman, Wilcox and Buell 1987; Wilcox 1987; Johnson, Tamney and Burton 1989). However, as long as these individuals have ideas that are congruent with those of the Christian Right, they are candidates for and can be counted as part of "the great pro-family coalition." For this reason, the focus here is not on racial diversity in the organizations of the Christian Right, but rather on those factors that help or hinder the appeal of the Christian Right's positions and electoral priorities within the African American community.

Theories of Evangelical Mobilization

Many scholars (Wuthnow 1989, 1988; Lipset 1982; Hunter 1983) have contended that the evangelical way of life is at odds with, and to a certain extent under siege from, the "rational" and scientific forces of modernity. One of the most popular and parsimonious explanations for the politicization of the Christian Right is that of lifestyle defense (Bruce 1988; Lorentzen 1980; Page and Clelland 1978). Lifestyle defense theory holds that, because evangelicals perceive a threat to the integrity of their way of life, they seek to have congruity between their beliefs and public policies. Plainly put, society is "going to hell in a handbasket," and evangelicals have politically mobilized to stop the descent.

According to lifestyle defense theory, mobilization is an entirely rational response to threat. Wald (1987) credited the return of the Christian Right to the political arena largely to evangelical concerns about lifestyle issues following the social upheaval of the 1970s. From this perspective, it is no wonder that in the 1990s "family values" are especially salient in the white evangelical community. Homosexuality, equal rights, abortion, and untraditional morality undermine and conflict with their understanding of the scriptural way of life. The perception of discrepancies between their religious beliefs and their perceptions of public policies encourages action on the part of evangelicals to reconcile these differences. Theoretically, if black evangelicals share such beliefs, they too will adopt policy positions similar to the rest of the evangelical community.

However, black evangelicals have not done so. Although a number of studies have found that conservative religious beliefs do predict conservative social positions (Driedger 1974; Wilcox 1990; Kellstedt and Smidt 1993), black evangelicals are not part of the electoral constituency of the Christian Right. Many researchers cite the uniqueness of the black religious tradition as an explanation for this divergence. But how exactly does the tradition act as a hindrance? Why does the link between conservative issue positions and conservative political positions not work in the black evangelical community?

Symbolic politics theory may offer some explanation. According to symbolic politics theory, ordinary citizens' attitudes are organized by long-standing predispositions like partisan identification, political ideology, racial prejudice, and values such as individualism, egalitarianism, and postmaterialism (Sears and Citrin 1985; Conover and Feldman 1981; Feldman 1983; Rokeach 1969). In a large number of studies, self-interest had much less influence on policy and candidate preferences than did long-standing predispositions (Sears, Lau, Tyler, and Allen 1980; Sears and Funk 1991). As Sears (1993, 120) explained, "the symbolic politics process is characterized by generally unthinking, reflexive, affective responses to remote attitude objects rather than by calculations of probable costs and benefits whether personal or not." The critical matter is how an issue hits someone at "gut level."

From this perspective, behavior is contingent on symbolic political attitudes. Several recent studies have found that feelings about major societal groups provide much of the substance of these attitudes (Jelen 1993, 1991a, 1991b; Conover 1985; Leege, Lieske, and Wald 1989; Guth, Jelen, Kellstedt, Smidt, and Wald 1988). Jelen (1993, 178) has demonstrated that "group related attitudes provide cognitive structures through which the political world can be simplified and understood" (see also Tajfel 1981). According to symbolic politics theory, it is not as important in explaining political behaviors and opinions to know how an issue affects an individual as it is to know symbolically what that issue means to him or her. Much of that processing rests on a person's affective evaluation of groups that he or she symbolically associates with that issue. Jelen (1991a, 121–22) has shown that "outgroup evaluations are considerably more potent as predictors than religious self identifications," concluding that "the application of religious beliefs to political issue positions requires identifying 'enemies' who provide a tangible source of opposition." Theoretically, if black evangelicals identify the same "enemies" and symbolically associate issues with them, then the political attitudes and behaviors of black evangelicals should be similar to that of white evangelical Christians.

Thus, in explaining the lack of support for conservative electoral objects among black evangelicals, two explanations are available. Either black evangelicals do not really perceive the same societal threat that white evangelicals do, or (even with the perception of threat) black evangelicals do not symbolically interpret the threat in the same way.

Assessing African American Political Opinions and Behavior

The data set for this analysis came from the 1992 American National Election Study (ANES) conducted by the Center for Political Studies and the Inter-University Consortium for Political and Social Research at the University of Michigan. A total of 2,485 voting eligible individuals were interviewed prior to the 1992 election and 2,255 were reinterviewed after that election. The total number of African Americans in the first panel was 318 and in the second panel 180. While it would be preferable to have larger numbers of African Americans in the survey, the ANES is used because it provides the best operationalization of evangelical respondents and allows for the kinds of comparisons between whites and blacks that are necessary for this analysis.

Dependent Variables

Since I am defining the constituency of the Christian Right as those who adopt conservative political attitudes toward electoral objects because of their conservative religious values, five political objects were utilized to assess conservative electoral actions and attitudes. In the first, a simple action measure, respondents were asked whether or not they voted in the 1992 presidential election for George Bush, the preferred candidate of the Christian Right. This operationalization is also included because it provides a strict measure of electoral mobilization. As voting is the cornerstone of political participation in the United States, the first step in evaluating whether conservative religious beliefs affect conservative political behavior is to look at their relationship to electoral participation.

However, because relatively low numbers of African Americans traditionally vote for Republican candidates, two other, more cognitive,
measures of support for political objects were used to assess the impact
of conservative religious beliefs on politics in the African American
community. Respondents were asked not only if they voted for Bush or
Bill Clinton, but how they felt about them as well. Support for each
candidate was measured via feeling thermometer scales adjusted for the
respondent's individual response pattern.[1] Party support and ideological
position were the final two cognitive measures of electoral objects used.
Several analysts (Lopatto 1985; Kellstedt 1989a; Wilcox 1989; Penning
1994) have noted the growing relationship between the Christian Right
and the Republican Party. Some assert that "evangelical Protestants . . .
are a fulcrum on which both present and future party alignments rest"
(Kellstedt, Green, Guth, and Smidt 1994, 309). Supporters of the Christian Right also tend to be more conservative than most Americans
across a broad range of issues. Green and Guth (1987) found conservative ideological congruence to be a strong predictor of support for the
Moral Majority, a Christian Right organization, among those that gave
to political action committees. Both party support and ideological position are measured on standard seven point scales. On each scale conservatives and Republicans represent the high end of the scale.

Operationalizing Evangelicals

A debate exists in the literature regarding the proper way to opera-
tionalize evangelicals. They can be identified on the basis of self-identification (Smidt 1988), on the basis of denomination (Lopatto 1985), or
on the basis of doctrine. However, self-identification categories are not
mutually exclusive and may not be clearly understood (Green and Guth
1988). Discrepancies may exist between a respondent's personal theological beliefs and the predominant theological beliefs of his or her
denomination (Wald, Owen, and Hill 1988). Exactly what doctrinal
components all evangelicals share is also open to debate (Kellstedt
1989b).
Operationalizing evangelicals among blacks presents special challenges. Even though a majority of African Americans hold evangelical
beliefs, less than 7 percent identified themselves as such in the ANES
data. The label "evangelical" is simply not salient in the African American community. The term touches on the historic separation between
black and white churches over the issue of slavery and segregation. To
some extent the word itself is a challenge to racial diversity in the Chris-

tian Right. One writer suggested that for most black churches the term itself is either "unknown and unused or so politically loaded that it should be called the 'e' word" (Sidey 1990).

Denominational operationalizations are also problematic. Almost 70 percent of churchgoing blacks belong to Baptist denominations (Lincoln and Mamiya 1990). Due to the lack of hierarchical structure in this family of denominations, Baptist churches tend to be much more theologically, organizationally, and financially independent than churches in other denominations. This is particularly true in the African American community, where charismatic leadership qualities and a "call from the Lord" have traditionally meant more than formal doctrinal training (Lincoln and Mamiya 1990). Because of the large number of black Baptists and the autonomy of black congregations, using denomination as the operationalization of evangelical may not fully or adequately capture this theological tradition.

Thus, a doctrinal measure of evangelicalism is employed in this study, as I assume that doctrine is the foundation of conservative religious beliefs and a predominant emphasis of evangelicalism (Kellstedt 1989b). Evangelicals, then, are identified as those who say that they have had a born-again experience *and* believe that the Bible is, at a minimum, the inspired Word of God. In the 1992 ANES survey, almost 50 percent of blacks and 30 percent of whites met this criteria.

Lifestyle Defense

According to lifestyle defense theory, the mobilization of the Christian Right is the result of a threat to their way of life. Conservative organizations such as the Moral Majority, Christian Voice, Roundtable, and National Christian Action Coalition in the 1980s, and groups such as the Christian Coalition, Family Research Council, and National Right to Life Committee in the 1990s, have used essentially the same set of issues to politicize evangelicals. Strong conservative positions on these issues are intended to combat the moral relativism that many members of the Christian Right believe is causing society to become increasingly removed from Judeo-Christian principles and perspectives (Shriver 1981). What is often described as the "family values" agenda can be divided into four broad components. These components include the issue of abortion, the rights of homosexuals, the status and role of women, and traditional morality in society. Although the politics of each of these issues is different, the Christian Right has united around them in an attempt to save America from, as Bill Bennett (1993) described, "a corruption of the heart, a turning away of the soul." To assess the veracity of the lifestyle defense theory, composite measures of each of these issues were constructed.[2]

In addition to these key social issues, controls were included for other issues understood to be important in electoral assessments. Differences between black and white evangelicals may be attributable to divergent positions on racial issues and the appropriate role of government in the economy. Because blacks tend to have much more liberal positions on these issues than whites, not taking these issues into consideration may lead to spurious results. Both economic and racial perceptions have long been offered as explanations for political behavior (Carmines and Stimson 1989; Kinder and Sears 1981). Additive indices of both the government's role in the economy[3] and racial issues[4] positions are included in order to evaluate these alternative explanations.

Symbolic Politics

According to symbolic politics theory, political actions and opinions are largely contingent on affective responses. Group evaluations provide the content for much of these responses. In operationalizing symbolic politics, this study focuses on affect toward groups most often associated with the social issues defined above. For abortion and status of women, attitudes toward the woman's movement generally and feminists specifically were evaluated. The affective component of positions on homosexual rights was measured as feelings for homosexuals. The affective component of moral traditionalism was operationalized as feelings toward conservatives and liberals, Democrats and Republicans. Society's responsibility to improve the position of blacks was compared to feelings toward blacks, and the affective component of the appropriate role of government was measured by feelings toward the federal government, Congress, Democrats, and Republicans. Each affective measure was assessed using a feeling thermometer. All thermometer ratings were corrected for positivity bias, and higher scores indicate warmer feelings toward the group. In addition to the above independent variables, controls are included for the standard political attitude and behavior predictors—specifically, these control variables included age, region, gender, partisan identification, and level of education.

Comparing Black and White Evangelicals

As other studies have found, these data confirm that conservative religious doctrine does indeed predict conservative social position for both black and white evangelicals. As table 7.1 records, on each social or moral issue position, doctrine was an important indicator of conservative issue positions for both blacks and whites. If threat is measured by the uniqueness of the evangelical perspective relative to the rest of society, one cannot conclude that black evangelicals are not disturbed by

TABLE 7.1
Black and White Evangelicals
Determinants of Issue Positions
Regression Coefficients

	Women's Rights	**Abortion**
Black Evangelicals	.73***	1.00***
Black Nonevangelicals	.20	.22
White Evangelicals	.74***	1.58***
White Nonevangelicals		
(constant)	1.84***	.81**
Adjusted R²	.12	.20

	Traditional Morality	**Homosexual Rights**
Black Evangelicals	1.09***	.28*
Black Nonevangelicals	.77	-.01
White Evangelicals	2.53***	.58***
White Nonevangelicals		
(constant)	-3.12***	1.31***
Adjusted R²	.24	.22

	Position of Blacks	**Government Role**
Black Evangelicals	-3.26***	-.89***
Black Nonevangelicals	-2.83***	-.63***
White Evangelicals	.13	.17*
White Nonevangelicals	10.67***	-1.52***
Adjusted R²	.27	.25

All issue positions coded toward conservative perspective. Controls included in each model for age, education, gender, region, and partisan identification.
*p < .05; **p < .005; ***p < .0005

contemporary societal values. On these traditional "family values," conservative doctrinal beliefs promote conservative issue positions in the black as well as in the white community.

However, black evangelicals, like the rest of black Americans, are also very concerned about the position of blacks in society and the need to maintain an activist government. In both cases, conservative doctrine predicted the most liberal policy positions. It may be that these issues represent a bigger threat to black evangelicals than do the the deterioration of family values. For whites, evangelical doctrine did not influence stances on the position of blacks but was a strong positive predictor of a more restrained role for the government.

Nonetheless, according to symbolic politics theory, it is not enough to know an individual's perception about the issue; one must also know how the individual symbolically interprets the issue. How an individual affectively responds to an issue is based largely on their evaluations of the group associated with the issue. Table 7.2 shows that issues do not resonate the same way in the black evangelical community as they do in the white evangelical community. The table displays each social issue with the affect toward the groups that would most logically be associated with it. The smaller number of black cases precludes relatively healthy correlations from achieving statistical significance. Still, the magnitude of the correlation between the issue and its related affectual group is, on every moral position, considerably weaker for black evangelicals than for white evangelicals. For instance, even given black evangelicals very conservative positions on women's role in society, that position does not translate or reflect back on their evaluations of either feminists or the women's movement—indicating that symbolically the issue does not mean the same thing for the two groups. Traditional morality is strongly associated with ideological affect for white evangelicals, but overall the relationship is much weaker for black religious conservatives. The correlation between homosexual rights and feelings toward homosexuals is stronger for black evangelicals, but still much less than the white evangelical correlation. Only with regard to the correlation between the abortion issue and affect toward feminists do white and black evangelicals come close to each other.

Table 7.2 also records the correlations between nonmoral social positions and their related affectual groups. As on moral issues, the association between the positions on the appropriate government role and related affectual groups was much stronger for white evangelicals than for blacks. Only with regard to the position of blacks in society and feelings toward blacks generally was the magnitude of the correlation for black evangelicals larger than the one for whites. On this issue the relationship for whites was not statistically significant.

TABLE 7.2
Black and White Evangelicals
Correlation Affect and Issue Position

	Black Evangelicals	White Evangelicals
Women's Role		
Feminists	.00	-.34***
Women's Movement	-.09	-.35***
Abortion		
Feminists	-.29**	-.35***
Women's Movement	-.22	-.40**
Traditional Morality		
Conservatives	-.06	.49***
Liberals	-.24	-.42***
Democrats	-.07	-.28***
Republicans	-.26	.33***
Homosexual Rights		
Homosexuals	-.34**	-.56***
Government Role		
Federal Government	.12	-.21*
Democrats	-.02	-.35***
Republicans	.18	.35***
Congress	.18	.42***
Position of Blacks		
Blacks	-.36**	-.18

All issue positions coded toward conservatism. On affectual scales, higher scores indicate warmer feelings toward the group.
*p < .05; **p < .005; ***p < .0005

This indicates that, symbolically, issues do not mean the same thing for the two communities. For black evangelicals, talking about the position of blacks in society is related to an individual's feelings toward blacks. For white evangelicals, they are two separate things. For white evangelicals, conservative positions on abortion are symbolically associated with cooler feelings toward the women's movement. For black evangelicals, they are almost entirely distinct. For white evangelicals, appealing to traditional morality is positively related to feelings about conservatives. For blacks, there is no relationship. According to symbolic politics theory, regardless of issue position, if issues are not interpreted the same way or they do not tap into the same things, the expectation that black and white evangelicals will act together is unlikely.

The affect of white and black evangelicals is very different. Table 7.3 makes clear that black and white evangelicals have significantly different feelings toward all groups except homosexuals. Conversely, black evangelicals have the same feelings as black nonevangelicals toward all groups except homosexuals and blacks. It is unclear why black evangelicals have slightly cooler feelings toward blacks than black nonevangelicals. It may be because teaching about loving one's neighbors discourages feelings of ethnocentricity. However, even with the distinction, black evangelicals are much more like other blacks than they are like white evangelicals. White evangelicals are separate from white nonevangelicals on every issue except feelings toward the federal gov-

TABLE 7.3
Black and White Evangelicals
Mean Score Affect

Affect	Black Non-E	Black Evan.	White vs Black Evan.	White Evan.	White Non-E
Feminists	.15	-1.5	***	-12.8***	-2.1
Women's Movement	15.2	12.4	***	-6.3***	5.3
Conservatives	-12.1	-10.4	***	3.9	-2.8
Liberals	-4.8	-1.0	***	-14.8***	-5.0
Democrats	10.2	5.5	***	-6.4***	0.46
Republicans	-21.3	-23.5	***	-.07***	-5.6
Homosexuals	-14.9	-24.6*		-28.7***	-14.3
Federal Govt.	-8.4	-7.0	*	-11.9	-10.7
Congress	-5.3	-3.6	*	-7.6	-8.4
Blacks	26.6	21.7*	***	7.1***	4.1

Zero represents indifference relative to other groups. Tests of significance relative to black nonevangelicals for black evangelicals and relative to white nonevangelicals for white evangelicals. Center column represents test between black evangelicals and white evangelicals. *p < .05; **p < .005; ***p < .0005

ernment. Not only on the basis of issues, but on the basis of affect as well, white evangelicals constitute a distinctive group. Affectively, black evangelicals are much like other blacks.

One of the chief reasons that these affections of black and white evangelicals are so different and that issues are not interpreted the same way by them is that doctrine does not impact the affect of black and white evangelicals in the same way. For whites, evangelical doctrine impacts almost every affectual position. As table 7.4 records, among whites, it was negatively associated with affect toward feminists, the women's movement, liberals, Democrats, homosexuals, the federal government, and Congress, while it was a positive predictor of feelings toward conservatives and feelings toward blacks. It is not surprising that evangelical doctrine would be a positive predictor of feelings toward blacks when one considers the evangelical teaching about equality before God. Still, as noted above, these positive feelings toward blacks are not highly correlated with positions on a belief in society's responsibility to improve the positions of blacks.

For blacks, evangelical doctrine was a much less consistent indicator of affect. It did make black evangelicals feel cooler toward homosexu-

TABLE 7.4
Black and White Evangelicals
Determinants of Affect
Regression Coefficients

	Feminists	Women's Movement	Conservatives
Black Evangelicals	-4.08	3.45	-1.94
Black Nonevangelicals	-2.39	5.97**	-3.57*
White Evangelicals	-8.73***	-10.20***	3.89***
White Nonevangelicals (Constant)	3.32	10.62***	-13.13***
Adjusted R^2	.16	.18	.25
	Liberals	Democrats	Republicans
Black Evangelicals	-.29	-4.68*	-7.90**
Black Nonevangelicals	-4.22*	.78	-5.23*
White Evangelicals	-7.15***	-3.38**	.24
White Nonevangelicals	5.93**	20.11***	-20.50
Adjusted R^2	.19	.36	.42
	Homosexuals	Federal Government	Congress
Black Evangelicals	-10.44***	1.60	-1.94
Black Nonevangelicals	-2.61	1.41	-3.57*
White Evangelicals	-11.78***	-2.06	3.89***
White Nonevangelicals	-20.04	-5.02*	-13.13***
Adjusted R^2	.18	.03	.25
	Blacks		
Black Evangelicals	19.17***		
Black Nonevangelicals	23.23**		
White Evangelicals	3.51***		
White Nonevangelicals	1.58		
Adjusted R^2	.20		

Controls in each model include age, education, gender, region and partisan identification.
*$p < .05$; **$p < .005$; ***$p < .005$

als and Democrats than other blacks. However, overall, doctrine was not as useful in helping them to identify "enemies" or tangible sources of opposition as it was in the white evangelical community. For whites, conservative religious doctrine orders both issue positions and feelings toward the groups logically associated with them. For blacks, it helps to determine the positions but does not have the same impact on the evaluation of groups.

Moreover, affect influences the evaluation of electoral objects—even after controlling for issue positions. Table 7.5 shows that overall affect is a much more important predictor than issue position.[5] Even though issues are perceived to be very important, when it came down to voting for George Bush, positions on abortion, homosexual rights, women's rights, society's responsibility to help blacks, and the appropriate role of government did not serve as statistically significant indicators of such a voting decision. Only moral traditionalism had an impact. On the other hand, many affectual measures contributed to the Bush vote. Likewise, with regard to partisan identification, ideology, feelings toward Bill Clinton, and feelings toward George Bush, affect was often a much more influential indicator than issue positions.

Is a Racially Diverse Christian Right Possible?

There are three important challenges to the Christian Right in trying to mobilize black doctrinal conservatives. First, doctrinally conservative blacks do not see themselves as evangelicals. Although this chapter did not focus on this issue, the fact that black born-again Christians do not self-identify as evangelicals reveals much about the lack of political consciousness around evangelicalism in the African American community. If they do not even identify themselves as evangelicals, they cannot be expected to mobilize behind an evangelical agenda or evangelical candidates.

Second, despite the fact that doctrine contributes to conservative views on moral-cultural issues, these issues are not interpreted the same way by black and white evangelicals. Because doctrine did not have much of an impact on affect, the feelings of blacks toward most social groups did not vary with conservative religious doctrine. Thus, no matter how strongly black evangelicals may object to the lifestyles of contemporary society, these objections are not as strongly attached to tangible sources of opposition in the form of identifiable social groups as they are in the white evangelical community. Consistent with symbolic politics theory, the data have shown that attitudes and actions

TABLE 7.5
Black and White Evangelicals
Determinants of Attitudes
toward Electoral Objects

Vote for Bush (logit coeffiicients)		Feelings for Bush (betas)	
Traditional Morality	.2041*	Government Role	.07*
Conservative Affect	.0267*	Homosexual Issues	.11**
Congressional Affect	-.0243*	Traditional morality	.08*
Democratic Affect	-.0516***	Conservative Affect	.16***
Federalist Affect	.0453***	Democratic Affect	-.15***
Republican Affect	.0659***	Federalist Affect	.09**
-2 Log Likelihood	387.189	Republican Affect	.42***
Cases Predicted		Black Evan.	-.06*
(Correctly)	89.0%	Black Nonevan.	.09***
		R^2	.61

Feelings for Clinton (betas)		Partisan Identification (betas)	
Congressional Affect	.09***	Government Role	.12***
Democratic Affect	.33***	Homosexual Issues	.08*
Liberal Affect	.15**	Black Effect	.07*
Republican Affect	-.20***	Conservative Affect	.14***
Women's Movement			
(Affect)	.09*	Democratic Affect	-.31***
White Evangelicals	-.08**	Homosexual Affect	.07*
R^2	.47	Republican Affect	.43***
		Women's Movement	
		(Affect)	.07*
		Black Evan.	-.06*
		Black Nonevan.	-.04*
		White Evangelicals	.06***
		R^2	.47

Ideology (betas)	
Abortion	.08*
Morals	.10*
Conservative Affect	.30***
Democratic Affect	-.07*
Liberal Affect	-.24***
Republican Affect	.10**
Black Nonevan.	.09*
R^2	.49

Models included all issue positions, all affectual positions, and
doctrine. Only statistically significant predictors are shown.
Models also included standard predictors of age, education,
region, and gender. The betas for these standard indicators are not
listed above.

toward electoral objects are highly contingent on the evaluation of social groups. The cognitive map that affect provides black evangelicals
is very different from the cognitive map that affect provides their white
evangelical counterparts—even around family values issues. Without
the same map, it is not surprising that they often end up in very different
places.

Third, while black and white evangelicals agree (at least in terms of
issue positions) on moral-cultural questions, there is very little agreement on social issues beyond that. The fact that black and white evangelicals have such different perceptions of the appropriate role of
government is particularly problematic, because the role of government
is an important indicator of attitudes toward electoral objects. This disagreement, coupled with the difference between black and white evangelicals toward society's responsibility to improve the position of
blacks, makes a common coalition difficult. It is unrealistic to expect
that black evangelicals would join the coalition of the Christian Right
without the Christian Right being at all sympathetic to these concerns.

In view of these challenges, are there opportunities for a racially diverse Christian Right? On what basis has the Christian Right decided
to stop conceding minorities to the political left (*Christian American*,
October 1993)? Why in the last few years have Christian political organizations made an unprecedented attempt to attract a minority following? The Christian Coalition has begun advertising on minority-owned
radio stations and sending its literature to black and Latino churches. It
highlighted several African American speakers at its annual "Road to
Victory" conference held in September 1996.[6] The Coalition has also
named Rev. Earl Jackson of the New Cornerstone Exodus Community
Church in Boston its National Director of Community Development;
his charge is to develop linkages with the African American community. The Traditional Values Coalition has marketed an antigay home
videocassette designed for an audience concerned about civil rights. A
black male narrator stresses the film's theme that gay rights are special
rights that elevate a lifestyle choice to the level of immutable racial
categories and thereby undermine the legitimate minority status of people of color. The Family Research Council (the lobbying affiliate of
Focus on the Family) hosted a roundtable discussion in May 1996, on
racial reconciliation and has named as vice president Kay Coles James,
a black antiabortion activist and prominent Republican. James Dobson's Focus on the Family has recently established a "Black Family
Ministry" and has aired several programs on its radio broadcast devoted
exclusively to black issues.[7] Why are they making these overtures?

The environment of racial reconciliation cannot be discounted. Even though there are many, like the Southern Christian Leadership Conference's Joseph Lowery, who believe that the Christian Coalition has contributed to a climate in which black churches have been burned,[8] there are others who are much more open to the reconciliation message of the Christian Right. While it is still true that 11:00 Sunday morning is the most segregated hour in the United States, increasingly some of the largest and fastest-growing churches in the country are racially mixed. These churches include: John Meares's Evangel Temple in Washington, D.C.; Rod Parsley's World Harvest Church in Columbus, Ohio; Benny Hinn's Orlando Christian Center in Florida; Dick Bernel's Jubilee Christian Center in San Jose, California; Joseph Garlington's Covenant Church of Pittsburgh, Pennsylvania, and Carlton Pearson's Higher Dimension Family Church in Tulsa, Oklahoma (*Charisma* April 1993: 9–12). The existence of these churches is made more notable by the fact that they maintain a high profile with television ministries and other media outlets that among other things, publicize racial inclusiveness. In addition, over the last few years, the expansion of Promise Keepers and the proliferation of interracial "campmeetings" and other religious conventions by leading Christian broadcasters have led to the type and level of interaction and exposure that might begin to counter the environment of distrust that is the legacy of evangelical racial and religious history.

The theme of racial reconciliation has been sounded in all parts of the evangelical community. It has found perhaps its most receptive audience in the charismatic or Pentecostal segment of that community (Diamond 1994). Pentecostals (like Christian Coalition founder, Pat Robertson) trace early Pentecostalism back to the Azusa Street Revival of 1906, which crossed both gender and racial lines. Although this inclusiveness was not sustained in the denominations that developed after the revival, Pentecostals see this diverse beginning as the original plan of God and an example of His true purpose for the church (Blumhofer 1994). In addition, Pentecostal doctrine has a particular emphasis on being a "new creature in Christ" and being in covenant with God through salvation, suggesting that those in covenant with God always have more in common than they do with those who are not saved (and, therefore, outside the covenant of God). In the black community, this teaching that God is for only those who are in relationship with Him contrasts sharply with liberation theology where God identifies with the oppressed (Cone 1969). According to Pentecostal logic, Christians, regardless of race, are one people who must live in accordance with the Word of God.

In this changing environment, new organizations of conservative black pastors and congregations are beginning to emerge in hopes of rivaling the traditional direction of civil rights organizations like the Southern Christian Leadership Conference. The Christian Leadership Conference, headed by Dr. Tony Evans of Dallas and the Fellowship of Inner City Word of Faith Ministries headed by Dr. Frederick Price of Los Angeles are two such efforts. In Atlanta the newly formed Fellowship of Metro Atlanta Churches seeks to balance the perspective of the Concerned Black Clergy, a liberal group of black pastors. What is significant about these developments is that the black church has always played a major political socialization role in the black community (Calhoun-Brown 1996; Harris 1994; Walton 1985). As these types of ministries socialize people, conservative issue positions linked to conservative affectual positions may begin to emerge, and the type of linkages between evangelical doctrine and conservative political attitudes and behaviors that currently do not exist in the African American community may be forged. Black churches have, in the past, turned out the vote for liberal causes; conservative socialization might be able to produce the same result for conservative causes.

Finally, the Christian Right has begun to develop better strategies for working politically with black evangelicals. In Georgia the Christian Coalition works closely with the Network of Political Active Christians (NPAC). NPAC, which has chapters in five states, is an organization of black evangelicals dedicated to "bring biblical relevance to the political arena" (*Balance* 2 August/September 1995, 12). Together with the Christian Coalition, NPAC has identified areas in which blacks and whites can work together. Both organizations strongly lobby on traditional issues like homosexuality and abortion, but have also moved into other areas where potential exists, such as school vouchers. Many large black churches have private schools that could benefit from a voucher program. Much like the Family Research Council or the Christian Coalition, NPAC faxes "issue alerts" to black churches in an effort to mobilize support for (or opposition to) particular public policies. Working with black evangelical political groups like NPAC and Life Education and Resource Network (LEARN), the Christian Right is able to gain entrance into churches that previously would not return its calls, refused to go to its meetings, declined information like its voter guides, and were almost completely closed to its message.[9]

It is these opportunities that lead those in the Christian Right to continue to make overtures to the black evangelical community. However, the history of racism and mistrust is much to overcome. Even around family values issues, where the best opportunities for joint mobilization exists, most blacks, whether evangelical or not, feel the same way about major societal groups associated with the issues. Because affect conditions behavior, the affect of black evangelicals would have to become more closely aligned with those of white evangelicals for common political mobilization to occur on a large-scale basis.

Notes

1. All respondents were asked to rate 20 different individuals and groups on a scale ranging from 1 to 100, where 1 indicated extremely cool feelings and 100 indicated extremely warm feelings. All scores were corrected for positivity bias by subtracting the mean score for all individuals and groups from the score for the group or individual in question (Wilcox, Sigelman, and Cook 1989; Knight 1984).

2. Composite measures were constructed from the questions below. On each measure the values of the variables that comprise the index were made to vary within a common range. Each index was coded such that higher scores indicate more conservative positions. The reliability for each of these indices is given in parentheses.

Abortion: Respondents were asked their opinions about spousal notification, parental consent, government funding, and the circumstances under which abortion should be legal (alpha = .69).

Homosexual Rights: Respondents reported their views on gays in the military, adoption of children by gay individuals, and laws to protect homosexuals from job discrimination (alpha = .67).

Status of Women: Respondents were asked whether they thought of themssleves as feminists, whether women should work together to improve their position, how often they felt a sense of pride in the accomplishments of women, how angry they were about the treatment of women in society and whether a woman's place was in the home (alpha = .52)

Moral Traditionalism in Society: Respondents were asked whether they believed candidates should display higher morals, whether Americans should believe in God, whether it is wrong to have sex with a nonmarital partner, whether one should have tolerance for people with different morals, whether morals should be adjusted to a changing world, whether new lifestyles were destroying society, and whether the country would be better off if traditional family ties were emphasized (alpha = .69).

3. A composite measure of attitude toward the appropriate role of government was created from a respondent's answer to whether the government should provide fewer (more) services to decrease (increase) spending and whether it should be the government's responsibility to guarantee people a job and a good

standard of living. Responses were coded so that higher scores indicate more conservative positions.

4. An additive index was created from the respondents' positions on the government's responsibility to help blacks, the pace of civil rights, the relative position of blacks in society, affirmative action, and quotas. The index was so constructed that higher scores indicate more conservative positions (alpha = .78).

5. Both affective evaluations and issues positions were included in this model. A tolerance test was conducted to ensure that multicollinearity was not a problem. No tolerance was below .40, indicating that multicollinearity was not a major obstacle with these data.

6. Road to Victory speakers included Kay Coles James, J. C. Watts, Star Parker, and Alan Keyes.

7. An example of such a program is "The Challenge of Finding the Right Mate" (Nov. 27, 1995). This broadcast dealt with the shortage of Christian men in the black community who were "marriageable." Other topics dealing with race or racial reconciliation include: "Men in the 1990s" (June 10, 11, 12, 1992); and "A Man and His Mission" (Feb. 18, 1993).

8. Statement by Joseph Lowery in response to call by Christian Coalition for Summit on Church Burnings, Atlanta, Georgia, June 16, 1996.

9. Much of this information comes from interviews with Georgia Christian Coalition Chairman, Jerry Keen, and Georgia NPAC President, Sherry Jackson.

References

Balance. 1995. Vol. 2 (August/September): 12.

Bennett, William. 1993. *Book of Virtues*. New York: Simon and Schuster.

Blumhofer, Edith. 1994. "For Pentecostals, a Move toward Racial Reconciliation. *The Christian Century* (April 27): 444–46.

Bruce, Steve. 1988. *The Rise and Fall of the New Christian Right*. Oxford: Oxford University Press.

Calhoun-Brown, Allison. 1996. "African American Churches and Political Mobilization: The Psychological Impact of Organizational Resources." *Journal of Politics* 58: 935–53.

Carmines, Edward G., and James A. Stimson. 1989. *Issue Evolution: Race and the Transformation of American Politics*. Princeton, N.J.: Princeton University Press.

Charisma. 1993. April: 9–12.

Christian American. 1993. October.

Cone, James. 1969. *Black Theology and Black Power*. New York: Seabury Press.

Conover, Pamela Johnston. 1985. "The Impact of Group Economic Interests on Political Evaluations." *American Politics Quarterly* 13: 139–66.

Conover, Pamela Johnston, and Stanley Feldman. 1981. "The Origins and Meaning of Liberal and Conservative Self Identification." *American Journal of Political Science* 25: 617–45.

Diamond, Sara. 1994. "Watch on the Right: Change in Strategy." *Humanist* 54: 34–36.

Driedger, Leo. 1974. "Doctrinal Belief: A Major Factor in the Differential Perception of Social Issues." *Sociological Quarterly* 15: 66–80.

Feldman, Stanley. 1983. "Economic Individualism and American Public Opinion." *American Politics Quarterly* 11: 3–30.

Green, John, and James Guth. 1987. "The Moralizing Minority: Christian Right Support among Political Activists." *Social Science Quarterly* 67: 598–610.

———. 1988. "The Christian Right in the Republican Party: The Case of Pat Robertson Supporters." *Journal of Politics* 50: 150-65.

Guth, James, Ted Jelen, Lyman Kellstedt, Corwin Smidt, and Kenneth Wald. 1988. "The Politics of Religion in America." *American Politics Quarterly* 16: 357–97.

Harris, Fredrick C. 1994. "Something Within: Religion as a Mobilizer of African American Political Activism." *Journal of Politics* 56: 42–68.

Hunter, James D. 1983. *American Evangelicalism: Conservative Religion and the Quandary of Modernity.* New Brunswick, N.J.: Rutgers.

Jelen, Ted. 1991a. *The Political Mobilization of Religious Beliefs.* New York: Praeger.

———. 1991b. "Politicized Group Identification: The Case of Fundamentalism." *Western Political Quarterly* 44: 209–19.

———. 1993. "Political Consequences of Religious Group Attitudes." *Journal of Politics* 55: 178–90.

Johnson, Stephen, Joseph Tamney, and Ronald Burton. 1989. "Pat Robertson: Who Supported His Candidacy for President?" *Journal for the Scientific Study of Religion* 28: 387–99.

Kellstedt, Lyman. 1989a. "Evangelicals and Political Realignment." In *Contemporary Political Involvement,* edited by Corwin Smidt, 99–117. Lanham, Md.: University Press of America.

———. 1989b. "The Meaning and Measurement of Evangelicalism: Problems and Prospects." In *Religion and Political Behavior in the United States,* edited by T. Jelen, 3–21. New York: Praeger.

Kellstedt, Lyman, John Green, James Guth, and Corwin Smidt. 1994. "Religious Blocs in the 1992 Election: The Year of the Evangelical?" *Sociology of Religion* 55: 307–26.

Kellstedt, Lyman, and Corwin Smidt. 1993. "Doctrinal Beliefs and Political Behavior: Views of the Bible." In *Rediscovering the Religious Factor in American Politics,* edited by David Leege and Lyman Kellstedt, 177–98. Armonk, N.Y.: M. E. Sharpe.

Kinder, David, and Donald Sears. 1981. "Prejudice and Politics: Symbolic Racism vs. Racial Threats to the Good Life." *Journal of Personality and Social Psychology* 40: 414–31.

Knight, Kathleen. 1984. "The Dimensionality of Partisan and Ideological Affect: The Influence of Positivity." *American Political Quarterly* 12 (July): 305–34.

Leege, David, Joel Lieske, and Kenneth Wald. 1989. Toward Cultural Theories of American Political Behavior: Religion, Ethnicity and Class Outlook. Paper presented at the annual meeting of the Midwest Political Science Association, April, Chicago.

Lincoln, C. Eric, and Lawrence Mamiya. 1990. *The Black Church and the African American Experience.* Durham, N.C.: Duke University Press.

Lipset, Seymour. 1982. "Failure of Extremism." *Society* 20: 48–58.

Lopatto, Paul. 1985. *Religion and the Presidential Election.* New York: Praeger.

Lorentzen, Louise. 1980. "Evangelical Lifestyle Concerns Expressed in Political Action." *Sociological Analysis* 41: 144–54.

Page, A., and D. Clelland. 1978. "The Kanawha County Textbook Controversy: A Study in Politics of Lifestyle." *Social Forces* 57: 265–81.

Penning, James. 1994. "Pat Robertson and the GOP: 1988 and Beyond." *Sociology of Religion* 55: 327–44.

Reed, Ralph. 1996. Speech given at Summit of African American Pastors, 18 June, Atlanta, Georgia.

Rokeach, Michael. 1969. *Beliefs, Attitudes and Values: A Theory of Organization and Change.* San Fransisco: Jossey-Bass.

Sears, David. 1993. "Symbolic Politics: A Socio-Psychological Theory." In *Explorations in Political Psychology*, edited by Shanto Iyengar and William McGuire, 113–49. Durham, N.C.: Duke University Press.

Sears, David, and C. Funk. 1991. "The Role of Self Interest in Social and Political Attitudes." In *Advances in Experimental Social Psychology*, Vol. 24, edited by M. Zanna, 2–91. Orlando, Fla: Academic Press.

Sears, David, and J. Citrin. 1985. *Tax Revolt: Something for Nothing in California.* Enlarged edition. Cambridge: Harvard University Press.

Sears, David, R. Lau, T. Tyler and H. Allen Jr. 1980. "Self Interest and Symbolic Policy Attitudes and Presidential Voting." *American Political Science Review* 74: 670–84.

Shriver, P. 1981. *The Bible Vote.* New York: Pilgrim.

Sidey, Ken. 1990. "What's in a Word?" *Christianity Today*, 5 February.

Sigelman, Lee, Clyde Wilcox, and Emmett Buell. 1987. "An Unchanging Minority: Popular Support for the Moral Majority, 1980-1984." *Social Science Quarterly* 68: 876–84.

Smidt, Corwin. 1988. "Evangelicals within Contemporary American Politics: Differentiating Between Fundamentalists and Non-Fundamentalist Evangelicals." *Western Political Quarterly* 41: 20– 60.

Tajfel, Henry. 1981. *Human Groups and Social Categories.* New York: Cambridge University Press.

Wald, Kenneth. 1987. *Religion and Politics in the United States.* 1st ed. New York: St. Martin's Press.

Wald, Kenneth, Dennis Owen, and Samuel Hill. 1988. "Churches as Political Communities." *American Political Science Review* 82: 531–48.

Walton, Hanes. 1985. *Invisible Politics*. Albany, N.Y.: SUNY Press.

Wilcox, Clyde. 1986. "Evangelicals and Fundamentalist in the New Christian Right: Religious Differences in the Ohio Moral Majority." *Journal for the Scientific Study of Religion* 25: 355–63.

———. 1987. "Religious Orientations and Political Attitudes: Variations within the New Christian Right." *American Politics Quarterly* 15: 274–96.

———. 1989. "Feminism and Anti-Feminism among White Evangelical Women." *Western Political Quarterly* 42: 147–60.

———. 1990. "Blacks and the Christian Right: Support for the Moral Majority and Pat Robertson among Washington, D.C. Blacks." *Review of Religious Research* 32: 43–56.

———. 1992. *God's Warriors: The Christian Right in Twentieth-Century America*. Baltimore: Johns Hopkins University Press.

Wilcox, Clyde, Lee Sigelman, and Elizabeth Cook. 1989. "Some Like It Hot: Individual Differences in Responses to Group Feeling Thermometers." *Public Opinion Quarterly* 53: 246–57.

Wilmore, Gayraud. 1983. *Black Religion and Black Radicalism*. Maryknoll, N.Y.: Orbis.

Wuthnow, Robert. 1988. *The Restructuring of American Religion: Society and Faith since World War II*. Princeton, N.J.: Princeton University Press.

———. 1989. *The Struggle for America's Soul: Evangelicals, Liberals and Secularism*. Grand Rapids, Mich.: Eerdmans.

8

Romancing the Jews:
The Christian Right in Search
of Strange Bedfellows

Kenneth D. Wald and Lee Sigelman

When I hear the words "Christian America," I see barbed wire.
—American rabbi (Cohen 1993, 12)

Of the various constituencies targeted for coalition by the conservative movement in general and the Christian Right in particular, none has proven as refractory as Jewish Americans. Jews have long been a pillar of political liberalism in the United States. Because Jewish economic self-interest seems so contrary to this pronounced liberalism, some political analysts have anticipated its erosion. In the face of continuing conflict between blacks and Jews, Jewish antipathy toward affirmative action, spreading anti-Zionist sentiments among leftists, and the courting of Jews by conservatives, Jews have seemed especially ripe for ideological and partisan conversion. Yet, they have largely resisted these advances, remaining steadfastly attached to the Democratic Party and more deeply tied to liberal causes than virtually any other segment of the public (Lipset and Raab 1995). As early soundings had suggested they would, Jews remained securely in the Democratic fold in 1996.[1]

In this chapter we explore the political estrangement between Jews and the Christian Right in the United States. We begin by documenting the chief political differences between Jews and the central element of the Christian Right, white evangelical Protestants.[2] After examining the sources of these differences, we probe more closely into the Christian Right's attempts to overcome tensions with Jews—attempts we believe are largely doomed to failure. We then consider the prospects for collaboration between Christian conservatives and certain subgroups within American Judaism. We conclude with some thoughts about the motives of the Christian Right in its ardent pursuit of the Jews.

The Great Divide

Early studies of opinion differences among religious groups in the United States documented a striking political convergence between Jews and Baptists, with the latter constituting then, as now, the single largest bloc of American evangelicals (Allinsmith and Allinsmith 1948). In terms of partisanship and support for various government efforts to promote income security, Jews and Baptists stood close together during the New Deal party system. Their coalignment was particularly striking in light of obvious differences between them in history, doctrine, and economic status. The Baptists' support for Democratic programs evoked little surprise, for Baptists, a predominantly working-class group, were seen as responding to economic need. Jewish liberalism, however, posed a puzzle, for it contradicted the fundamental rule of electoral politics that privileged groups favor conservative economic parties and policies.[3] Subsequent generations of observers have expressed no less wonderment about the fact that, in the words of one, Jews "earn like Episcopalians and vote like Puerto Ricans" (Himmelfarb 1985).

In the past half-century, Jews and evangelical Christians have parted company on almost the entire array of national social and political issues. Jews remain largely allegiant to liberal causes and candidates, ranking alongside African Americans as the most dependable component of the Democratic coalition. Evangelicals, by contrast, have emerged as one of the most conservative and pro-Republican voting blocs in the electorate (Kellstedt, Green, Guth, and Smidt 1994). The epitome of their transformation has been the rise of the Christian Right. In institutional terms, the Christian Right encompasses a number of national organizations that have attempted to educate Christians about their political rights and duties and, more specifically, to harness this energized political force on behalf of conservative policies and candidates. In compositional terms, evangelical and fundamentalist Protestants are the heart and soul of the movement for Christian conservatism, which is most marked in the realm of social policy—especially on the issues of abortion, gender roles, and sexuality—but increasingly extends to debates over foreign policy, economic concerns, and other issues.

From the moment the new manifestation of the Christian Right first emerged in the late 1970s, it was perceived as a potential threat to Jewish interests by leading Jewish organizations, which continue to keep a wary eye on it (Cohen 1993). Spokespersons for various Jewish organizations have contended that the movement stands for specific policies that would undercut Jewish standing in the United States. Many of the policies most ardently embraced by Christian conservatives—school prayer, school vouchers, the teaching of creationism—are perceived by Jews as instruments of Christianization rather than as expressions of support for "religion in general." The broader attempt to ground public policy in "biblical principles," the motto of Christian Right activists, is similarly perceived by many Jews as a code word for granting legal recognition and privilege to the particular religious vision of evangelical Christianity. Despite many attempts at dialogue, the institutional representatives of American Jewry continue to regard evangelical political activism as a hazard that bears watching (see Forman 1994; Moyers and Rifkind 1996). Does the Jewish constituency, known for its pride in denying any organization the warrant to speak authoritatively in its name, share the concerns of its institutional leaders?

The dimensions of the gap between Jews and evangelical Protestants become obvious when we examine their responses in a series of opinion surveys conducted since the late 1980s. Because Jews comprise such a small segment of the U.S. public, national surveys with samples the size of those employed in media polls, the American National Election Study, and the General Social Survey do not provide enough Jewish respondents for reliable analysis. Fortunately for present purposes, the American Jewish Committee (AJC) has funded a series of mail surveys of Jewish Americans, conducted by Market Facts, Inc. These constitute a rich data source on Jewish political and social attitudes and behavior, but on only one occasion (in 1988) have companion surveys of Jews and non-Jews been undertaken. The analyses reported below thus draw heavily on the 1988 AJC National Survey of American Jews and its non-Jewish counterpart, the 1988 AJC National Survey of American Public Opinion.[4]

In table 8.1 we contrast the partisan loyalties of self-identified Jews and evangelicals in three election years. Because of differences across the three surveys, we should not take at face value apparent trends over the 1988–94 period. Nonetheless, the overall patterns are clear and consistent. Compared to evangelicals, Jews are much more likely to be

TABLE 8.1
Jewish and Evangelical/Born-Again Protestant Voters
Party Identification in 1988, 1992, and 1994

	Jews	Evangelical/ Born-Again Protestants
1988		

Do you usually think of yourself as a:

	Jews	Evangelical/Born-Again
Strong Democrat	24.8%	16.8%
Democrat	34.8	14.6
Independent	25.7	24.9
Republican	9.0	20.5
Strong Republican	5.8	23.2

1992

No matter how you voted today, do you usually think of yourself as a:

Democrat	65.2%	23.2%
Independent	19.5	20.1
Republican	13.2	52.1
Something else	2.0	4.6

1994

No matter how you voted today, do you usually think of yourself as a:

Democrat	60.5%	22.0%
Independent	26.8	23.1
Republican	11.5	50.9
Something else	1.3	4.0

Source: 1988 American Jewish Committee, National Survey of American Public Opinion; 1992 Voter Research & Surveys General Election Exit Poll; 1994 Mitofsky International Exit Pole

Democrats and much less likely to be Republicans. Even Jews who are not Democrats are unlikely to be Republicans, remaining instead in the intermediate status of independents. Evangelicals display a far different pattern. In the 1988 survey, they were appreciably less Democratic and three times as likely as Jews to identify as Republicans. These differences were even sharper in the 1992 and 1994 exit polls. Thus, unlike the situation that prevailed during the 1940s, when they were partners in the New Deal Democratic coalition, Jews and evangelical Protestants are now core elements of rival party coalitions.

These differences in partisan identification have a behavioral as well as a psychological component. In all three presidential elections and in both congressional elections for which we report data in table 8.2, differences in candidate choice have been stark. Jewish voters have overwhelmingly preferred Democratic candidates, but evangelicals have been massively Republican. This difference is mirrored in assessments of the Democratic president who assumed office after the 1992 election. In surveys conducted in 1994 and 1995, 70 percent of Jews approved of Bill Clinton's job performance, while almost two-thirds of evangelicals were critical of the president. Overall, evangelicals seem to have become the single most loyal voting bloc in the Republican Party, while Jews, by virtue of their Democratic preference and high turnout, eclipse all other groups in their commitment to that party (Leege 1993). The measure of the partisan difference between the two groups is borne out in their reluctance to vote for coreligionists who cross party lines. Jewish voters frequently prefer more liberal non-Jewish candidates even in races against Jews (Leventman and Leventman 1976). The same dynamic seems to operate among evangelicals, although in this case the preference is obviously for conservative, not liberal, candidates; tellingly, Jimmy Carter and Bill Clinton, the evangelicals atop the Democratic tickets in 1976, 1980, 1992, and 1996, failed to attract a majority of their own religious community when pitted against nonevangelical, but more politically conservative, opponents.

In table 8.3 we focus on the ideological dispositions of the two groups, in the form of liberal versus conservative self-descriptions (an effective shorthand device for measuring differences across a wide array of issues on the public agenda). Again, the differences are striking. For Jews, the political center of gravity is center-left. The modal category for Jews is moderate or middle of the road, with a somewhat smaller proportion describing themselves as liberal and with Jewish liberals outnumbering conservatives by roughly three to one. Evangelicals

TABLE 8.2
Jewish and Evangelical/Born-Again Protestant Voters
Vote Choice and Presidential Approval in 1984, 1988, 1992, 1994, and 1994–95

	Jews	Evangelical/ Born-Again Protestants

1984
In the 1984 presidential election, did you vote for:

	Jews	Evangelical/Born-Again
Ronald Reagan	44.4%	81.0%
Walter Mondale	55.6	19.0

1988
Who did you vote for in the 1988 presidential election?

George Bush	33.0%	84.8%
Michael Dukakis	67.0	15.2

1992
In today's election for president, did you just vote for:

George Bush	11.0%	65.6%
Ross Perot	9.3	13.0
Bill Clinton	79.7	21.3

In today's election for U.S. House of Representatives, did you just vote for:

Democrat	79.0%	32.8%
Republican	21.0	67.2

1994
In today's election for U.S. House of Representatives, did you just vote for:

Democrat	71.0%	27.7%
Republican	29.0	72.3

1994–95
Do you approve or disapprove of the way Bill Clinton is handling his job as president?

Approve	70.9%	36.2%
Disapprove	29.1	63.8

Source: 1984 National Election Studies; 1988 National Election Studies; 1992 National Election Studies; 1994 National Election Studies; 1994–95 Pew Research Center for the People & the Press

TABLE 8.3
Jewish and Evangelical/Born-Again Protestant Voters
Ideological Identification in 1988, 1992, and 1994

	Jews	Evangelical/ Born-Again Protestants

1988

Which of these best describes your usual stand on political issues?

Very liberal	3.9%	0.5%
Liberal	28.7	8.6
Middle-of-the-road	46.1	31.9
Conservative	20.0	49.2
Very conservative	1.3	9.7

1992

On most political matters, do you consider yourself:

Liberal	40.3%	6.1%
Moderate	50.2	34.2
Conservative	9.6	59.7

1994

On most political matters, do you consider yourself:

Liberal	36.9%	7.1%
Moderate	50.0	35.5
Conservative	13.1	57.3

How much confidence do you have in government's ability to solve the major problems facing this country?

A great deal of confidence	17.8%	7.7%
Some confidence	54.6	39.1
Little or no confidence	27.6	53.2

Source: 1988 National Election Study; 1992 Voter Research Study (VRS); 1994 Mitofsky Exit Poll

are even more skewed, but to the right. In all three surveys, their modal category is not moderate or middle of the road, but conservative; in fact, approximately six evangelical Protestants in ten have consistently described themselves as politically conservative. The same difference shows up in terms of confidence in government's ability to solve the major problems besetting the country. Neither Jews nor evangelical Protestants express great confidence, but the differences are still substantial. Most Jews fall into the middle category of "some confidence" in government, but most evangelicals take the most antigovernment option available to them, volunteering "little or no confidence" in the ability of government to address national problems. No doubt these responses reflect the partisan loyalties of the two groups as well as their underlying ideological leanings. But this differential in confidence in government definitely underlines the greater willingness of Jews than of evangelicals to grant power to government. For example, according to the 1994–95 Pew surveys, Jews far surpassed evangelicals in support of government regulation of business, environmental protection, civil rights measures, and assistance to the needy.

These differences in political identity are associated with contrasting issue priorities. Respondents in the 1992 Voter Research Survey were asked to select from a list of issues the two that had most affected their voting decision. This information clarifies how differently Jewish and evangelical Protestant voters frame the political universe. What we label "economic security" incorporates the responses of those who said their votes were shaped by concerns about health care and the economy, while the "social issues" dimension includes those who singled out abortion or family values. In 1992 Jews were more than four times as likely to cite economic security concerns to explain their vote decision as to mention a social issue, but among evangelicals social issues substantially outstripped economic concerns (data not shown).

Of course, knowing that Jews and evangelical Protestants see different issues as important does not tell us where they stand on these issues. Table 8.4 shows that they stand far apart on abortion, by all odds the most heated of these issues. Whereas nearly two-thirds of Jews embrace the option closest to unrestricted abortion, an even larger percentage of evangelicals think abortion should be illegal in most or all circumstances. These differences extend to other social issues as well. On questions about censorship, pornography, and homosexuality, the gap between Jews and evangelical Protestants is comparable in magnitude to the disagreement over abortion (not shown), with Jews consistently more likely to embrace the liberal position on these contentious issues.

TABLE 8.4
Jewish and Evangelical/Born-Again Protestant Voters
Abortion Attitudes, 1988 and 1992

	Jews	Evangelical/ Born-Again Protestants
1988		

What do you think about abortion? Should it be:

	Jews	Evangelical/Born-Again Protestants
Legal as it is now	87.6%	19.5%
Legal only in such cases as saving the life of the mother, rape, or incest	11.1	61.1
Not permitted at all	1.3	19.5

Suppose your unmarried daughter told you she was pregnant and intended to have an abortion. Would you support her decision to have an abortion?

	Jews	Evangelical/Born-Again Protestants
Yes	76.5%	15.6%
No	5.5	61.3
Not sure	18.0	23.1

1992

Which comes closest to your position? Abortion should be:

	Jews	Evangelical/Born-Again Protestants
Legal in all cases	63.0%	9.5%
Legal in most cases	31.3	18.6
Illegal in most cases	5.0	48.5
Illegal in all cases	0.7	23.3

Source: 1988 American Jewish Committee, National Survey of American Public Opinion, 1988 National Jewish Committee, National Survey of American Jews; 1992 Voter Research & Surveys Exit Poll

On issues that have been less visible in recent campaigns—particularly foreign policy—differences between Jews and evangelical Protestants are readily apparent but less dramatic. Throughout the Cold War, evangelicals were among the staunchest anticommunists in the United States, and they have retained their hawkish views since then (Jelen 1994; Wald 1994). As can be seen in table 8.5, in 1988, they

TABLE 8.5
Jewish and Born-Again Protestant/Evangelical Voters
Foreign Policy Attitudes, 1988

	Jews	Born-Again/ Evangelical Protestants
Soviet human rights abuses should not obstruct progress toward U.S.-Soviet arms agreements.		
Agree	53.4%	35.1%
Not sure	19.0	33.5
Disagree	27.7	31.4
Soviet human rights abuses should not be a barrier to expanding U.S.-Soviet trade.		
Agree	35.4%	24.2%
Not sure	21.1	38.2
Disagree	43.5	37.6
President Reagan was right when he said that the Contra rebels in Nicaragua are "freedom fighters."		
Agree	22.3%	39.6%
Not sure	35.8	41.7
Disagree	41.9	18.7

Source: 1988 American Jewish Committee, National Survey of American Public Opinion, 1988 National Jewish Committee, National Survey of American Jews

were less trusting of the Soviet Union and more willing to embrace the Nicaraguan Contras than were Jews. Table 8.5 must be read carefully given the low levels of opinionation. Yet, even discounting those with no opinions, it is clear that Jews were much more enthusiastic than evangelicals about closer ties with the Soviet Union and much less committed to the Contra cause.

These differences recur across a broad array of issues. Virtually the only significant political issue on which Jews and evangelicals seem not to part company is affirmative action. To assess opinions on this issue, we created a preferential treatment scale composed of responses to the following set of questions: "Do you favor or oppose giving preference in hiring to each of the following groups? The handicapped; women; blacks; Hispanics; Jews; Asians." Among Jews, the issue of affirmative action has been extremely contentious because it conflicts with both the Jewish belief in meritocracy and perceived self- and group-interest (Wald and Sigelman 1995).[5] Considering the ferocious denunciations of racial preference by many Jewish activists, we might even expect this to be one case where Jews would exhibit more conservative attitudes than evangelicals. In fact, though, no significant difference emerged on the preferential treatment scale. Even on this issue, commonly identified as the wedge most likely to dislodge Jews from their characteristic liberal affinity, Jews appear more liberal than one might expect.

Are the Differences Real?

When two groups differ as fundamentally as Jews and evangelical Protestants do across a wide range of political issues and concerns, it is natural to ask whether the observed differences are, to some extent at least, spurious. Is it possible that these are not really differences between Jews and evangelical Protestants as much as they are, say, differences between richer and poorer, or more and less educated, people? Does religion really account for the opinion gap between Jews and evangelical Protestants, or does the explanation for these differences lie in the realm of other factors that happen to be associated with being a Jew or an evangelical Protestant?

It is by no means implausible to suppose that factors that often stratify American political attitudes—race, age, income, gender, and education—may account for a large share of the observed differences between Jews and evangelicals. Despite the substantial social gains evangelicals have made in the postwar era, they remain well below Jews in terms of average levels of income and education. They may also differ from Jews in age and sex distribution, although previous research has not yielded consistent findings on these dimensions. The evangelical label comprises a substantial nonwhite population, while American Judaism does not. We have already taken race into account by limiting our Jewish-evangelical comparisons to white respondents, but need to incorporate these other factors before dismissing spuriousness as an explanation for the differences observed above.

We assess the relative impact of religion and other social forces by considering 1988 respondents' reactions to four groups on the American left: the American Civil Liberties Union (ACLU), the National Organization for Women (NOW), the National Association for the Advancement of Colored People (NAACP), and Planned Parenthood. These four groups embody some of the most persistent cleavages between Jews and evangelical Protestants. In the rhetoric of the Christian Right, the ACLU represents secularism and irreligion, NOW stands for militant feminism, the NAACP is committed to aggressive and intrusive government programs, and Planned Parenthood symbolizes "abortion on demand." For Jewish liberals, by contrast, these groups symbolize, respectively, religious freedom, gender equality, racial justice, and reproductive freedom. Attitudes toward these groups thus constitute a convenient indicator of politically relevant value differences between Jews and evangelicals.[6] Not surprisingly, Jews significantly outscored evangelicals on this scale. In fact, the mean scale score for Jews (.099) is more than one standard deviation above that of evangelical Protestants (-.990). But does this difference hold up when other social factors that might explain attitudes toward these four groups are taken into account?

The answer is straightforward: the gap between Jews and evangelical Protestants in affect for the four groups in question is not bridged, or even reduced, by the imposition of statistical controls for age, sex, education, and income. In a multiple regression analysis in which age, sex, education, and income serve alongside a variable indicating Jewish versus evangelical Protestant identification as predictors of scores on the scale of affect for the four groups, the Jewish versus evangelical identification variable continues to exhibit a significant and powerful impact. Even after taking account of all the other factors, Jews outscored evangelicals by 1.11 (standard error = .107, p<.001) on the scale—virtually identical to the simple mean difference between Jews and evangelicals. In analyses not detailed here, parallel patterns emerge on two other attitude scales, measuring social liberalism and support for church-state separation, respectively.

These findings suggest that the political differences between Jews and evangelicals are not reducible to differences in the demographic and social composition of the two groups. Jews and evangelical Protestants do tend to differ from one another in terms of race, socioeconomic status, and demographic composition, but these differences do not even begin to account for the wide disparities between them in political outlook.

Toward Understanding Jewish-Evangelical Differences

Is the unwillingness of Jews to make common cause with the Christian Right wholly a function of their attitudinal differences with evangelical Protestants? Even though the political differences between the two groups are deep-seated and wide-ranging, these differences seem insufficient to account for the vehemence many Jews direct toward the Christian Right. For example, one Jewish commentator contends that Republican appeals to Christian conservatives reveal "the naked fascist face of those who claim to be the party of God" (Roiphe 1992). In the words of a respected national leader of Reform Judaism, "The Religious Right systematically pursues policies and engages in activities that endanger the fundamental rights enshrined in the Declaration of Independence and the Bill of Rights" (Saperstein 1994). The subtitle of its report on the Religious Right, "The Assault on Tolerance and Pluralism," accurately conveys the perspective of the Anti-Defamation League (Cantor 1994). In even less measured tones, the League's recent roster of hate groups lumps together "Religious Right extremists" with Louis Farrakhan, the Klan, Nazi skinheads, white supremacists, and the militia movement.[7] The quotation that opens this chapter further attests to the intense visceral Jewish reaction against the core idea of the Christian Right.

In our view, a key to understanding the roots of the political estrangement between Jews and evangelical Protestants is the recognition that Jewish resistance to much of the Christian Right agenda expresses a considerable degree of antipathy toward the core of the Christian Right itself. Symbolic politics theory suggests that preferences on policy issues are often determined not by the issue itself but rather by attitudes to the contending groups engaged in conflict (Sears, Lau, Tyler, and Allen 1980). In the same way that, for example, whites' attitudes to affirmative action appear to embody their views of African Americans and other groups affected by such policies, we believe that Jewish

Americans may react to the Christian Right in terms of how they regard the people who support the movement. For many Jews, especially those who regard fundamentalist Protestants negatively, the policies championed by the Christian Right may be rejected precisely because they appeal to Christian conservatives. The gulf between Jews and the Christian Right may run even deeper than the findings summarized above suggest.[8]

It may be useful to demonstrate the depth of the estrangement before attempting to explain it. The 1988 presidential campaign provided an excellent laboratory for these purposes, in the form of a natural experiment involving candidate preferences. That year the nomination contest in each party featured a prominent Christian minister who had never held public office—Jesse Jackson for the Democrats and Pat Robertson for the Republicans. Jackson and Robertson adopted very different poses before Jewish voters. Jackson was persona non grata with much of the Jewish community, considered suspect for his anti-Semitic rhetoric in 1984, his unwillingness to condemn the anti-Semitism of Louis Farrakhan, and his well-publicized embrace of Palestinian leader Yasser Arafat.[9] By contrast, Robertson went out of his way to appeal to Jewish voters. He embraced the cause of Israel with real fervor and pointedly denounced religious bigotry of any kind. So how did Jews react to two such different candidates, one of whom seemed to be prostrating himself before them while the other sometimes seemed to be spitting in their face?

Jews responded to Robertson's blandishments and Jackson's provocations by pronouncing a plague on both candidates' houses. In the 1988 survey, Jewish Republicans and Democrats were asked, respectively, how they would vote in November with and without Robertson and Jackson on the ticket. As table 8.6 demonstrates, without Jackson on the ticket, about three out of every four Jewish Democrats said they would vote Democratic. With him on the ticket, only about one in three said they would do so.[10] That dropoff is steep but hardly surprising in light of the widespread perception of Jackson as being hostile to Jews and Jewish causes. What is more striking is that Robertson's presence as the Republican vice presidential nominee would have done equivalent damage among Jewish Republicans. The 70 percent Jewish Republican support for the Republican ticket dropped to just 32 percent if Robertson were added as the vice presidential candidate, leaving two-thirds of Jewish Republicans in doubt about whether they would support their party in November.

These defection levels underline the difficulties faced by evangelicals

TABLE 8.6
Intended Presidential Vote of Jews, 1988

Democrats

Intended Vote	Without Jesse Jackson on ticket	With Jesse Jackson on ticket	Change
Democratic	77%	34%	-43%
Unsure	19%	34%	+15%
Republican	4%	31%	+27%

Republicans

Intended Vote	Without Pat Robertson on ticket	With Pat Robertson on ticket	Change
Republican	70%	32%	-38%
Unsure	23%	38%	+15%
Democratic	7%	30%	+23%

Source: National Jewish Committee, National Survey of American Jews

who would attempt to appeal to Jewish voters. Jews were apparently no less skeptical about an openly philo-Semitic evangelical, Robertson, than they were about a candidate who was widely regarded as an anti-Semite, Jackson. Sectarian reasons do not account wholly for these findings because the mention of Robertson as the vice presidential nominee also drove down Republican support among mainline Protestants and Roman Catholics.[11] Nonetheless, the Jewish reaction against Robertson was both sharper and more heavily based on concerns about his attitudes to questions of church and state. Even with Robertson on the ticket, a plurality of both Catholic (42 percent) and mainline Protestant (52 percent) Republicans said they would still vote Republican in November, and those who claimed they would leave the GOP mostly shifted into the "not sure" category. Among Jewish Republicans, a much higher percentage promised to "cross the aisle" by voting Democratic if Robertson were nominated, leaving an almost even partisan balance among those with a definite vote intention. Anxiety about preserving church-state separation appears to have driven these patterns.

Jewish Republicans who planned to defect in the event of a Robertson candidacy scored more than three times as high on our index of support for church-state separation as those who remained loyal to their party's ticket. Catholic and mainline Protestant defectors from Robertson also had higher separationist scores than the party loyalists among their co-religionists, but with lesser disparities than the Jewish Republicans. These findings suggest that evangelicals have a fundamental Jewish problem.

To understand Jewish distrust of Christian political initiatives requires some familiarity with the political culture of American Jewry. Contrary to those who explain Jewish political distinctiveness as the product of some universal impulse toward liberalism, the prevailing academic interpretation attributes Jewish political preferences to historical and situational factors (Hyman 1992).[12] In western Europe, Jewish emancipation was a left-wing project, resisted—sometimes violently—by the Catholic Church and other conservative social forces (Katz 1978). Accordingly, many Jewish immigrants brought with them to the United States a deep-seated suspicion of the motives and intentions of religious conservatives. This skepticism was reinforced by the Jewish perception of religious fundamentalists as "ignorant rednecks, cultural Neanderthals, and fanatical Bible-thumpers led by self-styled ministers out of the pages of Sinclair Lewis" (Cohen 1992, 4). Anti-Semitism could certainly be found among the genteel classes as well, but most Jewish Americans encountered it in its most virulent form from religious fundamentalists.[13] Scholarly research buttressed this experience by showing a strong correlation between sectarian Protestantism and belief in anti-Jewish stereotypes (Martire and Clark 1982). This tension has been accentuated by the Christian Right's attempts to tear down the wall of separation. Many Jews attribute the success and security of Jews in the United States to the unparalleled religious liberty they have enjoyed here, a liberty that they believe depends on maintaining a secular state that takes no official notice of religion. Accordingly, they have elevated the doctrine of church-state separation to near-sacred status. Believing that "public religion in the United States could never be truly neutral, for it always connoted an advantage to Christianity" (Cohen 1992, 5), they have taken reflexive alarm at the first signs of incursion. When Christian Right leaders attack the wall of separation as misguided or pernicious, they immediately and inevitably raise anxieties within the strongly separationist Jewish community.

The political strategists of the Christian Right, well aware of this history, have taken considerable pains to overcome it. As part of his fence-mending strategy, the Christian Coalition's Ralph Reed has frequently appeared before Jewish audiences to issue assurances that his movement represents no threat and no attempt to Christianize the United States (American Jewish Committee 1996). Indeed, Reed has purged his speeches of most "God talk," opting instead for a resolutely secular form of rights language. Following the example of Jerry Falwell some years earlier, the Christian Coalition has also assigned high policy priority to maintaining the security of the state of Israel. The Christian Right also delights in showcasing the occasional Jewish conservative who joins forces with it, much as the GOP does with prominent African Americans who stray across the partisan divide.

Despite such efforts, many Jews remain skeptical about the intentions of their would-be allies in the Christian Right. In the 1988 survey, nearly three-fifths of Jews viewed anti-Semitism as the norm among fundamentalist Protestants and fewer than 10 percent considered it rare. As table 8.7 shows, this was the highest level of anti-Semitism Jews perceived among the eleven groups they were asked about and more than double their estimate for Republicans and conservatives, the other

TABLE 8.7
Jewish Perceptions of Anti-Semitism among Eleven U.S. Groups in 1988

Democrats	7%
Liberals	10%
Republicans	23%
Conservatives	26%
Union Leaders	30%
Hispanics	36%
Mainstream Protestants	37%
Big Business	38%
Catholics	42%
Blacks	50%
Fundamentalist Protestants	58%

Note: Entry indicates the percentage of Jewish respondents who perceived "many" or "most" members of the group as anti-Semitic.
Source: National Jewish Committee, National Survey of American Jews

right-wing groups mentioned in the survey. But even if the carriers of social conservatism were not perceived as anti-Semitic, their policy agenda would still pose a major obstacle to a political alliance with Jews. For Jews, as we have noted, separation of church and state is not a compartmentalized value but a constitutive element in understanding of the political universe. Why, for example, do Jews identify themselves as liberals? Their attitude toward church-state separation holds the key. In a multiple regression analysis of Jews' self-placements on the liberal-conservative scale, income, gender, and education all contribute significantly, but their predictive power is dwarfed by that of support for church-state separationism. The same impact shows up—albeit indirectly, mediated through the power of ideology—on Jews' pronounced Democratic partisanship. These results suggest that Jews' political loyalties are defined to a substantial degree by the priority they assign to maintaining the secular character of the state. To a considerable degree, Jews are liberals and Democrats because they understand liberalism as a means of promoting separationism and see the Democratic Party as more sympathetic to Jefferson's high wall of church-state separation.

It could be argued, contrary to our interpretation, that what we have discovered is not an evangelical problem with Jews but a Jewish problem with evangelicals. After all, how obstinate can a people be, continually spurning the overtures of an avid suitor? However, this argument overlooks the continuity of the very behavior Jews find so troublesome among evangelicals. For every expression of philo-Semitism and embrace of religious pluralism by Christian Right leaders, Jews can identify equal and opposite expressions—Jerry Falwell's repetition of crude stereotypes about Jewish money-making, Mississippi Governor Kirk Fordice's exclusionist claims about Christian America, Pat Robertson's troubling embrace of crackpot conspiracy theories historically linked to anti-Semitism, the propensity of Christian Coalition officials to equate their constituency with "people of faith," the 1996 Southern Baptist Convention declaration calling for renewed efforts to proselytize Jews. These signs of exclusion and religious intolerance cannot be dismissed as the opinion of a few unrepresentative extremists. According to a recent national survey sponsored by the American Jewish Committee (Smith 1996), almost half the respondents who fit the "evangelical" profile endorsed a constitutional amendment "declaring that the United States is a Christian country" and nearly three-fifths believed that Jews still need to convert to Christianity.[14] Compared to other Americans, these evangelicals were more than twice as likely to insist on the Christian identity of the United States and the need for Jews to embrace

Jesus. They were also markedly less sympathetic to feminists, gays, atheists, immigrants, Moslems, and practitioners of Eastern religions, suggesting an animus to out-groups that seems exclusionary and intolerant. Whatever the explanation for these views, their prominence within the principal constituency of the Christian Right will assuredly undercut Ralph Reed's soothing words to Jewish audiences.

Does any issue have the potential to bridge the gap between Jews and evangelicals? Of all the issues on the current policy agenda or likely to emerge in the foreseeable future, the one with the greatest potential to do so is surely the cause of Israel. As part of the spread of dispensationalist theology in evangelical circles since the 1950s, evangelicals have come to vest great theological significance in the restoration of a Jewish state in the Middle East. Compared to other Christians, evangelical clergy, activists, and laity are much more supportive of Israel (Green, Guth, Smidt, and Kellstedt 1996, ch. 17).[15] Nonetheless, this issue does not seem particularly promising as a bridge to Jewish political cooperation. As many Jewish critics have noted, evangelical commitment to Israel is the outgrowth of a theological vision that requires Jewish ingathering and conversion to Christianity as a precondition of the Second Coming of Jesus. Even discounting this rather instrumental view of the Jews, the evangelical commitment to Israel has to this point been largely rhetorical. On bread-and-butter issues, such as Israel's annual foreign aid appropriation, social conservatives in Congress have failed to help or stood in opposition (Wald, Guth, Fraser, Green, Smidt, and Kellstedt 1996). Even more alarming to Jews, many evangelical activists were strongly attracted to Pat Buchanan during the 1996 GOP nomination campaign despite his clear anti-Israeli thrust and veiled anti-Semitism.

In sum, the barrier to Jewish-evangelical political cooperation is stronger than the issue-based disagreements between them. Jewish resistance to the Christian Right is rooted in both skepticism about its intentions and a stubborn sense that its policy objectives are diametrically opposed to Jewish interests. So long as Jews believe that Christian conservatism is not "good for the Jews," they will resist even the most fervent calls for brotherhood and tolerance, let alone the ardent courtship of those who hope for political union between this extremely odd couple.

Differentiation among Jews

To this point we have focused on differences between evangelical Protestants and Jews in general. The possibility remains, however, that the

Christian Right could manage to appeal to a specific subset of Jews. In *The Restructuring of American Religion*, Robert Wuthnow (1988) identified a fundamental shift from an essentially denomination-centered religious-political alignment to a system in which religious communities are likely to be rent by internal sociopolitical cleavages. Building on Wuthnow's interpretation, James Davison Hunter's (1991) "culture war" thesis posited that an "orthodox" worldview unites political conservatives of different faiths against "progressives" who are likewise recruited from various religious traditions. Hunter argues that the subscribers to each worldview are likely to develop more political commonalities with others who share their *weltanschauung* than with coreligionists who subscribe to the opposite worldview. Several political scientists and commentators have picked up on this theme, arguing that the traditional American-style system of political confessionalism (Catholics versus Protestants versus Jews) has been supplanted by an alignment more akin to a European-style secular versus religious cleavage (Green and Guth 1991). In this new alignment, conservatism is more likely to be associated with the level of religious commitment than with denominational affiliation.

In recent years American Judaism has unquestionably shown signs of increasing differentiation (Wertheimer 1993). The gaps among Orthodox, Conservative, and Reform Jews have taken on new significance, and those who are most committed to orthodoxy have occasionally exhibited a willingness to cooperate with Christian conservatives in crusades to restrict abortion rights, fight pornography, encourage state funding of religious schools, and promote other aspects of the conservative social agenda. The question, then, is whether the Christian Right agenda has the potential to split the ordinary political cohesion of American Jews.[16]

Applying the restructuring theory to Judaism is not quite as simple as using it to account for schisms within Christianity. In Christianity the concept of "religiosity" is normally equated with faithful religious observance and the maintenance of orthodox religious beliefs.[17] But in Judaism, a tradition more compatible with the liturgical model, the very concept of religious attachment is problematic. To begin with, the Jewish faith is less "church"-based than its Christian counterpart, allowing a larger role for private devotion, and Jewish religious behavior is not necessarily amenable to straightforward empirical measurement.[18] Compared to Christianity, especially in its Protestant formulations, Judaism is also less structured into distinctive theological camps. To further confuse the measurement issue, Judaism is often construed by its adherents as a civilization or peoplehood in which the distinctively religious element is but one, albeit a potentially very important, component. Ironically, the very religious freedom that characterizes Jewish life in the American Diaspora has reduced strictly religious behavior from the essential marker of Jewishness to one of many manifestations of Jewish identity.

To gain a clearer perspective on the Wuthnow hypothesis in the context of Judaism, it is useful to borrow from Lenski (1961) by considering measures of two different types of Jewish identification.[19] The first, communalism, taps the degree to which one is enmeshed in a network of Jewish social, organizational, and cultural ties. Operationally, it consists of responses to seven questions in the 1988 survey: "Of your three closest friends, how many are Jewish?"; "Do you belong to any Jewish organizations aside from a synagogue or synagogue-related group now?"; "Did you contribute $100 or more to the UJA/Federation in the past year?"; "Did you have a Christmas tree in 1987?"; "How close do you feel to other Jews?"; "How important would you say being Jewish is in your own life?"; and "Would you be upset if a child of yours married a non-Jew?" We standard-scored responses to these questions and summed them to form a composite scale (coefficient alpha = .777), which was itself then standard-scored. By contrast, associationalism taps into the kinds of ritual observance more commonly known as religiosity. It is measured here via responses to six survey questions: "How often do you attend religious services?"; "Do you use separate dishes at home for meat and dairy products?"; "Did you attend a Passover Seder at home or elsewhere this year?"; "Did you fast on Yom Kippur in 1987?"; "Did you light Chanukah candles in 1987?"; and "Do you think of yourself as Orthodox, Conservative, Reconstructionist, Reform, just Jewish, or not Jewish?" (with responses dichotomized into Orthodox versus other). Again, we standard-scored and then combined responses (coefficient alpha = .672) and then standard-scored the resulting scale. If the Wuthnow thesis applies to Judaism, we should observe increasing political conservatism at higher levels of both the communalism and associationalism scales.[20] However, other findings (Legge 1995) leave considerable room for doubt about whether this pattern should be expected to emerge.

To probe the applicability of the Wuthnow thesis, we have divided Jews into three categories apiece on the communalism and associationalism scales—low (one standard deviation or more below the mean for all Jews), medium (respondents within a standard deviation either way from the mean) and high (more than one standard deviation above the

Jewish mean)—and compared these groups in terms of partisanship, ideology, presidential vote, and scales representing church-state separation, liberal group affect, social values, and preferential treatment. There is no need to present the results of these analyses in detail, for their basic message is readily summarized: In not a single instance is Wuthnow's interpretation supported. The most common pattern is a lack of significant political differentiation associated with strength of Jewish involvement. Neither liberal-conservative self-placements nor opinions concerning preferential treatment are related to level of Jewish attachment on either communal or associational grounds. The social values scale is unrelated to communalism and presidential vote is unrelated to associationalism. In the few instances where intergroup differences are in evidence, they seem idiosyncratic. For example, affect for liberal groups (the ACLU, NOW, NAACP, and Planned Parenthood) was highest among those in the middle category of communal and associational identification and was somewhat lower among those in the low and high categories—a pattern for which we have no ready explanation. Most of the significant relationships in these analyses actually contradict the expectation of a conservatizing effect for Jewish involvement. Democratic identification increased with each increment of religious involvement and was significantly higher for both moderate and highly involved communal Jews than for those with minimal Jewish interaction patterns. The respondents with the lowest level of Jewish social ties also proved to be the most supportive of the Republican presidential candidate in 1988. The belief in church-state separation, which we have identified as the core Jewish belief affecting political loyalties, showed a strong increase as respondents became more involved in Jewish communal and religious ways.

These patterns provide little evidence that those Jews who are most intensely linked to the Jewish community—either by social interaction or religious behavior—are particularly amenable to the lure of the Christian Right.[21] Indeed, to the limited extent that they reveal evidence of political differentiation among Jews, these analyses tend to suggest that those Jewish groups who are most sympathetic to aspects of Christian conservatism are only marginally affiliated with the Jewish community. The lack of strong ties means that they are less likely to be mobilized politically by virtue of interaction with other Jews. By contrast, Jews who partake of Jewish life more actively exhibit the greatest attachment to the liberal tendency in terms of partisanship and belief in the priority of church-state separationism.

Prospects for Common Cause

Advocates of a Jewish-evangelical Christian political alliance will find little cause for rejoicing from this analysis. The vast majority of Jews have very different political outlooks and loyalties than the bulk of evangelicals and tend to take a jaundiced view both of evangelicals, the core constituency of the Christian Right, and of the movement itself. Small segments of the Jewish community may be available for coalition on a narrow, issue-by-issue basis, but we see little prospect of any but the most fragmentary cooperation.

These findings make us wonder why the Christian Right perseveres in wooing the Jews. With limited resources, it seems odd that a movement led by savvy strategists should invest time and energy in such a recalcitrant target. Of course, it may be that these efforts are not really all that significant. But more to the point, we suspect that the efforts of the Christian Right have a different ultimate purpose than attracting Jewish support.

One of the highest barriers to the political success of the Christian Right is the norm of religious tolerance and pluralism. That is, the Christian Right is shackled by widespread public resistance to imposing sectarian religious values in public policy. For all its deep commitment to theistic faith, the American public habitually draws a line at movements that seek to force a particular religious vision upon the wider community. The perception that movements like the Moral Majority or Pat Robertson's presidential candidacy had just such ambitions contributed significantly to their collapse. In its subsequent incarnation, the Christian Right has demonstrated a keen awareness of the self-imposed limits of triumphalism and has tried to learn from past mistakes (Moen 1994). The mission to the Jews, if we may call it that, may be less important for its stated objective of political coalition than for its contribution to fostering an image of tolerance. That is, it may well be more important for the Christian Right to be seen appealing to Jews than it is to attract them. Even if the effort bears little fruit in the way of political converts, it can still be deployed to answer critics who condemn the movement for religious insularity. No matter that Jews continue to look askance at their suitors; in spite of their resistance, they are useful nonetheless.

The problem with Jewish participation in common cause, at least from the Jewish perspective, is that the Religious Right is seen to be the Christian Right. Lest we leave the impression that these findings constitute evidence for the culture war hypothesis, it is important to note that we do not foreclose entirely the possibility of some common political interests between the two communities. As noted by even the most acerbic Jewish critics of Christian conservatism, Jews share with many evangelicals a sense of dismay about the erosion of personal responsibility, the pressures on the family unit, and the coarsening of American culture. Like evangelicals, many Jews insist on the relevance of religious conviction to public policy debate. Yet, even Jews who believe that the Religious Right has identified important questions cannot overcome a feeling that social conservatives have managed to reach exactly the wrong answers.[22]

Notes

For facilitating access to the data used in this study, we are grateful to Market Facts, Inc., and its research director, Sid Groenemann, Steven M. Cohen of the Hebrew University, the research staff of The Pew Research Center for the People and the Press, and the Roper Center for Public Opinion Research. Neither those who originally collected the data nor those who granted us permission to use it bear any responsibility for the way we have interpreted it. We also thank Arthur Berger of the American Jewish Committee for expeditiously providing some AJC reports and J. David Singer, Research Director, for granting us permission to analyze surveys conducted under AJC auspices. For helpful comments and suggestions, we thank the editors, the participants at the Calvin conference, Jerry Legge, and Geoff Levey.

1. According to the exit polls conducted by the Voter News Service, 80 percent of Jewish voters supported Bill Clinton in the 1996 presidential race. This compared to 37 percent of white Protestants, 48 percent of white Catholics, and just 26 percent of whites who claimed they belonged to the "Religious Right." We obtained these results from the "Politics Now" site on the World Wide Web at http://wwwl.politicsnow.com.

2. For a recent account of the Religious Right that stresses the centrality of evangelical Protestants, see Wilcox (1996). We exclude Roman Catholics and black Protestants from the core constituency of the Christian Right, the former because of differences in religious tradition and the latter because of a distinctive sociopolitical style that differs markedly from that of white Christian conservatism. We acknowledge that many evangelicals and fundamentalist Protestants do not subscribe to the agenda of Christian conservatism. In describing the core constituency of the movement as we do, we recognize that it exerts its strongest appeal on members of these groups, with no claim that all members embrace it or embrace all of its agenda.

3. As Fein (1988) and Ginsberg (1993) have argued, Jewish support for

liberalism may rest upon the perception and/or reality that Jews can do best, economically and socially, under the conditions of a liberal society.

4. We obtained these surveys from Market Facts with the permission of the American Jewish Committee. "Exit polls" (Election-Day surveys leaving the polls) have the virtue of drawing extremely large samples—enough to enable reliable estimates of the attitudes of Jews as well as evangelical Protestants. Accordingly, we also make use of the 1992 Voter Research & Surveys General Election Exit Poll and the 1994 Mitofsky International National Exit Poll, both of which we obtained from the Roper Center. Finally, in 1994 and 1995, the Pew Research Center for the People & the Press undertook a series of four surveys focusing on religious issues; the combined four-survey data set, obtained from the Pew Center, serves as our most recent data source.

It is no simple matter to define either Jews or evangelical Protestants. For Jews, we relied in each instance on self-identifications provided by the survey respondents. We classified as evangelical Protestants all self-identified Protestants who (a) in the AJC survey responded positively when asked whether they had personally had a "born-again" experience, or (b) in the 1992 exit poll checked a box to identify themselves as a "born-again Christian/Fundamentalist," or (c) in the 1994 exit poll checked a box to identify themselves as a "born-again/evangelical Christian," or (d) in the Pew Center surveys, responded positively when asked whether they would describe themselves as a " 'born-again' or evangelical Christian." We concede that these are imperfect means of identifying members of each group (see Jelen, Smidt, and Wilcox 1993). However, if, as we suspect, our measurement strategy has led us to identify as Jews and evangelical Protestants some who would not qualify under stricter criteria, then the effect should presumably have been to water down differences between the two groups. If this is so, failure to uncover major differences in social and political attitudes between Jews and evangelical Protestants could plausibly be attributed to problems in identifying members of the two groups; but if we detect major intergroup differences despite this measurement problem, we should be all the more prepared to take these differences seriously.

In any event, the numbers of Jews and white evangelical Protestants, thus identified, in each data set are as follows: in the 1988 AJC surveys, 1,293 Jews and 187 evangelical Protestants; in the 1992 exit poll, 305 Jews and 891 evangelicals; in the 1994 exit poll, 175 Jews and 852 evangelicals; and in the 1994–95 Pew Center surveys, 190 Jews and 2,324 evangelicals.

5. Describing affirmative action policies as "preferential treatment" may seem inaccurate, loaded, and harsh. In dealing with such essentially contested concepts, any choice of language is likely to inspire objections. We employ this phrase because that is how the survey questions were worded.

6. Responses to the groups, expressed on a continuum with options of "very favorable," "somewhat favorable," "mixed," "somewhat unfavorable," and "very unfavorable," were coded so that a higher score indicated a more positive view of the group. The items were standard-scored and then combined

in a composite measure (alpha = .745) that was itself standard-scored to a mean of zero and standard deviation of one.

7. Undated mailing from the Anti-Defamation League, July 1996.

8. In our view this does not signify religious hostility, but rather a strong sense that the political agenda of Christian conservatives constitutes a fundamental threat to American Jews.

9. Having learned from his mistakes, Jackson later made overtures to Jewish voters. What is interesting is that many Jewish voters remain sympathetic to the civil rights agenda in spite of their perceptions that many African Americans entertain anti-Semitic opinions. For example, in the Pew Center surveys, Jewish respondents were far more likely than evangelical Protestants to attribute persisting black economic problems to discrimination, and far less likely to blame blacks themselves for such problems.

10. By contrast, Democratic support among white evangelical Democrats would drop from 72 percent to 49 percent in the event Jackson were nominated for Vice President.

11. Among nonevangelical Protestant Republicans, Robertson lowered the Republican vote intention from 85 percent to 52 percent and similarly reduced Roman Catholic partisan loyalty from 78 percent to 42 percent. The mention of Robertson as the vice presidential candidate left preferences basically unchanged among Republican evangelicals; 67 percent said they would vote Republican, and 65 percent did so when Robertson was identified as the vice presidential candidate.

12. For an interesting recent attempt to provide an explanation that includes both internal and external factors, see Levey (1995,1996).

13. Jews perceive proselytizing aimed at them as anti-Semitic, an insight that helps explain why they regard evangelicals so negatively. Whatever the motivations of those who seek converts, Jews perceive these efforts as a continuation of the Holocaust by peaceful means.

14. To be classified as part of the Religious Right, a respondent had to meet the following four criteria: endorse a literal view of the Bible, report a "born-again" religious experience, indicate an attempt to evangelize others, and identify as a social and/or political conservative. About 14 percent satisfied all these criteria.

15. In some respects, the evangelical/born-again community actually outstrips Jewish respondents in support for expansionist Israeli policies. In the 1988 AJC survey, born-again Protestants were less supportive than Jews of talks with the PLO in the event that organization recognized Israel and reduced terrorism. They were also less likely to report feeling troubled by the policies of the Likud government. Upon closer inspection, however, these differences really reflect the low levels of opinionation among this segment of the matched sample. Very large proportions of born-again white Protestants—38 percent in the PLO question and 49 percent on the Likud policies—selected the "not sure" response option. Among those with opinions, evangelicals were still more

hawkish than Jewish respondents, but not by much. During the first author's stay in Israel in 1990–91, the "International Christian Embassy," an unofficial group that espouses fundamentalist Christianity, frequently condemned the Jewish peace movement and urged the Likud to adopt even more aggressive policies in defense of Israeli claims to the West Bank and Gaza. According to the 1996 AJC surveys, evangelicals were more pro-Israel than the rest of the American population and, by a 72 percent to 43 percent ratio, more likely to agree that "Jews have a right to the land of Israel, since it was promised to them by God." Relatively few American or Israeli Jews cite the Bible as the basis of land claims.

16. The scales are slightly tilted against confirming the Wuthnow hypothesis with this sample because the prime Jewish exemplars of traditionalism, the ultra-orthodox or *haredim*, are unlikely to participate in opinion surveys. Concerned primarily with maintaining their own subcommunity, these Jews might find common cause with the Christian Right on such matters as school vouchers. For two reasons, though, their omission does not pose a severe threat to testing the culture war hypothesis on Jews. First, unlike their Israeli counterparts who have intervened to obtain direct state benefits and urge the state to follow Jewish law, the American ultra-orthodox have refrained from playing a conspicuous public role (Heilman 1992). Second, the Jewish sample does contain a significant number of the Modern Orthodox who have increasingly embraced the social values of ultra-orthodoxy. If Jewish political attitudes are indeed stratified by religious commitment, that pattern should be observed in these data.

17. Despite most efforts to portray Christian commitment as multidimensional, in empirical analyses it usually reduces to a single factor dominated by orthodox religious beliefs (Roof 1979). The Jewish pattern appears to be more differentiated.

18. In the Jewish tradition, piety and righteousness are often equated with the performance of mitzvot, a term that is only loosely equated with "good deeds" (Hertzberg 1996). (It is telling that ancient Hebrew does not contain a word for "religious" and modern Hebrew uses language that refers more to adherence to the law than to belief.) In a classic example of transvaluation, many Jews understand this to mean that Judaism is defined essentially by acts of charity (Sklare and Greenblum 1967). Whatever the accuracy of that understanding, such a definition does not facilitate operationalization in the survey setting.

19. For a parallel analysis of Israeli Jews, see Wald and Shye (1995).

20. As indicated by the correlation of +.55 between them, the two forms of Jewish identity are not orthogonal.

21. We cannot really determine whether the Wuthnow hypothesis of inner group differences based on religiosity holds for the non-Jews in this sample, because we lack both comparable measures of communal and associational involvement for non-Jews and a sufficient number of non-Jewish respondents.

Nonetheless, when we stratified Jewish political attitudes solely by frequency of synagogue attendance—the type of measure used in studies that support Wuthnow's argument with predominantly Christian samples—it did not discriminate effectively among Jews.

22. If they were familiar with it, Jews might recommend that evangelicals attend to the doctrine of "civil peace" associated with Catholic theologian John Courtney Murray (1960). Murray advised Catholics to appreciate and venerate a political system that had allowed them an unparalleled degree of religious freedom. The price of maintaining such a system is the need to tolerate behavior by others that their own faith deemed sinful. If Catholics insisted on applying Church doctrine to U.S. society, Murray feared, they might well encourage other groups to impose sectarian policies on Catholics.

References

Allinsmith, Wesley, and Beverly Allinsmith. 1948. "Religious Affiliation and Politico-Economic Attitudes: A Study of Eight Major U.S. Religious Groups." *Public Opinion Quarterly* 12: 377–89.

American Jewish Committee, Philadelphia Chapter. 1996. Philadelphia: American Jewish Committee.

Cantor, David. 1994. *The Religious Right: The Assault on Tolerance and Pluralism in America.* New York: Anti-Defamation League.

Cohen, Naomi. 1992. *Jews in Christian America.* New York: Oxford University Press.

———. 1993. *Natural Adversaries or Possible Allies? American Jews and the New Christian Right.* New York: American Jewish Committee.

Fein, Leonard. 1988. *Where Are We? The Inner Life of America's Jews.* New York: Harper and Row.

Forman, Lori. 1994. *The Political Activity of the Religious Right in the 1990's: A Critical Analysis.* New York: American Jewish Committee.

Ginsberg, Benjamin. 1993. *The Fatal Embrace: Jews and the State.* Chicago: University of Chicago Press.

Green, John C., and James L. Guth. 1991. "The Bible and the Ballot Box: The Shape of Things to Come." In *The Bible and the Ballot Box*, edited by James L. Guth and John C. Green, 207–25. Boulder, Colo.: Westview Press.

Green, John C., James L. Guth, Corwin E. Smidt, and Lyman A. Kellstedt. 1996. *Religion and the Culture Wars: Dispatches from the Front.* Lanham, Md.: Rowman & Littlefield.

Heilman, Samuel. 1992. *Defenders of the Faith: Inside Ultra-Orthodox Jewry.* New York: Schocken.

Hertzberg, Arthur. 1996. "My God, Myself." *Hadassah Magazine* (November): 74.

Himmelfarb, Milton. 1985. "Another Look at the Jewish Vote." *Commentary* (December): 39–44.

Hunter, James Davison. 1991. *Culture Wars: The Struggle to Define America.* New York: Basic Books.

Hyman, Paula E. 1992. "Was There a 'Jewish Politics' in Western and Central Europe?" In *The Quest for Utopia: Jewish Political Ideas and Institutions Through the Ages*, edited by Zvi Gitelman, 105–18. Armonk, N.Y.: M. E. Sharpe.

Jelen, Ted G. 1994. "Religion and Foreign Policy Attitudes: Exploring the Effects of Denomination and Doctrine." *American Politics Quarterly* 22: 382–400.

Jelen, Ted G., Corwin E. Smidt, and Clyde Wilcox. 1993. "The Political Effects of the Born-Again Phenomenon." In *Rediscovering the Religious Factor in American Politics*, edited by David C. Leege and Lyman A. Kellstedt, 199–215. Armonk, N.Y.: M. E. Sharpe.

Katz, Jacob. 1978. *Out of the Ghetto: The Social Background of Jewish Emancipation, 1770–1870.* New York: Schocken.

Kellstedt, Lyman A., John C. Green, James L. Guth, and Corwin E. Smidt. 1994. "Religious Voting Blocs in the 1992 Election: The Year of the Evangelical?" *Sociology of Religion* 55: 307–26.

Leege, David C. 1993. The Decomposition of the Religious Vote: A Comparison of White, Non-Hispanic Catholics with Other Ethnoreligious Groups, 1960–1992. Paper delivered to the annual meeting of the American Political Science Association, Washington, D.C.

Legge, Jerome, Jr. 1995. "Explaining Jewish Liberalism in the United States: An Exploration of Socioeconomic, Religious and Communal Living Variables." *Social Science Quarterly* 76: 124–41.

Lenski, Gerhard. 1961. *The Religious Factor: A Sociologist's Inquiry.* New York: Doubleday.

Leventman, Paula Goldman, and Seymour Leventman. 1976. "Congressman Drinan, S.J., and His Jewish Constituents." *American Jewish Historical Quarterly* 66: 215–48.

Levey, Geoffrey Brahm. 1995. "Values, Interests and Identity: Jews and Politics in a Changing World." In *Studies in Contemporary Jewry*, Vol. 11, edited by Peter Y. Medding, 64–85. New York: Oxford University Press.

———. 1996. "The Liberalism of American Jews: Has It Been Explained?" *British Journal of Political Science* 26: 369–401.

Lipset, Seymour Martin, and Earl Raab. 1995. *Jews and the New American Scene.* Cambridge: Harvard University Press.

Martire, Gregory, and Ruth Clark. 1982. *Anti-Semitism in the United States: A Study of Prejudice in the 1980s.* New York: Praeger.

Moen, Matthew C. 1994. "From Revolution to Evolution: The Changing Nature of the Christian Right." *Sociology of Religion* 55: 345–57.

Moyers, Bill, and Robert S. Rifkind. 1996. *The Stakes in the Fight for the First Amendment.* New York: American Jewish Committee.

Murray, John Courtney. 1960. *We Hold These Truths: Catholic Reflections on the American Proposition.* New York: Sheed and Ward.

Roiphe, Anne. 1992. "Bush and the Party of God." *Jerusalem Report* (8 October): 54.

Saperstein, David. 1994. "With Friends Like These, We Don't Need Enemies." *Moment* 19 (October): 49–51, 76.

Sears, David O., Richard R. Lau, Tom R. Tyler, and Harris M. Allen. 1980. "Self-Interest vs. Symbolic Politics in Policy Attitudes and Presidential Voting." *American Political Science Review* 74: 670–84.

Sklare, Marshall, and Joseph Greenblum. 1967. *Jewish Identity on the Suburban Frontier.* New York: Basic Books.

Wald, Kenneth D. 1994. "The Religious Dimension of American Anti-Communism." *Journal of Church and State* 36: 483–507.

Wald, Kenneth D., and Samuel Shye. 1995. "Religious Influence in Electoral Behavior: Institutional and Social Forces in Israel." *Journal of Politics* 57 (May 1995): 495–507.

Wald, Kenneth D., and Lee Sigelman. 1995. Jews' Views of Preferential Treatment: The End of Tribalism? Paper presented to the annual meeting of the Society for the Scientific Study of Religion/Religious Research Association, 26–29 October, St. Louis, Missouri.

Wald, Kenneth D., James L. Guth, Cleveland R. Fraser, John C. Green, Corwin E. Smidt, and Lyman A. Kellstedt. 1996. "Reclaiming Zion: How American Religious Groups View the Middle East." *Israel Affairs* 2: 147–68.

Wertheimer, Jack. 1993. *A People Divided.* New York: Basic Books.

Wilcox, Clyde. 1996. *Onward Christian Soldiers?* Boulder, Colo.: Westview Press.

Wuthnow, Robert. 1988. *The Restructuring of American Religion.* Princeton, N.J.: Princeton University Press.

Part IV

Cross-National Perspectives
of the Christian Right

9

Divided by a Common Religion: The Christian Right in England and the United States

J. Christopher Soper

The role of religion in England and the United States is a study of contrasts. England has an officially established Church, the state liberally funds private religious schools, and there is formal religious worship and instruction in state-run schools. The United States, by contrast, has a strong tradition of church-state separation, it is unlawful for the state to fund private religious schools, and the Supreme Court has barred state-sponsored religious exercises from the public schools. Given these differences, one might logically conclude that the social and political impact of religious groups was much greater in England than in the United States. This could not be farther from the truth.

While some have argued that the state has removed religion from the public square in the United States (Carter 1993; Neuhaus 1984), religious groups continue to have a profound political influence. American political parties are divided along religious lines and social issues remain central to the debate of both parties. Politicians liberally deploy the language of the scriptures, and religious interest groups are politically significant. Religion has maintained an important public political role in England, yet religion is not the basis for party cleavage and social issues are peripheral to party politics. Politicians almost never discuss religion, and religious interest groups have only a marginal impact on public policy. It is not surprising, therefore, that the Christian Right has found more fertile soil in the United States than in England.[1]

In this chapter three factors are identified that help explain these differences and highlight a key irony between the Christian Right in the two nations. The most significant contrasting factors between the countries are (1) the social and religious conditions that produce a very different market for conservative Christian politics, (2) divergent policies in each state on social and religious issues that have affected the rise of a Christian Right movement, and (3) political and institutional structures that provide dissimilar opportunities for organized interest groups to have a political impact. In each of these areas, conditions in the United States have fueled the rise of the Christian Right, while circumstances have muted a similar movement in England. Religionists sympathetic to the Christian Right are numerous in America, they perceive a genuine threat from the state in terms of public policy related to religious issues, and there are many opportunities for organized groups to express their views through political institutions. By contrast, there are few active religionists in England, the state is far from hostile to organized religious groups, and the political system provides few opportunities for groups to have a political impact.

The central irony in this comparative analysis is that the U.S. Christian Right has mobilized a powerful social movement and gained access to, but little influence among, decision makers, while the reverse is true in England. In this latter context, there is only a negligible Christian Right movement, yet religious leaders have both access to and some influence over key areas of public policy. The Anglo-American contrast is important not only for what it reveals about the political successes and failures of the American and British Christian Right, but also for what it teaches about the political opportunities and incentives for religious group mobilization provided by different political cultures (Soper 1994).

Social and Religious Factors:
The Market for the Christian Right

The most obvious contrast between England and the United States that affects Christian Right political activism involves the rates of religious membership and activity in the two nations. In terms of church membership and attendance, Britain is among the most secular countries in the industrialized world and America one of the least. The majority of the British population are "nominal" Christians, people who claim to believe in God, profess to be Anglicans, but are religiously inactive. According to a 1995 survey, 55 percent of the British consider themselves to be religious and 57 percent say they believe in heaven. In addition, the Church of England has baptized about half of the country's total population. However, only 14 percent report attending religious services once a week or more, and church membership rates have been falling rapidly for the past several decades in England, from 22 percent of the population in 1970 to 11 percent in 1990. In the United States, by contrast, 82 percent of respondents said they considered themselves to be religious, 84 percent believe in heaven, and 44 percent reported attending church once a week or more (Ladd 1995).

Not only is there a larger religious market in the United States than in England, but the composition of church membership is also significantly different in the two countries. Church membership in England comes primarily from the nonsectarian, nonevangelical Anglican and Roman Catholic churches. There has been an evangelical renewal in Britain, particularly within the Church of England, but a liberal perspective still dominates the theology and politics of the main Protestant churches (Bebbington 1989; Hylson-Smith 1988). Although they have grown rapidly in recent years, Baptist, independent evangelical Protestant, fundamentalist, and Pentecostal churches (the core of Christian Right support in the United States) are small with only 800,000 members among them out of a total population of nearly 50 million (Briereley and Longley 1993). By contrast, church membership remains high in the United States, and evangelical and fundamentalist churches are a significant percentage of the total. The evangelical Southern Baptist Church is the largest Protestant denomination in the country with over 15 million members; survey research shows that approximately 23 percent of the U.S. population are white, evangelical Protestants (Pew Research Center 1996).

The relative influence of evangelicalism has had a dramatic impact on the fortunes of Christian political movements in the two countries. American evangelicals have historically competed aggressively and successfully in the religious marketplace for church members and social influence (Hatch 1989). Beginning with the fundamentalist controversy in the early part of the twentieth century, American evangelicals and fundamentalists have militantly opposed modernism with the development of their own set of social, educational, and religious institutions. These subcultures have shielded an evangelical worldview from secular challenges and made it possible for activists and leaders to gain the skills necessary to engage the world. In recent years, the evangelical leadership has become adept at using the latest communications technology to organize supporters through a well-integrated network of churches, radio and television programs, and schools. According to a 1996 survey (Pew Research Center 1996), pluralities of Americans watch religious programs and/or listen to religious radio shows (43 percent) or listen to Christian music (45 percent).

The story is far different in England. British and American evangelicals were part of a single transatlantic movement from the time of the Puritans to the end of the nineteenth century, but they parted company with the rise of American fundamentalism (Marsden 1977). Fundamentalism never took hold in England. British evangelicals did not respond militantly to the modernist challenges of the early twentieth century nor did they develop their own independent institutions. In recent years, British evangelicals have begun to form their own organizations, including seminaries, missionary organizations, and even the first Christian cable television station, but they do not have the general impact on the churches and culture that their American counterparts do (Gledhill and Frean 1995).

With a subculture well established, American evangelicals were in the ideal position for political mobilization when social and political change challenged their moral views in the 1960s and 1970s. The liberalization of abortion and divorce laws, the proliferation of pornographic material, the greater social acceptance of homosexuality, the removal of religious expression from the public schools, and a perceived attack on religion itself threatened the traditional religious views of evangelicals. Evangelical discontent with these changes sprang from their religious ideology and provided the impetus for the formation of political organizations to combat what believers saw as America's moral decay. Over the next two decades, evangelicals provided the bulk of support for organizations such as Moral Majority, Traditional Values Coalition, Concerned Women for America, Christian Coalition and Family Research Council, to name a few. Despite the intention of group leaders to expand the movement to include orthodox Jews, conservative mainline Protestants, and traditional Catholics, they have largely been unable to move beyond their evangelical membership. Evangelicals themselves are not politically monolithic, but they are so numerous in America that the Christian Right has been able to become a significant social and political movement simply by mobilizing a portion of them and not going beyond this core religious support.

The mobilization of the Christian Right in America has demonstrated that, under the right circumstances, regular churchgoers lend themselves splendidly to political mobilization. From a resource perspective, committed people with shared beliefs who gather frequently in the same place are ideal for political activism (Gilbert 1993). The Christian Coalition, for example, uses evangelical and fundamentalist churches to distribute campaign literature and recruit group members. Television and radio stations and independent schools have also been a key to the success of movement activists because they provide additional opportunities to contact a sympathetic audience. An evangelical ideology is also an important "resource" as it provides a powerful link between orthodox Christian beliefs and conservative political views—particularly on social issues—and nurtures believers in the efficacy of political action. According to a 1996 survey, a higher percentage of white evangelicals (70 percent) than any other religious tradition believed that churches should express their views on social and political issues (Pew Research Center 1996).

British evangelicals share the religious ideology and social issue conservatism of their American counterparts, but they are not as well placed for political organization. There is a Christian Right in Britain, and evangelicals have been instrumental in the formation of several political organizations including LIFE, SPUC (Society for the Protection of Unborn Children), CARE (Christian Action Research Education), and the National Viewers and Listeners Association. And, from an ideological standpoint, there is a great similarity between the protest groups formed on both sides of the Atlantic. As with American organizations, the intent of these British groups is to represent religious beliefs and defend deeply held values, particularly on the issue of abortion. But, without the resources of a large religious base or a network of institutions, it has been more difficult for group leaders there to recruit members and have a strong political impact. The simple fact that there are far fewer people sitting in church pews on a typical Sunday, listening to Christian radio stations, or attending Christian colleges limits the capacity for this kind of mobilization in England. The Christian Right in England has had more success expanding beyond its evangelical base to include Anglicans and Roman Catholics, but this has occurred largely out of necessity. Leaders of the Anglican and Roman Catholic churches have important access to policy makers on educational and moral issues, which has meant that the fledgling Christian Right has had to make overtures beyond its natural religious constituency in order to have any political impact.

Policy Factors: The Demand for the Christian Right

England is far more secular than the United States, yet there is less of a sense of hostility to religion in Britain. The state generally accommodates organized religious groups and affirms the idea that churches have an important cultural and social function to play. In terms of public policy, the state-owned British Broadcasting Corporation annually gives the churches hundreds of hours of time for religious broadcasting, religious schools receive state aid, and religious exercises and instruction are part of the curriculum in state-run schools. Even in their moments of wildest fancy, Ralph Reed and the other leaders of the Christian Right could not possibly imagine winning these concessions from the American state.

The religion offered in English institutions is rarely evangelical, but by retaining a formal role for religion in public life, the British state has minimized the criticism so prevalent among American evangelicals that the state is hostile to organized religion. The Christian Coalition, the Traditional Values Coalition, Concerned Women for America and other groups within the Christian Right have successfully appealed to group members by claiming that the American state is antagonistic toward religion. The argument is plausible given (1) Supreme Court decisions of the early 1960s that removed prayer and Bible reading from the public schools and eliminated virtually all state aid to religious schools, as well as (2) changing social values that challenge traditional religious norms. Ironically, the "threat" felt by the Christian Right in the United States from public officials is part of the reason that they have been better able than their British counterparts to organize a social movement. The perception that the state has done nothing to stop the demise of conservative religious values—that the state actually opposes the values and lifestyle of conservative Christians—has been a key factor in explaining the rise of the Christian Right movement in the United States (Wilcox 1992).

It is more difficult for religionists in England to sustain the argument that the state is hostile to religion when policy, in certain key areas, benefits churches. The state in England has not departed from its traditional support for religious schools nor abandoned its commitment to religion in state-supported schools. Since a challenge to a group's values is a key factor for an emerging social movement, the absence of such a threat deprives English evangelicals of a central argument in favor of forming a Christian Right political movement.

A final policy difference between the countries that is worth noting is the role played by the established Church of England.[2] It enjoys a level of social and political influence that cannot be explained by its minimal legal privileges and limited number of active congregants. While only five percent of the British population are active members of an Anglican church, such membership is concentrated in the middle and upper classes. This helps to explain how the Anglican Church has come to have significant representation in the upper echelons of the nation's political, legal, and cultural institutions (Medhurst and Moyser 1988). In addition, there is a widespread assumption that the Church of England and its bishops who sit in the House of Lords will have a role in major pieces of moral legislation. The church has used its status to blunt some, though certainly not all, of the secular attacks on religion. There has been a liberalization of abortion, pornography, homosexuality, and divorce laws in the past several decades, but the church has often been a moderating force on these issues. On abortion, for example, the law requires that a woman seeking an abortion must obtain the consent of two physicians. Church leaders also won concessions from the government on a 1995 bill that would have automatically allowed no-fault divorces after a waiting period of twelve months; the bill was amended to allow spouses with strong religious views to claim additional hardship in their attempts to block a divorce.

Political and Institutional Factors: The Opportunities for the Christian Right

The different market and demand for conservative politics in England and the United States does not by itself explain the influence of the Christian Right in the two countries. Britain's religious community is relatively small, but the political interest groups formed by the Christian Right are among the largest in the nation. This is particularly true for the pro-life organizations SPUC and LIFE, which have 47,000 and 35,000 members respectively, and are in the top ten percent in membership among British promotional interest groups. There is no British equivalent to the 1.5 million-member Christian Coalition, although the fast-growing Movement for Christian Democracy is a multi-issue organization that has twice as many members as the National Union of Mineworkers and more adherents than the Socialist Workers' Party (Glass 1995).

The most dramatic contrast between the two countries comes from the partisan political impact of the Christian Right. British groups have initiated some political debate on such issues as abortion, pornography, divorce, and Sunday closing laws, but they have had almost no influence within the dominant political parties. American organizations, by contrast, have initiated much debate on a variety of public policy issues, and they have now become a key constituency within the Republican party.

The Christian Right in England has been frustrated in its efforts as much by the paucity of opportunities for meaningful activism that Britain's relatively centralized political system affords it as by its small size. The British system is centralized in three important respects: it is a unitary state, with a parliamentary system, and a tradition of strong political parties. The success of the U.S. Christian Right, by contrast, is as much attributable to the multiple points of access that America's decentralized polity gives organized interest groups to penetrate the political process as it is with the size of the evangelical constituency. The American state is decentralized in having a federal polity, a division of authority at the national level, and weak political parties. As many scholars have noted, institutions shape the capacity of organized groups to affect public policy, and each of these institutional factors has influenced the ability of Christian Right organizations in both countries to politicize their social issue discontent and influence public policy on moral issues (Weaver and Rockman 1993).

Because of Britain's unitary polity, local political authorities lack real independence and have little role in the policy-making process. The local bodies that do exist are constitutionally subject to the will and dictates of a sovereign Parliament that can, and has, created and abolished local governments through legislation. On two key Christian Right issues, abortion and education, for example, local government simply implements policy that Parliament or a government department makes. From the standpoint of organized interest groups of the Christian Right, this means that there is little incentive to "capture" or even lobby local or regional governments because the power to decide policy does not reside there (Cochrane 1993).

The importance of state and local governments in America's federal system stands in stark contrast to Britain's unitary polity. Local government units in the United States have political significance and autonomy on the social issues about which the Christian Right cares most deeply: abortion, pornography, and religion in the public schools. This creates a powerful incentive for Christian Right mobilization at the local level, which is precisely what has occurred there. The Christian Coalition, as an example, claims to have 48 state and 1,400 local chapters; the Family

Research Council has 26 state affiliates (Green 1995). The Christian Right has used its grassroots support at the state and local levels to help win victories in school board races, gay rights initiatives, and restrictions on access to abortion services and funding. In the world of pressure-group politics, nothing succeeds like success; because the American Christian Right has demonstrated a capacity to affect political outcomes they have been better able than the British Christian Right to mobilize group members. British groups are less able to mobilize support at the local level because the issues that they care most deeply about are national political issues. It is difficult to imagine the Christian Right in the United States becoming as politically salient as it is without a federal political system at its disposal.

Models of interest group politics in Britain often note that, in order to be most effective, interest groups direct their effort toward the institutions that dominate the policy-making process: the executive branch and the Whitehall Street bureaucracy (Richardson 1993). The prime minister and the cabinet make public policy; the other branches of government do not share that power. Members of Parliament (MPs) are expected to vote as instructed by their party whip on any government bill, which means that a government with a healthy majority in the House of Commons can do just about anything it wants. The ideal situation for an interest group in a system dominated by the executive branch is for the group to have access to the government departments that set public policy. The centralized nature of the policy-making process can facilitate reform, but only if an interest group has this influence within Whitehall (Pierson and Smith 1993).

In some cases the government does negotiate directly with the churches, particularly on educational issues where the Church of England and the Roman Catholic Church have performed a role in designing legislation (Waddington 1985). The Christian Right, however, has had little or no success penetrating the executive or bureaucratic arenas or eliciting support from key political elites. While she was in office, Margaret Thatcher ignored the wishes of conservative Christian interest groups, and actually opposed the Christian Right on such issues as Sunday closing laws and abortion; she had little or no electoral incentive to respond to these voters, who were neither numerous nor willing to abandon the Conservative Party on moral issues alone. The Christian Right's best opportunities for a policy impact have come when they have joined forces with the more powerful Anglican and Roman Catholic Churches.

Political parties are another potential conduit for interest group activism. The Labor Party is not at all sympathetic to social issue conservatism or religious activism; when Tony Blair became the leader of the Labor Party in 1994, party activists were shocked and somewhat dismayed to discover that he was a committed Christian (Aitken 1996). The Conservative Party is theoretically a more natural home for conservative Christians. The Church of England has famously been described as the Tory Party at prayer, indicating the close historical alliance between the Church and the Conservative Party. According to a 1992 survey of Conservative Party members, a strong link exists between party and church involvement, with 70 percent of party members claiming regular church attendance (Whiteley, Seyd, and Richardson 1992).

The important point of political cleavage in the British party system is not religion, however, but social class.[3] Moral issues are not generally part of the debate within the Conservative Party, and recent attempts to introduce a social agenda have been ineffectual. In 1993 Prime Minister John Major launched his "back-to-basics" campaign at the Conservative Party conference and called for a return to such traditional values as respect for the family, personal responsibility, and self-discipline. To American ears this seems innocuous, but party members opposed the campaign and the press ridiculed it—gleefully exposing the moral indiscretions of various Conservative government ministers. Major eventually abandoned his campaign, claiming that he never intended the focus to be primarily about personal morality (Macintyre 1994). Major's attempt to switch priorities from economic to social policy failed because most voters, even most Conservative voters, do not expect the parties to emphasize moral issues. The Conservative Party does not have an official position on abortion, for example, and only one-third of the party members surveyed in 1992 believed that a future Conservative government should make abortions more difficult to obtain (Whiteley, Seyd, and Richardson 1992, 54).

The British electoral system also works to the disadvantage of pressure groups like the Christian Right. British elections are "party centered," meaning that parties, not candidates, are the dynamic element in a campaign. British parties control virtually all the resources candidates desire and most of the sanctions they fear. Voters do not choose party candidates for the general election in political primaries; instead a small number of party leaders select candidates in each of the local constituencies. In addition, the party finances and organizes the campaign, which means that candidates do not need to raise money from individuals and organized groups. Candidates who win a general election remain dependent upon the party while in office. The party controls nearly all the rewards that a member of Parliament seeks while in office, which helps to ensure party cohesion. All the features of the British electoral system work to create a set of incentives that link legislators more closely to national party than to the local constituency, and make interest group appeals to individual MPs almost a hopeless strategy.

In the absence of support from Whitehall's bureaucrats or the political parties, groups have tried to bypass the parties and exert their own pressure on individual members of Parliament. The Christian Right has been able to initiate public debate on a number of moral issues through private members' bills (Marsh and Read 1988). These bills are unique in British politics because they are unwhipped, which means that MPs are free to vote according to their conscience. This provides a limited opportunity for pressure groups to lobby members of Parliament, who are free of the normal pressure to vote the party line.

Abortion was decriminalized in 1967 through a private members' bill, and there have been several attempts to restrict abortion services using this legislative tactic. The most recent effort was by David Alton in 1988. His bill called for an upper time limit of eighteen weeks of pregnancy beyond which abortions would not be allowed except in extreme cases. Public opinion polls showed that a majority of the nation supported the bill, and pro-life organizations engaged in one of the largest lobbying efforts in recent years. The bill passed the Second Reading in the Commons by a vote of 296 to 251, but it ran out of time when it returned to the House for its final approval. Opponents used delaying tactics to block the bill's progress, and the Conservative government refused to grant extra time to work the bill through the House. Prime Minister Thatcher argued that it was Conservative Party policy not to provide government time to private members' legislation, but pro-life groups countered that the decision was implicitly a political choice in favor of the status quo. The bill's failure reflects the executive dominance of the British system; in the end the government determined the bill's outcome with its refusal to provide extra time.

Pro-life organizations have grown increasingly frustrated with their inability to change the legal status of abortion in England, and they have recently vowed to promote a U.S. style grassroots action against abortion (Brown 1995). What these groups fail to appreciate, however, is that Britain's unitary polity, parliamentary system, and strong political parties combine to create a political environment in which it is very difficult for pressure groups to initiate such a campaign. In the absence of elite and party support, there are few opportunities in Britain's centralized polity for interest groups like the Christian Right to initiate policy change. Christian Right organizations, which had a limited base of support to begin with, have largely been unable to exert influence on social issues or become a key constituency within one of the major political parties. In fact, a recent analysis reveals that, even with regard to voting on private members' bills dealing with homosexuality and capital punishment in the House of Commons, party affiliation remains the main determining factor for the way a MP votes (Read, Marsh, and Richards 1994).

The American Christian Right has had a dramatically different impact on U.S. party politics. Evangelicals were an attractive target for Ronald Reagan when he ran for President in 1980. They were a significant part of the electorate, with a plurality of them Democrats, but the Democratic Party's social issue liberalism dissatisfied them. The GOP attracted Christian Right support with conservative positions on abortion, religion in the public schools, and family values, and over the next several elections, evangelical identification with the Republican Party and support for its candidates increased (Smidt 1993). By the 1994 midterm elections, white, evangelical Christians, the core constituency for the Christian Right, represented 20 percent of the total electorate and voted for Republican house candidates by a margin of 76 to 24 percent (Soper 1996).

The support of Republican elites helped to legitimate the Christian Right and increased the publicity surrounding the social issues of abortion and family values. Yet, in terms of public policy, very little changed at the national level, and the Christian Right gradually turned its attention to state and local politics to press its case. The movement has matured politically and become more adept at using the opportunities that America's decentralized polity affords organized interest groups (Moen 1992). A key feature in that mobilization has been the effort by the Christian Right to penetrate the Republican Party. Unlike Britain's parties, American political parties are decentralized and weak, and thereby open to the grassroots mobilization of organized pressure groups. The porousness of American parties has provided the ideal context for Christian Right political activism, particularly at the state and local levels where turnout in party elections is low and conservative Christians have been able to win important party posts. The Christian Right has committed time and resources and turned out for party organizational elections to which few party members generally pay attention. As a result, the Christian Right has been able to achieve a "dominant" influence in eighteen state Republican Party organizations and a "substantial" influence in thirteen more (Persinos 1994).

The Christian Right has used its newfound strength within the GOP in a number of ways. First, the movement has helped to shape the party's platform at the state and national levels. The 1996 Republican Party platform retained the party's commitment to a constitutional amendment that would bar abortions, despite the fact that the party's presidential nominee, Bob Dole, publicly called for a message of tolerance on abortion in the platform. Second, the Christian Right has helped to nominate sympathetic candidates in Republican Party primary elections. In 1994 Christian Right voters proved to be a decisive constituency in the nomination of Oliver North (R-VA) and David Beasley (R-SC), and in 1996 the pro-life movement specifically, and the Christian Right more generally, aided in the successful Senate primary campaigns of Ronna Romney (R-MI) and Sam Brownback (R-KS).

What is even more significant is that social issues, and religion, are a significant point of cleavage between the two main political parties in the United States. The social issues that British parties ignore— abortion, family values, and homosexuality—are central to the discussion of American political parties, particularly the Republican Party (Kellstedt, Green, Guth, and Smidt 1994). In part, these issues are important in the United States because the Christian Right has had more opportunities to make them salient. Republican Party elites at the state level are powerless to stop this kind of insurgency movement within the party, despite the fact that the Christian Right has intensified tensions between socially moderate and conservative wings of the GOP (Hertzke 1993).

The "capture" of some state Republican Party organizations by the Christian Right has, however, been of limited value. Certainly it has been an important symbolic victory for the Christian Right, but the very weakness of American parties limits what any group can accomplish when it "controls" a political party. In contrast to England, American elections are candidate centered, not party centered, meaning that candidates, not parties, are the dynamic element of the campaign. American political parties do not control the nomination process, nor do they provide candidates with the essential resources for a campaign: money and personnel. In this context, Christian Right dominance of state Republican party organizations does not translate directly into political victories, as it would in England where the parties command both the nomination and electoral process. Even at the national level, there is no guarantee that Christian Right mobilization within the GOP will translate directly into public policy if the party wins the presidency. In 1996, for example, Bob Dole claimed not to have read the party's platform that the Christian Right worked so hard to write. There is no guarantee that a future Republican president would feel any more bound than Dole by the party doctrine on abortion should he or she win the election in 2000.

The Christian Right has recognized the limitation of party activism, however, and stepped into the vacuum created by weakened political parties by providing resources directly to candidates and mobilizing voters on their behalf (Green, Guth, and Hill 1993). In political primary elections, for example, leaders of the Christian Right have recruited candidates who shared their goals, or supported the party candidate who comes closest to the social issue conservatism of the movement. Nomination politics often pitted purists and pragmatists within the movement but this struggle was a luxury the Christian Right in Britain did not have because the electoral rules of the game shut them out of the decision-making process. The Christian Right has also used its resources to aid Republican Party candidates in the general election. In 1994 the Christian Coalition distributed over thirty million voter guides for the election. It is difficult to measure the influence of this activism, but several candidates closely identified with the Christian Right and the Christian Coalition won office in 1994, including Senator Rick Santorum (R-PA) and Representatives John Lewis (R-KT), Robert Dornan (R-CA), J.C. Watts (R-OK) and Steve Largent (R-OK), to name a few (Rozell and Wilcox 1995).

An important difference between England and the United States is that the executive branch does not dominate the policy-making process in the United States, as in England, but instead it shares authority with the courts and Congress. The fact that the three branches of the national government share power in the United States increases the opportunities for Christian Right political action. In addition to lobbying at the state and local level, then, the Christian Right in the United States has had multiple points of meaningful access at the national level.

Christian Right organizations have used the courts as a vehicle for policy change by initiating litigation on abortion and school prayer. This is an avenue that is simply not available to British groups because British courts do not stand in a position analogous to U.S. courts; they do not have the power to overturn parliamentary laws and thereby shape public policy. American courts, by contrast, have the power of judicial review, and are a key mechanism for policy innovation in the political process. On abortion, for example, the U.S. Supreme Court has repeatedly ruled that individual states have some discretion to determine the grounds under which abortions are performed within their borders, although states cannot outlaw abortions. As a result, states have become battlegrounds on abortion over such issues as the use of public funding to pay for abortions for poor women, mandatory waiting periods for women seeking an abortion, and parental consent for minors who want an abortion.

In contrast to the British Parliament, both houses of the U.S. Congress help to make public policy. The President and the legislature are elected separately, and both the Senate and the House can initiate or block legislation, propose amendments to existing bills, or bargain with other institutions. It makes perfect sense, therefore, for the Christian Right to lobby members of the House and Senate because individual legislators have some power over the policy-making process. Add to this the fact that America's electoral system makes politicians reliant more on individual voters or organized groups within their constituency than on the party, and it becomes apparent why groups work so hard to curry the favor of legislators. This is in direct contrast with England where electoral laws and party discipline shield individual MPs from their local constituency. Appeals to members of Parliament through private members' bills are a sign of the weakness of the Christian Right because the executive, not the legislature, dominates the policy-making process.

Contacts with legislators have paid dividends for the U.S. Christian Right. In 1996 members of Congress with close ties to the Christian Right introduced three major pieces of social legislation. Representatives J.C. Watts (R-OK) and James Talent (R-MO) introduced the American Community Renewal Act. The bill would have established school vouchers for use at religious and other private schools. A second feature would have allowed religious organizations to administer certain welfare programs on behalf of the government and with taxpayer funds, and barred the federal government from discriminating against religious organizations in receipt of public money on the basis of the group's religious character. This is very similar to the welfare bill passed by Congress in 1996 that included an amendment introduced by Senator John Ashcroft (R-MO) that sought to make more use of religious social service organizations than is done today. Senator Charles Grassley (R-IA) and Representative Steve Largent (R-OK) introduced the Parental Rights and Responsibilities Act that would have given parents the right to challenge any service for their children— including education and health care. Finally, in July 1996, Speaker of the House Newt Gingrich, Majority Leader Dick Armey, and Judiciary Committee Chairman Henry Hyde agreed to place on a "fast track" a constitutional amendment that would allow tax money to go to private religious schools. The access that the Christian Right has to policymakers in the legislative process is unmistakable.

Table 9.1 summarizes the differential consequences that flow from these market, demand, and institutional factors that help to shape the nature of Christian Right activity in the United States and England. As the table suggests, social and political factors have contributed to the formation of an important Christian Right movement in the United States, and a relatively small one in England.

Activism and Influence: The Impact of the Christian Right

While an "open" political system has created more opportunities for U.S. Christian Right political activism than has England's "closed" polity, it has not ensured a greater overall policy impact. The irony for a social movement like the Christian Right is that the very features of the American political system that make it relatively easy for it to gain access to the policy-making process (federal polity, weak political parties, division of authority at the national level), make it difficult for the movement to secure a uniform national policy on social issues. The mobilization of the Christian Right in the United States has spawned a countermobilization, intensified conflict on social issues, and created a stalemate on abortion, religion in the public schools, and other social issues. This is perfectly consistent with America's pluralistic and decentralized system where interest groups compete and often "capture" different parts of the state. The U.S. Christian Right has gained all sorts of access to the political process, but it is not apparent that they have had all that much influence on public policy.

Ironically, the centralized nature of British political institutions, which have made it very difficult for the Christian Right to gain access to the policy-making process, would, if the Christian Right controlled them, make it easier for them to implement policy reform than their American counterparts. The Education Reform Act of 1988 demonstrates what can happen when the executive branch supports an interest group's cause. In 1988 the Conservative Party introduced the Education Reform Bill to decentralize the educational system by giving parents more power in the governance of local schools and more choice in what school their children would attend (Feintuck 1994). In addition, the bill included two key goals of the Christian Right in the United States: public aid to religious schools and religious worship in state-run schools.[4] The bill preserved the system of public finance for church

TABLE 9.1
Comparing the American and British Christian Right
Institutional Arrangements and Social Movement Activism

	United States	England
Market		
Size of market	Large	Small
Target Constituency		
Primary	Evangelicals	Evangelicals
Secondary	Mainline Protest.	Anglicans
	Roman Catholics	Roman Catholics
Grievances	High	Low
Institutional Structures		
Federal v. Unitary	Larger Opportunity Structure	Smaller Opportunity Structure
Presidential v. Parliamentary	Larger Opportunity Structure	Smaller Opportunity Structure
Weak v. Strong Party System	Larger Opportunity Structure	Smaller Opportunity Structure
Forms of Action		
Primary	Electioneering Lobbying Party Mobilization	Private Members' Bills Attempted Contacts with Ministries that Design Legislation
Secondary	Litigation	Electioneering
Expected Outcome of Movement Activity	Significant	Small

schools that had been in place since the end of the nineteenth century and strengthened the state's commitment to religious education by requiring (1) religious instruction in state-run schools that would "reflect the fact that the religious traditions in Great Britain are in the main Christian whilst taking account of the teaching and practice of the other principal religions represented in Great Britain," and (2) a daily act of worship of a "broadly Christian character" (Gower 1990, 17). There was intense minority opposition to the bill, but the government did not waver and it easily became law.

Christian Right organizations supported the religious provisions of the bill, but the government hardly considered these groups in its deliberations. What was more significant was that the hierarchies of the Church of England and the Roman Catholic Church supported the bill, and, as previously noted, these churches are key players in educational policy in that they have access to and influence over educational policymakers. The Christian Right wisely joined forces with these more powerful religious lobbies, and they won a political victory as the state maintained its policy of providing aid to religious schools and having religious education and worship as part of the curriculum in state-run schools. But, despite its impact on party politics and its access to policymakers that it has worked so hard to secure, the American Christian Right is still not very close to winning on either of these policy issues.

Conclusion

Evangelical Christians in the United States and England formed political organizations to combat the legalization of abortion, the relaxation of divorce and homosexual laws, and the perceived attack upon organized religion in increasingly secular cultures. Religionists on both sides of the Atlantic shared a social issue conservatism and a willingness to become politically involved. Here the similarities end. While the Christian Right in the United States has become a politically significant force in myriad ways, the Christian Right in England has had little political impact. The main reasons why similar movements have had different outcomes are that evangelicals are more numerous in the United States than in England, sympathetic state policy in England has muted the calls for a Christian Right movement, and America's decentralized polity has provided the Christian Right with more opportunities to flex its political muscle than has Britain's centralized system.

The U.S. Christian Right will continue to be a more imposing political force than its English counterpart both because it represents a larger constituency and because American groups will be able to take advantage of a political system that encourages their activism. Ironically, however, the American Christian Right might never "win" on some of the policy issues that the Christian Right in Britain can currently take for granted, including prayer in the state-run schools and public aid to private, religious schools. America's decentralized political system will make it very hard for the Christian Right to win decisively on these issues, and the United States lacks the model of state accommodation to religion that England has historically adopted. The Christian Right in the United States will continue to have a greater social and political impact than in England, but in terms of public policy the movement might not have much more to show for it.

Notes

1. The United Kingdom is composed of the three countries of England, Scotland, Wales, plus Northern Ireland. This chapter focuses on England, which is by far the largest of these countries with a population of 48 million out of a total United Kingdom population of 57.5 million.

2. The Church of England is the established church in England only; the Church of Scotland is the established church in Scotland; Wales and Northern Ireland do not have an established church.

3. The exception to this is Northern Ireland where the major parties remain divided along religious lines.

4. The Christian Coalition includes both of these policies in its ten-point Contract with the American Family.

References

Aitken, Ian. 1996. "Is Tony Promising Pie in the Sky?" *New Statesman and Society*, 12 April.

Bebbington, D.W. 1989. *Evangelicalism in Modern Britain*. London: Unwin Hyman.

Briereley, Peter, and David Longley, eds. 1993. *United Kingdom Christian Handbook* 1992/93. London: MARC Europe.

Brown, Colin. 1995. "Anti-Abortion MPs Seek to Tighten Laws." *The Independent*, 8 March.

Carter, Stephen L. 1993. *The Culture of Disbelief*. New York: Basic Books.

Cochrane, Allan. 1993. *Whatever Happened to Local Government*. Philadelphia, Pa.: Open University Press.

Feintuck, Mike. 1994. *Accountability and Choice in Schooling*. Philadelphia, Pa.: Open University Press.

Gilbert, Christopher P. 1993. *The Impact of Churches on Political Behavior*. Westport, Conn.: Westview Press.

Glass, Suzanne. 1995. "A Matter of Life and Death." *The Independent*, 15 October.

Gledhill, Ruth, and Alexandra Frean. 1995. "Christian TV Station to Start Next Year." *The Times*, 17 May.

Gower, Ralph. 1990. *Religious Education at the Primary Stage*. Oxford: Lion Educational Trust.

Green, John C. 1995. "The Christian Right and the 1994 Elections: An Overview." In *God at the Grass Roots: The Christian Right in the 1994 Elections*, edited by Mark J. Rozell and Clyde Wilcox, 1–18. Lanham, Md.: Rowman & Littlefield.

Green, John C., James L. Guth, and Kevin Hill. 1993. "Faith and Election: The Christian Right in Congressional Campaigns, 1978–1988." *Journal of Politics* 55: 80–91.

Hatch, Nathan O. 1989. *The Democratization of American Christianity*. New Haven, Conn.: Yale University Press.

Hertzke, Allen D. 1993. *Echoes of Discontent*. Washington, D.C.: CQ Press.

Hylson-Smith, Kenneth. 1988. *Evangelicals in the Church of England*. Edinburgh: T&T Clark.

Kellstedt, Lyman A., John C. Green, James L. Guth, and Corwin E. Smidt. 1994. "Religious Voting Blocs in the 1992 Election: The Year of the Evangelical?" *Sociology of Religion* 55: 307–26.

Ladd, Everett Carl. 1995. "Every Country is Unique, But the U.S. is Different." *The Public Perspective* 6 (April/May): 14.

Macintyre, Donald. 1994. "Tories in Turmoil: True Roots of 'Back to Basics' are Unearthed." *The Independent*, 12 January.

Marsden, George. 1977. "Fundamentalism as an American Phenomenon: A Comparison with English Evangelicalism." *Church History* 46: 215–32.

Marsh, David, and Melvyn Read. 1988. *Private Members' Bills*. Cambridge: Cambridge University Press.

Medhurst, Kenneth, and George Moyser. 1988. *Church and Politics in a Secular Age*. Oxford: Clarenden Press.

Moen, Matthew C. 1992. *The Political Transformation of the Christian Right*. Tuscaloosa: University of Alabama Press.

Neuhaus, John Richard. 1984. *The Naked Public Square*. Grand Rapids, Mich.: Eerdmans.

Persinos, John F. 1994. "Has the Christian Right Taken over the Republican Party?" *Campaigns and Elections* 15 (September): 21–24.

Pew Research Center. 1996. *The Diminishing Divide: American Churches, American Politics*. Washington, D.C.: The Pew Research Center.

Pierson, Paul, and Miriam Smith. 1993. "Bourgeois Revolutions? The Policy

Consequences of Resurgent Conservatism." *Comparative Political Studies* 25: 487–520.

Read, Melvyn, David Marsh, and David Richards. 1994. "Why Did They Do It? Voting on Homosexuality and Capital Punishment in the House of Commons." *Parliamentary Affairs* 47: 374–86.

Richardson, Jeremy J. 1993. "Interest Group Behavior in Britain: Continuity and Change." In *Pressure Groups*, edited by Jeremy J. Richardson, 86–99. Oxford: Oxford University Press.

Rozell, Mark J., and Clyde Wilcox, eds. 1995. *God at the Grass Roots: The Christian Right in the 1994 Elections*. Lanham, Md.: Rowman & Littlefield.

Smidt, Corwin E. 1993. "Evangelical Voting Patterns: 1976-1988." In *No Longer Exiles*, edited by Michael Cromartie, 85–117. Washington, D.C.: Ethics and Public Policy Center.

Soper, J. Christopher. 1994. *Evangelical Christianity in the United States and Great Britain*. New York: New York University Press.

———. 1996. "The Politics of Pragmatism: The Christian Right and the 1994 Elections." In *The Midterm Elections of 1994*, edited by Philip A. Klinkner, 115–24. Boulder, Colo.: Westview Press.

Waddington, Robert. 1985. "The Church and Educational Policy." In *Church and Politics Today*, edited by George Moyser, 221–55. Edinburgh: T&T Clarke.

Weaver, R. Kent, and Bert A. Rockman, eds. 1993. *Do Institutions Matter? Government Capabilities in the United States and Abroad*. Washington, D.C.: The Brookings Institution.

Whiteley, Paul, Patrick Seyd, and Jeremy Richardson. 1992. *True Blues: The Politics of the Conservative Party*. Oxford: Clarendon Press.

Wilcox, Clyde. 1992. *God's Warriors: The Christian Right in Twentieth-Century America*. Baltimore, Md.: Johns Hopkins University Press.

10

The Christian Right under
Old Glory and the Maple Leaf

Dennis R. Hoover

"Will a Religious Right Rise in Canada?" This rhetorical question serves as the title of Brian Stiller's commentary column in a recent issue of *Faith Today*, a Canadian evangelical magazine akin to *Christianity Today* in the United States (Stiller 1996). As president of the Evangelical Fellowship of Canada (EFC), Canada's version of the National Association of Evangelicals in the United States, Stiller is well placed to assess the character and potential of theologically conservative Christianity in Canada. Observing the rise in the United States of a largely evangelical "Christian Right,"[1] Stiller is prompted to consider whether a similar social movement will emerge north of the forty-ninth parallel.

Stiller's answer is negative but qualified: "I sense that it won't, at least not in the same way" (1996, 70). In contrast to the United States, where populist morality politics is an abiding feature of political life, Canada is not thought to provide conditions (religious, cultural, institutional) favorable to the rise of an American-style Christian Right. This conclusion is in line with the established conventional wisdom, one that enjoys an impressive scholarly pedigree (Simpson 1994; Lipset 1990; Simpson and MacLeod 1985; Wallis and Bruce 1985; Schwartz 1981; Clark 1968).

On the one hand, Stiller's skepticism concerning the prospects for a Canadian Christian Right seems quite justified. Yet, it is also ironic that Stiller would ask *whether* a Christian Right is forming in Canada, for as president of the fast-growing and increasingly politically active EFC, many Canadians would assume that Stiller *is* the Christian Right in Canada, or at least one of its most important spokespersons. For instance, one recent analysis of the lesbian and gay rights movement in Canada lists the EFC, Focus on the Family Canada, REAL (Realistic, Equal, Active, for Life) Women, the Salvation Army, and the Pentecostal Assemblies of Canada as constituent members of the Canadian "New Christian Right" because of their joint opposition to gay rights in a recent court case (Herman 1994).

Indeed, recent years have witnessed a growth in EFC's political role. In addition to overseeing a phenomenal expansion and invigoration of the EFC since 1983 (Stackhouse 1993), Stiller has facilitated a broadening of EFC's institutional vocation so as to embrace "political witness." For example, magazine advertisements for the EFC began in the 1980s to highlight EFC's lobbying activity. One ad featured a picture of Stiller posing with the prime minister, with accompanying text announcing that EFC had become a "strong, credible voice to government, media, and the public at large" (EFC n.d.). In addition, since 1989, Stiller has raised the political profile of Canadian evangelicalism still further, hosting an issues-oriented television talk show on Vision TV, a national cable channel. And perhaps most importantly, in 1996 the Toronto-based EFC opened a lobbying office in Ottawa, the nation's capital (Harvey 1996).

How can Stiller's skepticism concerning the Christian Right in Canada be squared with the emerging movement of which he and the EFC are a part? Here it is important to emphasize the nuanced nature of Stiller's argument; Stiller acknowledges that many Canadian Christians are concerned about "moral drift," but assures his readers that the response of Canadian Christians is unlikely to approximate that of U.S. Christians. Stiller, distancing himself and other Canadian Christians from the Christian Right in the United States, points up a distinction regarding the *character* of conservative Christian politics in North America that, if valid, removes the appearance of disingenuousness from his commentary. In comparison to the U.S. Christian Right, which is said to be aggressive, predominantly "right-wing," and large enough to entertain nationalistic, millennial pretensions, conservative Christians in Canada are, according to Stiller and other observers, more moderate, politically diverse, accepting of their minority status within Canada's famously pluralistic society, and, in a word, "irenic" (Rawlyk 1996; Harvey 1996; Marshall 1992; Stackhouse 1993; Redekop n.d.; Noll 1992).

This chapter will suggest that Stiller is reasonable to insist that, while conservative Christian politics per se are not somehow "unCanadian," the large-scale, aggressively conservative activism of certain contemporary Christian Right groups in the United States is not easily exportable to Canada. I will develop this argument in three ways.

First, I suggest that, in light of recent developments, conventional wisdom concerning the "exceptionally" American nature of Christian Right mobilization is due for revision. The extent to which theologically conservative Christians are politically mobilized in Canada must be reappraised and put into comparative perspective. I argue that the Canadian Christian Right can no longer be characterized as "underdeveloped" (Cuneo 1989; Menendez 1996) in proportion to the pool of likely "recruits" available in each country. Second, more than anecdotal and impressionistic evidence must be marshaled for the claim that, on average, the political temperament of the Canadian Christian Right is more moderate than that of the U.S. counterpart. I argue that evidence does support this characterization.

The third and final section of this chapter engages the deeper question of explanation. Just what explains the particular scale and character of the Canadian Christian Right as compared to the more familiar American Christian Right? I contend that two factors (namely, different configurations of religious groupings in each nation, and different features of each nation's political/regulatory structure) are the most important, though by no means the only, factors explaining the relative size and character of the Canadian Christian Right.

Assessing and Comparing the North American Christian Right

There are at least three levels at which to assess the extent of Christian Right mobilization: individual activism, advocacy organizations, and partisan behavior/institutionalization. At the individual level, the most straightforward approach is simply to estimate what percentage of each population identifies with the label "Christian Right." A recent Angus Reid survey is ideal for this purpose, as it put identical questions about religion and politics to 3,000 Americans and 3,000 Canadians (Angus Reid Research Group 1996). This survey revealed that 18 percent of Canadians feel somewhat or very close to the "Christian Right," while 34 percent of Americans feel this way. As a proportion of population, then, the size of the Christian Right in the United States is roughly twice the size of its Canadian counterpart. However, the U.S. population is ten times larger than the Canadian. As such, in absolute figures the

American to Canadian ratio of Christian Right sympathizers is roughly 19:1.

These figures are only suggestive, of course, since the meaning of "Christian Right" may not be entirely clear to respondents, nor consistent from one respondent to the next. More importantly, this measure does not reveal whether a respondent has "cognitively mobilized" (Inglehart 1990) his or her general affinity, translating it into specific actions and/or preferences.

Table 10.1 addresses this issue by comparing figures for various forms of political activism within national populations and national subpopulations of Christian Right sympathizers. These figures suggest that Canadian Christian Right sympathizers lag somewhat behind their American counterparts in activism. However, it is important to note that in neither the American nor Canadian milieu does identifying with the Christian Right lead to levels of activism that are significantly above or below national averages. In other words, Canadian Christian Right sympathizers engage in somewhat lower levels of activism than American Christian Right sympathizers, but this would appear to be a function

TABLE 10.1
United States and Canada Participation in Political Activities in 1995 and 1996
by Country and "Christian Right Sympathy"

Political Activity	U.S.	U.S. CR	Canada	Canada CR
Worked for a Party or Candidate in an Election	9	11	9	9
Contributed Money to a Candidate or Party	25	24	15	15
Contacted a Politician about an Issue with a Question or a Request	43	43	37	38
Attended a Public Meeting on Town or School Affairs	50	50	40	37

Source: Angus Reid Group: Green, Guth, Kellstedt, and Smidt 1996

simply of being average Canadians, rather than a function of "undermobilization." Both U.S. and Canadian Christian Right sympathizers exhibit unremarkable levels of activism in comparison to their respective national norms.

These data are illuminating, yet they do not reveal the extent to which Christian Right sympathizers favor a distinctly *religious* influence on the political process. Canadian and American Christian Right sympathizers may be participating at rates similar to their fellow citizens, yet the extent to which participation is related to religious motivations remains unclear. Again, available figures from the 1996 Angus Reid Research Group study provide some insight on this issue. Significantly, nearly identical percentages of U.S. and Canadian Christian Right sympathizers, 78 percent and 74 percent respectively, agreed that "It is essential that traditional Christian values play a major role in U.S./Canadian politics." Altogether, 56 percent of U.S. respondents agreed with this statement, as did 45 percent of Canadians.

Furthermore, U.S. evangelicals, mainline Protestants, and Catholics who were *both* "highly committed" religiously *and* sympathetic to the Christian Right displayed levels of approval for religious influence similar to their Canadian counterparts. Three-quarters or more of each of these three subgroups in each country agreed that "Christians should get involved in politics to protect their values." Roughly parallel levels of agreement were also reported in response to the statement, "My religion is very important to my political thinking." High-commitment evangelicals registered the highest degree of support for religious influence, with mainliners and Catholics less so.

To be sure, the actions and opinions of discrete, unorganized individuals expressing an abstract sympathy for the Christian Right are not what most people first think of when they ponder the Christian Right. Rather, it is one or both of two phenomena that come to the fore: (1) formation of advocacy organizations and/or (2) partisan behavior and institutionalization. How does the contemporary Christian Right in Canada stack up against the Christian Right in the United States on these dimensions?

On the former score, it is worth reiterating that Stiller's EFC represents only one manifestation of an overall pattern of accelerating advocacy group formation among evangelicals and other theologically conservative Christians. As in the United States, liberalization of abortion laws, which in Canada first occurred in 1969, served as the initial spark igniting sustained countermobilization. Lay Catholics took the lead in this regard, forming antiabortion groups such as the Campaign Life Coalition.

Conservative Protestants appear to have played a minor role in Canada's abortion conflicts of the 1970s. Lingering animosity between evangelicals and Catholics (grounded in long-standing theological and ecclesiastical differences, ethnic, linguistic, and regional cleavages, and recurring conflicts over parochial schools) undoubtedly contributed to an initial evangelical reticence to join in a cause that, despite evangelicals' own opposition to abortion, was still viewed as essentially a "Catholic issue."

However, throughout the course of the 1980s, Catholics and evangelicals (especially Reformed evangelicals) progressively abandoned their mutual suspicion, joining hands on the front lines of the abortion conflict (Cuneo 1989). This was particularly true in the wake of a 1988 decision by the Supreme Court of Canada, the end result of which has been an even greater deregulation of abortion than that achieved by *Roe v. Wade* (1973) in the United States. Canada's 1969 abortion law was criticized by the antiabortion movement as a rubber stamp procedure preventing few abortions, but its presence in the criminal code nonetheless maintained the appearance of restraint (Morton 1992). In 1988 Canadian evangelicals awoke to the realization that legally, abortion was now a completely legitimate procedure in Canada. Current research indicates that between one-quarter and one-third of the membership of Canadian antiabortion groups is now evangelical rather than Catholic (Hoover 1997).

For the most part, the broader range of moral issues usually associated with the Christian Right—the so-called "pro-family" or "family values" agenda—did not produce organizational advocates until the 1980s. One exception is Renaissance Canada formed in 1974 by Baptist minister Ken Campbell. Due to his penchant for high-publicity tactics and his personal friendship with Jerry Falwell, Renaissance Canada was for a time thought to be Canada's answer to the "Moral Majority." This equivalence is dubious, however, since Campbell's organization was formed five years prior to Falwell's and has never been as central to the Canadian Christian Right as the Moral Majority was to the U.S. movement. Still, Campbell was a leader in urging Canadian evangelicals to join the antiabortion movement.

Throughout the 1980s and 1990s, Campbell and antiabortion groups have been joined by increasing numbers of advocacy organizations. Some of these, such as the EFC, are explicitly evangelical, while others are attempting to build a tacit coalition of evangelicals and Catholics. One of the earliest examples of the latter to form (1983) was REAL Women, which staunchly opposes most aspects of the feminist movement, and claims over 50,000 members.

By the mid-1980s, REAL Women was joined by Focus on the Family Canada (FOFC), a sister organization to the huge U.S. group run by James Dobson. Along with the EFC, FOFC has quickly become a "hub" organization for newly politicized evangelicals and, more generally, the "pro-family" movement. It maintains contact with some 150,000 Canadians, broadcasts commentary on over 400 radio stations, and publishes *Citizen*, a political issues newsletter. Furthermore, since 1988, FOFC has sponsored annual national conferences of "pro-family" activists and sympathetic members of parliament (MPs). In the early 1990s, it also began organizing local "Community Impact Committees" in order to increase its political clout.

The 1990s have witnessed a continuation of this trend toward larger numbers of ambitious advocacy organizations. For example, a Canadian Center for Law and Justice, modeled after the American Center for Law and Justice, was formed in 1993 to concentrate solely on fighting battles for religious broadcasting and "pro-family" values in the courts. In that same year, Canada's first "think tank" devoted to conservative moral and religious concerns, the Centre for Renewal of Public Policy, was formed. Finally, in 1996, separate provincial and national organizations were formed, modeled after the powerful Christian Coalition in the United States. In fact, the provincial organization went so far as to borrow the name, calling itself the Christian Coalition of British Columbia. At the national level, an organization called Citizen Impact was recently formed (Fieguth 1996b). Citizen Impact's leader, Jack Baribeau, has attended the U.S. Christian Coalition's meetings, but has also pledged to adapt the model to Canadian conditions (Fieguth 1996a). Accordingly, it was decided that to label the group as explicitly "Christian" would be less effective in the Canadian milieu than it has been in the United States.

Clearly, then, the past fifteen years have witnessed a remarkable upturn in conservative Christian advocacy in Canada. In 1996 *Faith Today* identified twelve Canadian evangelical parachurch groups that had both (1) budgets over $150,000 and (2) primarily political mandates (Ryan 1996). Similarly, a recent doctoral thesis found a total of fourteen conservative Christian political groups active at the national level (Hoover 1997).

How does this organizational expansion and diversification compare to the more familiar U.S. mobilization that dates from the 1970s? A partial answer to this question can be gained by comparing data from a 1996 survey of conservative Christian groups in Canada (Hoover 1997) with statistics drawn from previous studies of U.S. religious interest groups (Weber and Jones 1994, Hofrenning 1995). Table 10.2 compares the number of national advocacy groups in each country that are supported largely by evangelicals and other conservative Christians. It also presents statistics on the membership, budget, and staff of these groups.

The data show that U.S. evangelical groups are clearly larger, more numerous, and endowed with more resources than Canadian groups. This contrast is put in a different light, however, when it is recalled that the United States contains nineteen times as many Christian Right sympathizers as does Canada. None of the above comparative ratios, however, approach 19:1. As such, it would appear inappropriate to characterize the Canadian Christian Right as "undermobilized." In fact, at least on some measures, it could be argued that the young Canadian movement has more fully mobilized its "resources" than the American movement.

Finally, the comparative status of the Christian Right in the United States and Canada can be assessed by examining the extent to which the movement has resulted in partisan behavior and/or institutionalization in each country. In the United States, the Christian Right has not formed its own political party, but its activist penetration of the Republican Party is widely noted (Persinos 1994; Green, Guth, and Fraser 1991; Rozell and Wilcox 1995). Furthermore, the American Christian Right is often credited with facilitating a major realignment of evangeli-

TABLE 10.2
United States and Canada
Advocacy Groups Organizational Statistics

	United States	Canada	U.S-Canada Ratio
Number of National Organizations	34	14	2.4:1
Mean Membership	626,116	49,750	12.6:1
Median Membership	75,000	18,500	4.0:1
Mean Staff	15.89	13.38	1.2:1
Median Staff	10	3	3.3:1
Mean Budget	$5,374,800	$1,159,875	4.6:1
Median Budget	$1,200,000	$ 315,000	3.8:1

Note: Dollar amounts given in U.S. dollars
Source: Hoover 1997; Weber and Jones 1994; Hofrenning 1995

cal voting behavior in favor of the Republican Party (Kellstedt, Green, Guth, and Smidt 1995; Smidt 1993).

By contrast, in Canada the relationship between Christian Right mobilization and the party system is more complex. Christian Right activists in Canada maintained ties to the Progressive Conservative (PC) Party's Family Caucus when that party was in power at the federal level in the 1980s and 1990s. However, as both the Progressive Conservatives and Liberals, Canada's historically dominant parties, are largely pragmatic rather than consistently ideological entities, Christian Right activists have been able to find allies within the Liberal Party as well.

More recently, Christian Right activists have established connections to sympathetic elements of the new Reform Party. Though the party is national, it is strongest in western Canada. Indeed, the Reform Party (RP) itself has sometimes been referred to as an "evangelical party," even though it eschews any explicit religious identity, and instructs its MPs to follow a strictly "populist" (in the radical democratic sense) decision procedure regarding moral issues in the House of Commons; they are instructed to vote the "consensus" of their riding (constituency), and only invoke their own judgment when that consensus is clearly lacking (Flanagan 1995).

Still, the evangelical cast of the Reform Party has been evident from its inception in 1987. The party's founder, Preston Manning, as well as its first elected MP, Deb Grey, are both quite open about their evangelical faith commitments (Manning 1992). In the 1993 federal election, which saw the Liberal Party come to power and the ruling Progressive Conseratives reduced to only two seats, the Reform Party achieved a significant breakthrough. On the strength of 100,000 party members, the Reform Party earned 18.7 percent of the vote and elected fifty-two MPs, approximately two-fifths of whom are evangelical (Mackey 1995). The de facto conservatism of the party on moral issues revealed itself in 1996, when the Reform Party opposed the Liberals' (ultimately successful) plan to add "sexual orientation" to the Canadian Human Rights Act as a prohibited ground for discrimination.

Manning is heir to a tradition of evangelical populism (primarily of an economic, rather than cultural-moral sort) in western Canada that stretches back to the Depression era (Simpson and MacLeod 1985). In Saskatchewan, evangelicals played leading roles in a movement of agrarian socialism that led to the formation of the modern New Democratic Party (Rawlyk 1990). Connections to evangelicalism proved to be tenuous, however, as the party became more obviously secular and liberal in orientation.

The Social Credit movement of Alberta (and later British Columbia), on the other hand, exhibited more durable ties to evangelicalism. The party was founded by an eccentric radio evangelist, William "Bible Bill" Aberhart, who was succeeded by Ernest Manning, Preston Manning's father. After Aberhart's passing, the party shed some of its "leftist" populism (Rawlyk 1990) and became more traditionally conservative. The present-day Reform Party is largely in the vein of conservative populism, though divisions exist between moderates (including Manning) and "new right" conservatives (Flanagan 1995).

Social Credit has maintained only a very minor presence at the federal level. However, at the provincial level conservative Christians appear to have remained a small but important part of broader coalitions electing Social Credit governments in Alberta and British Columbia. For example, it has been argued that evangelicals supported the election of the Social Credit government of Bill Vander Zalm (a self-described "fundamentalist Catholic") in British Columbia in 1986, as well as his subsequent effort to de-insure abortion in public health plans (Burkinshaw 1995). Since leaving office, Vander Zalm has become a leader in the fledgling Christian Coalition of British Columbia.

Other than a tiny Social Credit/Christian Freedom Party organized at the federal level in the late 1980s (now under Ken Campbell's wing), the only other explicitly Christian party in Canada is the Christian Heritage Party, formed in 1986. This party initially appeared to hold the potential for pulling together the disparate elements of the emerging Canadian Christian Right into a single political force. In the 1988 election, it received 100,000 votes on the strength of 20,000 members. However, the party's flirtation with a radical "Christian Reconstructionist" philosophy, in combination with an internal leadership shakeup and the rise of the Reform Party, led to a reversal of fortunes. By the time of the 1993 election, the Christian Heritage Party's membership had slipped to 5,000, and, in the election, it received only 30,000 votes.

Given the great differences between the U.S. Christian Right's penetration of the Republican Party and the Canadian Christian Right's connections to diverse political parties, direct comparisons of levels of institutionalization are difficult to make. Suffice it to say that with respect to party organizations in both countries, a broad social movement based in the conservative Christian community has made its presence known.

However, with respect to individual voters' partisanship, the Angus Reid survey data do allow direct comparisons to be made. Table 10.3 presents the voting intentions as of 1996 for decided voters in each nation as a whole and for Christian Right sympathizers.

TABLE 10.3
United States and Canada Individual Voting Intentions
by Country and "Christian Right Sympathy"

	U.S.	U.S. CR		Canada	Canada CR
Clinton	54	43	Liberal	55	52
Dole	32	45	PC	15	17
Perot	7	7	Reform	12	22
Other	6	6	Other	2	3
			Bloc	7	0
			NDP	8	5

Source: Angus Reid Group: Green, Guth, Kellstedt, and Smidt 1996

U.S. Christian Right supporters were more Republican than Democratic in presidential voting intentions, bucking the national trend, which was heavily in President Bill Clinton's favor.[2] Other polling has shown even stronger relationships between conservative Christian groups and Republican partisanship (Kellstedt, Green, Guth, and Smidt 1995). In Canada the evidence is more difficult to interpret. Over half of Canadian Christian Right sympathizers chose the Liberal Party, and 5 percent even went for the largely secular and socialistic New Democratic Party. The two parties of the "right" in Canada, the Progressive Conservative and Reform Party, together drew only 39 percent of the vote. On one level, this would seem to suggest that conservative Christians in Canada do not lean as consistently to the partisan "right" as their American counterparts.

Yet viewed in comparison to Canadians as a whole, the Canadian Christian Right is distinctive for its above-average support for the Reform Party. The proportion of Christian Right sympathizers who favored the Reform Party was almost twice the national proportion. Therefore, even though the Reform Party denies that it exists to make any particularly religious appeals, there does appear to be an empirical basis for the conclusion that Christian Right sympathizers lean disproportionately toward the Reform Party.

Strictly speaking, therefore, the above evidence suggests that the answer to Stiller's query, "Will a Religious Right rise in Canada?" is "Yes, and it is already rising." Stiller, therefore, too quickly discounts the Christian Right's chances in Canada. Yet his argument is more nuanced than those who argue that "the religious right is un-Canadian."

Dennis R. Hoover

Rather, Stiller means to draw a distinction between the "American-style" Christian Right and the kind of political aspirations that committed Canadian Christians may have. The implication is that Christian Right mobilization does not come in only one mold, and that a Canadian Christian Right will be distinctly Canadian, or at least distinct from the American variety. The second section of this chapter investigates whether available evidence does, in fact, reveal whether the Canadian Christian Right is politically distinctive.

A "Moderate Moral Majority?"

In 1981 Ken Campbell took care to describe his constituency to *The Globe and Mail* as Canada's *moderate* moral majority (Simpson and MacLeod 1985). Is this a distinction without a difference? Stiller suggests that conservative Christians in Canada are less politically "right-wing" than U.S. Christians. Contemporary usage of "right-wing" usually connotes three characteristics: (1) traditional moralism, (2) intolerance for diversity, and/or (3) "new right" views on economics and welfare. As noted, the sine qua non of the Christian Right perspective in any era is conservatism on issues of personal morality. As such, it is not surprising that the Canadian and American Christian Right are, on the whole,[3] largely indistinguishable in their traditionalism on "moral issues" like abortion and homosexuality. Advocacy groups and party activists in both countries, even those sometimes described as "evangelical progressives," usually take positions ranging from moderately to extremely conservative on these issues.

Significant differences, if any, would have to be found on one or both of the latter two dimensions of "right-wing" conservatism. On these dimensions, it does indeed appear that members of the Canadian Christian Right are generally more moderate than their American counterparts.

On the question of diversity and sensitivity to minorities, for instance, suggestive evidence comes from a 1996 survey of thirty-five prominent Canadian evangelicals. Each of these individuals holds a position of leadership within advocacy groups or parties sponsored (or disproportionately supported) by conservative Protestants (Hoover 1997). Seventy-one percent of this leadership cadre disagreed with the goal of "reducing the number of immigrants and refugees in Canada"; 72 percent claimed to "support aboriginal rights." Furthermore, these leaders had no strong consensus that prayer should be brought back to public schools. In fact, they were evenly split on the issue, with 42 percent agreeing and 42 percent disagreeing. Sixty-nine percent opposed forming an *explicitly* Christian political party. The 1996 Angus Reid data shed comparative light on this issue domain as well. When asked if they would prefer to have neighbors of their own race, 18 percent of Canadian Christian Right sympathizers agreed, while 24 percent of the U.S. counterparts agreed.

On economic issues, directly comparable evidence is not abundant. However, one result from the Angus Reid Research Group report showed 73 percent of the Canadian Christian Right agreeing that the environment must be protected even if doing so costs money and/or jobs, while 58 percent of their U.S. counterparts agreed. Another indicator of Canadian distinctiveness in this area is that one of Canada's conservative Protestant interest groups is a 17,000-member *labor union*. In the United States, union organizing is not a prominent object of evangelical reformist energy. Still further suggestive evidence comes from the survey of Canadian evangelical leaders (Hoover 1997). Sixty percent of these activist leaders agreed with the goal of increasing "government protection of the environment"; the same proportion favored increasing "government help for the needy." Interestingly, only 18 percent agreed with the "new right" goal of decreasing regulatory burdens and taxes on corporations.

Though not directly comparable, evidence that is nonetheless suggestive of greater conservatism among Christian activists in the United States comes from a 1990 to 1991 survey of rank-and-file members of eight Christian advocacy groups (Smidt, Kellstedt, Green, and Guth 1994). The survey included groups ranging from evangelical progressive (Evangelicals for Social Action) to evangelical moderate (National Association of Evangelicals) to evangelical right (Focus on the Family, Americans for the Republic, Concerned Women of America). About one-third of the respondents agreed that government must help the needy even if taxes must be raised; less than one-half agreed that the environment must be protected even if it is costly. Although this level of "progressivism" may be higher than some might have predicted, in Canada such conservative Christian activists appear to exhibit even stronger progressive tendencies. For instance, rank-and-file activists within the antiabortion wing of the Canadian Christian Right (which, it should be remembered, is more Catholic than the broader "pro-family" Christian Right) defy "new right" stereotypes on some issues. A 1986 to 1987 survey of subscribers to *The Interim*, Canada's main antiabortion publication, asked respondents whether they thought the government should put more effort, the same effort, or less effort into various activities. Results were then compared to a separate national poll. Interestingly, the percentage of antiabortion activists who wanted more government effort expended on "helping the poor" (77 percent) and on "assisting the unemployed" (37 percent) *exceeded* the reported figures for all Canadians (64 percent and 36 percent respectively) (Erwin 1993).

Explaining Differences between the Christian Right in the United States and Canada

The final section of this chapter addresses the issue of how the differences between these two instances of Christian Right mobilization can be explained. Two key differences have been brought into relief. First, even though it appears that the Canadian Christian Right is no longer undermobilized in relation to its "base" of Christian Right sympathy, this "base" is still tiny by comparison with the United States. Second, the character of the Canadian Christian Right is more moderate.

Many factors could be cited as partially involved in producing the observed differences. However, the two most important variables are considered here, namely, the influence of religious traditions/groupings and the influence of political opportunity structures. Each of these factors will be considered in relation first to the issue of movement magnitude and then to the issue of movement character. The aim is not to unpack these factors comprehensively, but only to highlight specific differences on these dimensions that seem relevant.

First, the most obvious explanatory factor relevant to movement size is the huge difference in the proportions of each nation made up by committed Christians generally, and evangelicals specifically. Once again the Angus Reid data are helpful. While 76 percent of Americans and 68 percent of Canadians said they think of themselves as a Christian, the United States has, in absolute numbers, approximately eleven times the number of self-described Christians as does Canada. However, the ratio of "high-commitment" Christians (Protestants and Roman Catholics combined) in the United States compared to Canada is substantially larger at roughly 17:1. Furthermore, 25 percent of Americans but only 11 percent of Canadians are evangelicals, which in absolute terms translates into a ratio of 22:1. With these figures in mind, it is not surprising that Christian Right sympathizers are nineteen times more numerous in the United States as in Canada.

The second factor is part of what social movement theorists refer to as "political opportunity structure" (Kitschelt 1986). This refers to the ways in which different constitutional and regulatory frameworks shape mobilization. At a very general level, Canada's parliamentary system of government with disciplined parties has worked to centralize power in the hands of provincial and federal cabinet members, premiers, and prime ministers. The extent of this elite concentration of power is even greater than that found in Great Britain (Franks 1987), and has worked to reduce the incentives for interest groups to mobilize (Pross 1975). This is no less true for advocacy by religious groups than that by other groups (Redekop 1985).

More specific elements of Canada's political opportunity structure have also had important restraining effects on Christian Right mobilization, situations never encountered by the American Christian Right. One difference concerns the jurisdictional division of authority over some of the most common Christian Right issues. While both the United States and Canada have federal systems, in Canada the criminal code, including the law governing issues such as prostitution and abortion, is a *national* matter. Unlike the United States, therefore, regional concentrations of interest in regulating certain behavior will not translate into local regulations. For example, the city of Calgary attempted to restrict prostitution in 1983, and the province of Saskatchewan tried to institute its own abortion regulations in 1984, but both attempts were ruled unconstitutional on jurisdictional grounds (Landes 1995).

A second specific difference is that the Canadian context is much less conducive to religious broadcasting enterprises, which in the United States have proven to be important catalysts for Christian Right mobilization. For the most part, the contrast results from a confluence of two long-standing problems faced by Canadian religious broadcasting. First, with only rare and quite recent exceptions, Canada's broadcasting authority has maintained a strict policy of denying broadcasting licenses to religious broadcasters (Simpson 1985). They can buy time on commercial stations, but without a broadcast license it is difficult to attract a consistent audience that can serve as a necessary financial donor base. More specifically, without the consciousness-raising and fundraising tool of large broadcasting ministries, Canada's would-be movement entrepreneurs are seriously handicapped in comparison to U.S. entrepreneurs such as Pat Robertson.

These particular problems are further compounded by the fact that Canada is geographically contiguous with the much larger United States, and that 90 percent of Canadians live within one hundred miles of the U.S. border. As such, producers of Canada's religious culture are vulnerable to the same fate as many other aspects of Canadian culture— colonization by the U.S. market. The proximity of the two nations means that many U.S. religious broadcasters can be seen and heard in Canada, which not only funnels money south of the border (Stackhouse 1993), but also militates against the formation of an indigenously Canadian "movement consciousness" (Simpson and MacLeod 1985).

Therefore, it is the religious composition of Canadian society and its political opportunity structure that are key to explaining the comparatively small size of its Christian Right. These same two broad factors are also crucial in the analysis of the final question considered in this chapter: What explains the distinctively Canadian, which is to say "moderate," character of the Canadian Christian Right?

First, one can look to religious factors that differentiate the Christian Right in the United States from that in Canada. In short, the balance of theological traditions within the Canadian Christian Right and, more specifically, within Canadian evangelicalism, might plausibly be related to a moderating influence. According to the 1996 Angus Reid survey data, among Canadians, roughly equal numbers of evangelical Protestants, mainline Protestants, and Roman Catholics identified with the Christian Right, while in the United Sates, evangelical Protestants accounted for over half of such identifiers. Since both mainline Protestant and Catholic groups have long-standing traditions of progressive teaching on some socioeconomic justice issues, it may be the case that the higher prevalence of these groups within the ranks of the Canadian Christian Right predisposes the Canadian Christian Right to more acceptance of communal or collectivist approaches.

Religious groupings are perhaps even more clearly relevant in relation to evangelicalism. Two conservative Protestant traditions, Anabaptist and Reformed, are notably "overrepresented" within Canadian evangelicalism as compared to U.S. evangelicalism. Anabaptists (the "peace church" tradition that includes Mennonites) may comprise as much as 10 percent of Canadian evangelicals, but they are less than 1 percent of American evangelicals (Jacquet 1993; Bibby 1987). Likewise, Reformed (Calvinist) conservative Protestants, many of whom in Canada have Dutch ancestry, are numerically small, but they are still a proportionately larger component of the Canadian than American Christian Right. Both these communities harbor long-standing traditions of liberalism on social justice issues, and both have leavened the broader transdenominational evangelical movement in Canada with their influence.[4]

Similarly, the fact that Baptists and fundamentalists are less frequently found among the leaders and activists within Canadian than American evangelicalism also explains much about the question of character of evangelicalism in the two countries. Baptists comprise a larger plurality (46 percent) of all evangelicals in the United States, while in Canada they comprise approximately one-fifth of the evangelical total (Green, Guth, Kellstedt, and Smidt 1992; Bibby 1987; *Christian Week* 1996). And, many Canadian Baptists are more "mainline" in style than are most U.S. Baptists (Hiller 1978). Fundamentalism too has touched a smaller proportion of Canadian Baptists than U.S. Baptists, as fundamentalism was a comparatively minor phenomenon in Canadian Protestantism generally (Stackhouse 1993). For example, two beliefs common among fundamentalists are that the Bible must be taken literally, word for word, and that the world will end in a battle of Armageddon between Jesus and the Antichrist. These beliefs, for example, commanded 55 percent and 42 percent agreement, respectively, among all Americans in 1996, while, in Canada, only 28 percent and 17 percent expressed such agreement, respectively.

Surveys have indicated that fundamentalist evangelicals are the most likely to support a thoroughgoing right-wing agenda (Beatty and Walter 1988; Wilcox 1986), so their relative absence in Canada is not without potential political significance. Moreover, many Canadian evangelicals are quite insistent that they not be confused with fundamentalists, who are thought to be largely an American idiosyncracy. An illustration of this Canadian sentiment occurred during Canada's election campaign when a major media outlet described Preston Manning of the Reform Party as a "fundamentalist." Brian Stiller wrote a letter of protest, asserting that "to call a Canadian evangelical a fundamentalist is like calling an African-Canadian a 'nigger.' " (Harvey 1993). The media outlet changed its policy so that "fundamentalist" would only be used to describe those who chose to describe themselves accordingly.

Finally, in addition to these religio-cultural influences, it is also possible to identify key elements of the political opportunity structure that have had a hand in shaping the character of Canadian Christian Right behavior. Two features of this structure might be mentioned here: (1) the strategic effect of the number of "access points" for activism and (2) the expressive effect of broadcasting regulations, or the lack thereof. Other "rules of the game" could also be underscored, but these two differences are among the most obvious.

First, the Canadian state, with its rather elitist methods of dealing with interest groups and social movement organizations, allows for civil forums of communication, such as parliamentary committees and special commissions, but can and often does greet populist "outsider" tactics with polite indifference (Pyrcz 1985; Galipeau 1989). This is not to suggest that street protest, petition drives, and the like are not tried by the Canadian Christian Right, particularly its antiabortion wing (Cuneo 1989). Yet, the failure of these methods is testimony to the ultimate reality that painstaking, discrete cultivation of elite allies in cabinet and/ or the higher reaches of the bureaucracy is still necessary.[5] To put it simply, deferential respect for elites might be not so much an indelible Canadian personality trait as it is simply the price of *admission* to the Canadian policy process.

Second, in addition to Canada's nearly total ban on the granting of religious broadcasting licenses, there are regulations in place that temper the content of the message Canadian religious broadcasters are permitted to send during the air time they buy from commercial stations. Regulations prevent the presentation of "abusive comment" directed at a broad range of groups. Stations considering whether to sell time to an evangelical broadcaster thus must contend with the question of whether the broadcaster will make religiously and/or morally judgmental statements, which end up being ruled "abusive" to other religions, women, or homosexuals, and which invite regulatory sanction. Some Canadian evangelical broadcasters claim to have had programs pulled for this very reason. As a result, some raise money in Canada, but buy time on U.S. border stations that beam into Canada in order to circumvent regulatory inhibitions (Hoover 1997). Moreover, the few amiable personalities that make up Canadian evangelical broadcasting are not inclined toward aggressive fund-raising or political mobilizing (Nelles 1989). However, it is again difficult to know how much of this more moderate behavior among the Canadian Christian Right should be credited to a political culture of moderation or simply to the Canadian regulatory regime.

A Growing Convergence?

Although the Christian Right has far fewer sympathizers in Canada, in recent years it has achieved a level of mobilization that, in most respects, is more than proportionate to the United States when adjustments are made to account for the difference in scale. At the individual level, both the American and Canadian Christian Right exhibit average levels of political activism, and both are largely in favor of religious influence, particularly Christian influence, in politics. At the organizational level, both have produced a range of advocacy groups. Finally, at the level of partisan behavior and institutionalization, both have exhibited distinctive relationships to their respective party systems, although in Canada the relationships are more complicated.

A Canadian Christian Right of relatively recent vintage has thus developed in Canada. In many respects, it is a parallel movement to the American Christian Right, taking ideological and organizational inspiration, and in some cases financial assistance,[6] from its more mature U.S. counterpart. Yet, as Stiller and other Canadian leaders insist, it is a movement congruent with the particular constellation of religious and political conditions that prevail in Canada's "peaceable kingdom." Whether the contemporary Christian Right in Canada will prove to be a way station en route to the "Americanization" of Christian politics in Canada is a question that requires further research. On the basis of the recent interest group and public opinion research consulted for this chapter, however, it would appear that the Canadian Christian Right will not anytime soon lose its comparatively more irenic quality.

Notes

1. Space limitations preclude a full consideration of definitional issues. At a minimum, however, the label "Christian Right" demands that the subject be both "Christian" religiously and "Right" politically. This chapter presumes that, religiously, the Christian Right is predominantly a phenomenon of evangelical Protestants, though sympathetic mainline Protestants and Roman Catholics are sometimes allied. Politically, this chapter assumes that the Christian Right is by definition conservative about traditional morality (for example, "family values" issues), but not necessarily about other issues. Theologically orthodox Christians have at times been reactionary, nationalistic, militaristic, "new right," and so on, but at other times they have been champions of emancipation, peace, progressive social reform, and populist economics (Hertzke 1993; Hoover 1992).

2. The Republican bias of Christian Right sympathizers would have undoubtedly been even stronger had African American Christian Right sympathizers, who remain loyal to the Democratic Party, been analyzed separately, which is the usual practice in studies of conservative Christian political behavior.

3. The characterizations of movement character in this chapter aim at the "central tendency," admittedly ignoring individual cases that "deviate" from the norm, cases that would require a longer work to address.

4. My 1996 survey of evangelical leadership in Canada revealed that the top three most frequently claimed denominational family affiliations were: Re-

formed (20 percent of respondents), Anglicans (17 percent), and Anabaptists (14 percent).

5. The advent of judicial review in Canada, which accompanied constitutional repatriation and the adoption of the Charter of Rights and Freedoms (analogous to the U.S. Bill of Rights) in 1982, has in some respects allowed interest groups to use the courts to circumvent the slow process of Canadian parliamentary democracy (Morton 1992). However, the groups succeeding through this method are mostly liberal opponents of the Christian Right.

6. Those Canadian groups with U.S. precursors, it should be emphasized, usually benefitted from start-up capital from the United States, but in subsequent years became more self-sufficient. None of the groups responding to my survey (Hoover 1997) reported any direct budgetary relationship to U.S. sources.

References

Angus Reid Research Group, involving the Queen's University George Rawlyk Research Unit, the Institute for the Study of American Evangelicals, John Green, James Guth, Lyman Kellstedt, and Corwin Smidt. 1996. "God and Society in North America." Media presentation document.

Beatty, Kathleen Murphy, and B. Oliver Walter. 1988. "Fundamentalists, Evangelicals, and Politics." *American Politics Quarterly* 16: 43–60.

Bibby, Reginald. 1987. *Fragmented Gods*. Toronto: Stoddart.

Burkinshaw, Robert. 1995. *Pilgrims in Lotus Land: Conservative Protestantism in British Columbia, 1917–1981*. Montreal and Kingston: McGill-Queen's University Press.

Christian Week. 1996. "Baptists, Baptists, and More Baptists." 5 November, 3.

Clark, S. D. 1968. "The Religious Sect in Canadian Politics." In *The Developing Canadian Community*, edited by S. D. Clark, 131–46. Toronto: University of Toronto Press.

Cuneo, Michael W. 1989. *Catholics against the Church: Anti-Abortion Protest in Toronto, 1969–1985*. Toronto: University of Toronto Press.

Erwin, Lorna. 1993. "Neoconservatism and the Canadian Pro-Family Movement." *Canadian Review of Sociology and Anthropology* 30 (3): 401–19.

Evangelical Fellowship of Canada. n.d. "It's Time We Stood Up for What We Believe." *Faith Today*. Advertisement.

Fieguth, Debra. 1996a. "Quiet Canadians Question Politics: Canadians Want to See Political Change, But Not with an American Approach." *Christian Week*, 8 October, 1, 4.

———. 1996b. "Christians Try for United Political Front." *Christian Week*, 3 December, 2.

Flanagan, Tom. 1995. *Waiting for the Wave: The Reform Party and Preston Manning*. Toronto: Stoddart.

Franks, C. E. S. 1987. *The Parliament of Canada.* Toronto: University of Toronto Press.

Galipeau, Claude. 1989. "Political Parties, Interest Groups, and New Social Movements." In *Canadian Parties in Transition,* edited by Alain Gagnon and A. Brian Tanguay. Toronto: Nelson Canada.

Green, John, James Guth, and Cleveland Fraser. 1991. "Apostles and Apostates?: Religion and Politics among Party Activists." In *The Bible and the Ballot Box,* edited by James Guth and John Green. Boulder, Colo.: Westview Press.

Green, John, James Guth, Lyman Kellstedt, and Corwin Smidt. 1992. National Survey of American Evangelicals: Preliminary Report. Akron, Ohio: Ray C. Bliss Institute of Applied Politics, University of Akron.

Harvey, Bob. 1993. "Media Backs off Fundamentalist Stereotyping." *Christian Week,* 30 November, 1.

———. 1996. "Evangelicals Open Ottawa Office without U.S. Extremes." *Ottawa Citizen,* 23 March.

Herman, Didi. 1994. *Rights of Passage: Struggles for Lesbian and Gay Legal Equality.* Toronto: University of Toronto Press.

Hertzke, Allen D. 1993. *Echoes of Discontent.* Washington D.C.: CQ Press.

Hiller, Harry. 1978. "Continentalism and the Third Force in Canadian Religion." *Canadian Journal of Sociology* 3: 183–207.

Hofrenning, Daniel. 1995. *In Washington But Not of It.* Philadelphia, Pa.: Temple University Press.

Hoover, Dennis R. 1992. The Political Mobilization of the American Evangelical Left. Ph.M.. Politics thesis, University of Oxford.

———. 1997. Conservative Protestant Politics in the U.S. and Canada. Ph.D. thesis, University of Oxford.

Inglehart, Ronald. 1990. *Culture Shift.* Princeton, N.J.: Princeton University Press.

Jacquet, Constant H. 1993. *Yearbook of American and Canadian Churches.* Nashville, Tenn.: Abingdon Press.

Kellstedt, Lyman, John Green, James Guth, and Corwin Smidt. 1995. "Has Godot Finally Arrived? Religion and Realignment in 1994." *The Public Perspective* 6: 18–22.

Kitschelt, Herbert. 1986. "Political Opportunity Structures and Political Protest." *British Journal of Political Science* 16: 57–85.

Landes, Ronald G. 1995. *The Canadian Polity: A Comparative Introduction.* Scarborough, Ontario: Prentice Hall.

Lipset, Seymour Martin. 1990. *Continental Divide.* London: Routledge.

Mackey, Lloyd. 1995. "Evangelicals a Quiet, Steady Presence in Parliament." *Christian Week,* 3 January, 8.

Manning, Preston. 1992. *The New Canada.* Toronto: Macmillan.

Marshall, Paul. 1992. "Religion and Canadian Culture." In *Shaping a Christian Vision for Canada,* edited by Aileen Van Ginkel, 1–24. Markham, Ontario: Faith Today Publications.

Menendez, Albert. 1996. *Church and State in Canada*. New York: Prometheus Books.

Morton, F. L. 1992. *Pro-Life vs. Pro-Choice: Abortion and the Courts in Canada*. Norman: University of Oklahoma Press.

Nelles, Wendy. 1989. "Canadian TV Ministries: Higher on Hope than Hype." *Christianity Today* 33 (5): 46–47.

Noll, Mark. 1992. *A History of Christianity in the United States and Canada*. Grand Rapids, Mich.: Eerdmans.

Persinos, John F. 1994. "Has the Christian Right Taken over the Republican Party?" *Campaigns and Elections* 15 (September): 21–24.

Pross, J. Paul, ed. 1975. *Pressure Group Behaviour in Canadian Politics*. Toronto: McGraw-Hill Ryerson.

Pyrcz, G. 1985. "Pressure Groups." In *Liberal Democracy in Canada and the United States*, edited by T. C. Pocklington, 341–73. Toronto: Holt, Rinehart and Winston.

Rawlyk, George. 1990. "Politics, Religion, and the Canadian Experience." In *Religion and American Politics*, edited by Mark Noll. New York: Oxford University Press.

———. 1996. *Is Jesus Your Personal Saviour? In Search of Canadian Evangelicalism in the 1990's*. Montreal and Kingston: McGill-Queen's University Press.

Redekop, John. n.d. Canadian Evangelical Thought: Roots and Varied Fruits. Unpublished paper, Wilfred Laurier University.

———. 1985. The Role of Religious Pressure Groups in the Canadian Political System. Paper presented at the annual convention of the Canadian Political Science Association, 31 May, Montreal.

Rozell, Mark J., and Clyde Wilcox, eds. 1995. *God at the Grass Roots: The Christian Right in the 1994 Elections*. Lanham, Md.: Rowman & Littlefield.

Ryan, Bramwell. 1996. "The Parachurch: Complement, Competitor, Co-Worker." *Faith Today* 13 (November–December): 20–26.

Simpson, John H. 1985. "Federal Regulation and Religious Broadcasting." In *Religion/Culture: Comparative Canadian Studies,* edited by William Westfall, Louis Rousseau, Fernand Harvey, and John Simpson, 152–63. Ottawa: Association for Canadian Studies.

———. 1994. "The Structure of Attitudes toward Body Issues in the American and Canadian Populations." In *Abortion Politics in the United States and Canada*, edited by Ted Jelen and Martha Chandler, 145–60. Greenwood, Conn.: Praeger.

Simpson, John H., and Henry G. MacLeod. 1985. "The Politics of Morality in Canada." In *Religious Movements: Genesis, Exodus, Numbers*, edited by Rodney Stark. New York: Paragon.

Smidt, Corwin. 1993. "Evangelical Voting Patterns: 1976–1988." In *No Longer Exiles*, edited by Michael Cromartie, 85–117. Washington, D.C.: Ethics and Public Policy Center.

Smidt, Corwin, Lyman Kellstedt, John Green, and James Guth. 1994. "The Characteristics of Christian Political Activists: An Interest Group Analysis." In *Christian Political Activism at the Crossroads*, edited by William Stevenson, 133–71. Lanham, Md.: University Press of America.

Stackhouse, John G., Jr. 1993. *Canadian Evangelicalism in the Twentieth Century*. Toronto: University of Toronto Press.

Stiller, Brian. 1996. "Will a Religious Right Rise in Canada?" *Faith Today* (May–June): 70.

Wallis, Roy, and Steve Bruce. 1985. "Sketch for a Theory of Conservative Protestant Politics." *Social Compass* 32: 58–61.

Weber, Paul, and Landis Jones. 1994. *U.S. Religious Interest Groups*. Westport, Conn.: Greenwood.

Wilcox, Clyde. 1986. "Evangelicals and Fundamentalists in the New Christian Right." *Journal for the Scientific Study of Religion* 25: 355–66.

11

The Transformation of the Christian Right in Central America

Anne Motley Hallum

One of the most important phenomena in modern Central America is the growth of Protestantism on a massive scale. It is estimated, for example, that eight to ten thousand Catholics in Latin America convert each day as the region becomes less and less Catholic (*Latinamerica Press*, 26 September 1996, 3). The evangelical percentage of the population in virtually every Central American country has reached double digits,[1] ranging from a low of 10 percent in Costa Rica to a high of at least 25 percent in Guatemala (see table 11.1 below). In view of this

TABLE 11.1
Evangelicals in Central America

Country	Population (millions)	Percent Evangelical
Costa Rica	3.5	10.0
El Salvador (2)	6.0	25.0
Guatemala (3)	9.5	25.3
Honduras	5.2	10.5
Nicaragua (3)	3.8	20.0

Source: *Latinamerica Press*, 8 February 1996, 6. Numbers in parenthesis indicates the number of Christian political parties or named political movements.

217

growth, Protestantism provides at least the potential for the development of a significant Christian Right movement in Central America. This chapter focuses on the degree to which this potential is being realized and the political implication of such change.

To begin, then, it is important to recognize that the phrase, "success of the Christian Right" implies more than the success of Protestantism; it implies that right-wing political goals and objectives are succeeding in the region under the auspices of evangelical Christianity. But any assumption that the growth of evangelicalism in Central America is necessarily associated with the success of a Christian Right is highly problematic because the political orientation of evangelicals varies dramatically in Central America, depending upon the local context, and depending upon the class basis of the majority of the membership of different churches.

If political direction, ideology, and theology were simply imposed on Central Americans by North American missionaries representing Christian Right views, then Protestantism would lack a resonance with the people so crucial to its continued growth. Moreover, the evidence is strong that by now most of the local churches have found their autonomy from a North American religious-political agenda. Local Protestants lead their own churches, form their own umbrella organizations and seminaries, and practice a developing theology. Significantly, they will soon send out more missionaries than they receive (Siewert and Kenyon 1995).

This chapter, then, focuses on the transformation of the Christian Right in Central America when it confronts the realities of particular countries. It begins with an overview of the "missionary wave" of the 1980s that advanced Protestantism in Central America, addressing both the theological and structural reasons for Protestant success. This discussion includes an analysis of the three major categories of Protestants in the region: traditional or historic churches, Pentecostals, and Neo-Pentecostals. Then the relationship between Protestants and politics in Nicaragua, particularly during the October 1996, national elections is examined. Protestants there are not part of a monolithic Christian Right supporting the political status quo, but are battling instead for governmental access and reform. The term *evangelical* is used in this chapter as it is used throughout Latin America—as a synonym for the less familiar "Protestant." It refers to *all* non-Catholic Christians except Mormons and Jehovah's Witnesses who practice distinctive theologies.

Evangelical Missionary Patterns

A series of evangelical "missionary waves" from North America to South America has occurred over the past century, though the missionary wave to Central America of the 1980s has the most relevance for the present discussion. During this same decade, the Christian Right brand of evangelicalism was experiencing an upsurge in the United States, and this translated into more missionary efforts and resources directed toward Latin America. In particular, Ríos Montt's coup d'etat in Guatemala in 1982 received enthusiastic support from many evangelical Protestants in the States, largely because he was an evangelical. During this period, Costa Rica and Honduras also experienced an influx of missionaries from conservative churches. In contrast, after the Sandinista victory in 1979, the political setting in Nicaragua became unfriendly for many U.S. evangelicals as they were assumed to be against the revolution. As a result, many left. Missionaries from liberal U.S. mainline denominations, however, were eventually welcomed to work in Nicaragua after the revolution.

It was also during the 1980s that probably the most blatant use of religion in support of U.S. right-wing purposes occurred, particularly with regard to support for the Nicaraguan Contras against the Sandinista government. The popular Sandinista revolution toppled the Somoza regime in 1979. But, with the election of Ronald Reagan in 1980 and the Cold War division of the world into camps of good and evil, the young Sandinista government was quickly designated an enemy of the United States. By 1982, all U.S. aid to Nicaragua had been terminated (Barry and Preusch 1988). The facts of the subsequent counterinsurgency led by the United States in Nicaragua are well documented.

But, where do evangelicals fit into the scenario? While the United States was helping to organize the Contras near the Honduran and Nicaraguan borders, many conservative U.S. evangelical groups were also beginning to offer their support. The most prominent of these were Pat Robertson's "700 Club," Jimmy Swaggart's Missions in Motion, and the Christian Emergency Relief Teams (CERT). For example, in 1985, Swaggart flew over a Miskito Indian refugee camp in Honduras, booming his message about Christ and communism throughout the area, while dropping candy from his plane for children (Barry and Preusch 1988). Pat Robertson raised money by preaching against the evils of Marxism on his Christian Broadcast Network, claiming that the Contras were "God's Army." And, David Courson of CERT stated in his direct

mail that the "Sandinistas are determined to eliminate all Christians.
. . . Thousands of people have been brutally murdered because they
would neither deny Christ nor submit to the brutal demands of the Sandinistas" (Barry and Preusch 1988, 225). Lieutenant Colonel Oliver
North of the U.S. National Security Council staff was a central player
in this extensive campaign among U.S. evangelicals to build a private
support network for the contras, a campaign that was reviewed during
U.S. Senate investigative hearings in 1987. These various provocative
fund-raising activities complemented White House policy, which
sought to weaken the Sandinista government, and were a deliberate effort to undermine the Boland Amendment passed by the U.S. Congress
prohibiting military aid to the Contras.

Given such examples, it is not surprising that observers have often
assumed that the success of evangelical Christianity in Central America
also enhances the political goals of the "Christian Right" with such
countries. However, evangelical missionaries are not cut from one cloth.
Many have worked for "leftist" social reforms and even revolutionary
ends, just as many have opposed or ignored reformist policies. Furthermore, the long-term impact of the actions of such American evangelical
Christian Right leaders described above should not be exaggerated; the
members of the evangelical churches in Central America are not passive
objects who incorporate the ideology of North Americans passing
through. It is ludicrous to think that Jimmy Swaggart's sermon from a
helicopter while delivering candy had much effect on the campesinos
other than brief entertainment. If anything, the blatant U.S. manipula-
tion of the missionaries had a negative impact on their credibility and
influence. But these often crude interventions are not the missionary
efforts that have more significantly influenced Central America. The
long-term, committed evangelicals and now-nationalized churches they
encouraged are the sources of an authentic movement. Thus, analysis
should largely ignore the dramatic episodes described above and instead
study the goals, practices, and ideologies of Central American evangelicals.

For example, many evangelical churches in the region have provided
valuable assistance to neighborhood programs that mobilize people
rather than pacify them. An *Asambleas de Dios* preacher who works
also as a labor leader in Guatemala for electrical workers described to
this author the efforts of some evangelical organizations in spring 1989
to call for a just wage in Guatemala. Their efforts only resulted in ha-
rassment and intimidation from the government and the bombing of one
church. Even during the Riós Montt presidency in 1982, Protestants

were not immune from terrorism. In El Quiché thirty members of a Pentecostal church were killed while at worship because they were suspected of radicalism (Martin 1990). The indiscriminate attacks continue, as in the murder of Presbyterian human rights workers Manuel Saquic and Pascual Serech in 1995 in Guatemala and subsequent death threats to their coworkers at the Maya Cakchikel Presbytery. Terrorism persists in Nicaragua as well, where the *El Diario* newspaper reported in July 1995 that rearmed Contra groups ("recontras") attacked members of the United Pentecostal Church who were on their way to celebrate the sixteenth anniversary of the Sandinista revolution. The evangelicals are not a monolithic, conservative mass linked to the Christian Right; rather, they are autonomous and their political orientations depend upon the local context. They may elect to enter into protest movements, or they may attempt to remain apolitical and provide safe haven for members seeking refuge from violence, if that is what is needed at the time. In either case, the active evangelical laity often includes religious free thinkers who resist control by either U.S. founding missions or by U.S. government agencies. Evangelicals in such a decentralized, autonomous system can be more assertive, more reactionary, more radical, and more independent than predicted. Ultimately, the political direction that individual churches take is up to them.

Protestantism in Central America

Protestantism in the region is incredibly diverse, but we can identify three broad categories to aid in our understanding. In point of fact, the contradictory analyses about Protestants in Central America that I have encountered usually exist because of a failure to distinguish between and among categories of such Protestants.

1. Traditionalists. The Traditionalists include the historic Protestant churches that began sending missionaries at the turn of the century. Today, they are the smallest of the three major Protestant groups. Nevertheless, they have more influence than their numbers would indicate because their leaders are likely to disseminate published works on society and politics as well as sermons and theology. These evangelicals are the American Baptists, the Presbyterians, Methodists, Episcopalians, Lutherans, and a few other smaller denominations. They do not usually engage in the emotional worship style of faith healing and glossolalia (speaking in tongues from the Holy Spirit). These Traditionalists also refer to themselves as the "progressive" branch of Protestantism in Central America, and are more likely to be ecumenical than other Protestants in terms of their association with liberation theology Catholics. As progressives, they are also more likely than other Protestants to protest human rights violations in a direct way. Leaders of these particular denominations tend to be transnational, often networking with international human rights organizations and such groups as the Latin American Council of Churches.

2. Pentecostals. Pentecostals are concentrated in the poorest urban areas and in rural sectors. They are fundamentalists theologically (for example, they believe in Biblical inerrancy and in the importance of personal "born-again" experiences for religious conversion), but they also participate in highly charged worship services, which include much singing, faith healing, and glossolalia. A few Pentecostals require a speaking-in-tongues experience for full membership in their church. A large majority of Central American Protestants are Pentecostals; for example, they make up around 80 percent of Nicaraguan Protestants. They are by far the fastest-growing category of evangelicals and include many denominations and nondenominational faith missions.

The Assemblies of God denomination deserves special mention because it is the largest evangelical denomination in El Salvador, Guatemala, and Nicaragua, and is very strong in Honduras as well. It could be called the wellspring of the powerful Pentecostal branch of Protestantism. It began as an imported missionary church, like all such Protestant churches, but after roughly a sixty-year presence, it is now thoroughly nationalized in each Central American country. It is associated with thousands of individual churches across Central America, mostly in poor rural areas, but their precise number is virtually impossible to ascertain because churches may sprout in any available site without official registration. While local churches are self-supporting, the Assemblies of God organization runs dozens of primary schools, Bible schools, clinics and service centers throughout the region, largely financed by Jimmy Swaggart Ministries based in Missouri. Swaggart is still the most famous leader of the Assemblies of God in Central America, gaining popularity through his broadcasts, crusades, and revivals. However, the personal scandals concerning Swaggart that were publicized in 1985 have discredited him. Ironically, Swaggart's disgrace probably accelerated the growth rate of local churches as they sought to become more autonomous from the U.S. organization and relied more fully on indigenous pastors and administrators than foreign missionaries. In fact, the national superintendent of the *Asamleas de Dios en Guatemala* was adamant during an interview that his denomination was completely independent of Jimmy Swaggart as well as the United States.

3. Neo-Pentecostals. The Neo-Pentecostals are found primarily in urban areas and have grown in number among working-class, middle-class and upper-class professionals. Their leaders are frequently trained in the United States. They are different from the Pentecostals in their attitude toward material well-being. To generalize, one way the poorest Pentecostals adapt to their situation is by denying the importance of the material world. On the other hand, the Neo-Pentecostals believe that God will reward good Christians with material wealth. The Neo-Pentecostals are the most upwardly mobile of the three groups, and they are far more numerous in Guatemala than in Nicaragua. But it should also be noted that the majority of these Neo-Pentecostals were already in the middle and upper classes when they converted from Catholicism. They include such churches as Frontera Cristiani, El Shaddhai, Maranatha, the megachurch Hebron, the Full Gospel Businessmen's Fellowship, and the Elim Church (more working-class members). One careful observer of these categories speculated that many members of the Neo-Pentecostal groups were wealthier Catholics who converted because they felt betrayed by liberation theology's attacks on the economic system (Smith 1995). Because of class distinctions, they have little contact with the majority of Pentecostals who are among the urban and rural poor.

Of these three groupings, the Neo-Pentecostals are most sympathetic to the growth of the Christian Right because their middle- and upper-class experiences often match the political and social goals of the Christian Right. For instance, a fascinating recent dispute in Guatemala involving Neo-Pentecostals sounds familiar to observers of the Christian Right in the United States. Citing the "moral decomposition" of the nation's youth, the Guatemalan First Lady Patricia Escobar Dalton attempted to implement a series of classes on moral values and religion in public high schools. Neo-Pentecostal pastors supervise the selection and training of the teachers, as well as the design of the curriculum. The Guatemalan Bishop's Conference (CEG) and the Conference of Evangelical Churches (CIEDEG), both of which are progressive and ecumenical religious organizations, have issued strong statements condemning the proposed classes for their selective, conservative reading of the Scriptures and for their proselytizing nature. What is especially interesting about this church-state debate is that Escobar is a Catholic but conservative ideologically. (*Latinamerica Press*, 21 November 1996, 1, 8). She is siding with Neo-Pentecostals in her educational proposal against the Guatemalan bishops because she apparently agrees with their "Christian Right" ideology, if not necessarily their theology. Neo-Pentecostals have consistently been the Protestants in Guatemala closest to the higher echelons of political life.

Thus, the most significant division among the three categories is between the Neo-Pentecostal churches and the others because that fissure occurs along class lines. But this surface fragmentation has actually been an advantage for the growth of the Protestant movement, because it is spreading through the process of decentralization as people "shop" in the new religious marketplace. If people cannot find something they like, they can, and frequently do, establish a brand new church that is meaningful and comfortable to them. Thus, one reason for the rapid spread of evangelicalism is the ease of forming new churches. Today, there are at least one hundred different Protestant denominations or nondenominational faith missions in each country (including at least three hundred in Guatemala).

Field observation reveals the close interaction among the variety of Pentecostals—for instance, in the binding symbolism of referring to all fellow evangelicals as "brothers" and "sisters." As one minister in El Salvador explained his beliefs:

> I don't care if the Lord is coming or if He will scratch everything with one simple act of His will, or if it will be a process. I don't care. What I need to care about is being closer to Him. And if I'm closer to Him, everything will be for the good. So I'm not worried about that. Yes, we have a statement about the Rapture, but we work with a lot of churches, so we don't really teach that. (Nuncio 1995).

This lack of concern about precise theology was a typical response in interviews with religious leaders and church members and mirrors the lack of concern about written doctrines or creeds. Declining denominationalism is not only a phenomenon found in Latin America. Robert Wuthnow (1988) has argued, for example, that there is a restructuring of religion occurring in the United States in which similar groups across different denominations are emphasizing their religious, social and political common ground rather than doctrinal differences (as in the preceding example of the President's wife and Neo-Pentecostals in Guatemala).

One neglected factor in analyses of the success of both Pentecostalism and Neo-Pentecostalism is the role of music. When evangelical beliefs and priorities are set to music, they are even more unifying and powerful, particularly for attracting and holding younger members. One Protestant liberation theologian dismayed by the anti-intellectualism of the Pentecostals said the music was "like a drug" (Minerva 1993). But another observer, a minister with the Christian Missionary Alliance, noted that "the music fits the hearts of the people. Music is 80 to 85 percent of the message" (Whitman 1995). In Nicaragua, people want to convert old movie houses into massive "God is Love" churches, which would hold popular worship services with music syncretic with Latin music—an idea imported from Brazil. Evangelical services are often standing room only, with all the anticipation and excitement of rock concerts with spirituality. In nations where majorities of the population face oppressive poverty and millions have been displaced to alien urban settings, such events are uplifting respites.

The political implications of this religious movement are modest at present, but widespread Protestantism is a potential threat to the status quo because it challenges existing worldly powers in a way that has been recognized since the Reformation. The belief in an unmediated contact with the Deity and the common availability of the Bible were ancient challenges to the authority of the Roman Catholic Church. Thus, the Protestant Reformation emphasis on a "priesthood of all believers" who could discern the will of God through engagement with Scripture, guided by the Holy Spirit, provided the rationale for empowerment of both individuals and communities of faith—and still does. Its social power is manifest when individuals engage in interactive, interdependent religious communities. Importantly, emphasis on a personal, unmediated relationship with Christ is a unifying element of evangelical beliefs, a point of deep and widespread agreement.

It does not require much of an analytical stretch to ascertain egalitarian and democratizing aspects of elevating lay church members to a "priesthood." The most obvious examples of such democratization in a Central American context are the leadership opportunities in Pentecostal Churches that are available to the poorest, illiterate members who have eloquence and "gifts from the Spirit." Unlike the hierarchical demands of Catholicism or the seminary requirements of some mainline Protestants, most evangelical congregations only require their pastor to have spiritual gifts. This is a highly flexible system, appropriate for a society in which a majority of the people are poor and illiterate. Even women—who are often excluded from male-dominated church institutions—can gain authority in these churches through their biblical expertise or through spiritualism. For instance, the most respected member this author met at the Church of the New Jerusalem in a small town in

Guatemala was not the pastor, but a woman who regularly practiced faith healing and speaking in tongues. This movement is not only non-hierarchical but the theology elevates the poorest individuals to persons in direct contact with God. It is difficult to imagine a more empowering belief system, an empowerment that could eventually spill over into the political arena.

Local context shapes not only the religious and political activities but also religious scholarship. Again, the people are not simply objects absorbing a prepackaged message. Rather, they are actively reforming a theology even as they respond. Nicaraguan theologian Benjamín Cortes explained, "Evangelical theology in Latin America is being developed. It's a blend of Protestant liberation theology plus Catholic liberation theology plus evangelical theology—plus the Nicaraguan experience" (Cortes 1993). Protestantism in Central America may have roots in evangelical Protestantism in the United States, but it is now being transformed in these countries even in the deepest theological sense. Andrew Walls (1987, 15) of the Yale Divinity School provides this perspective on the significance of the movement for the development of Christianity:

> Within a very short period of time, the conditions which have produced the phenomena characteristic of Christianity for almost a millennium have largely disappeared. After centuries in which the norms by which Christian expression have been tested have arisen from the history and conditions of the Mediterranean world and of the lands north and east of it, the process has been transferred into a new and infinitely more varied theatre of activity. The conditions of African and Melanesian life, the intellectual climate of India, the political battlegrounds of Latin America, increasingly provide the context within which the Christian mind is being formed. The process is already beginning to produce changes in Christian priorities, and in the structure of Christian thought, practice and government. Indeed, most of the discernible changes in Christianity since 1945 come from this fundamental southward shift.

Progressive Pentecostals in Nicaragua

What is the potential of Protestantism, then, for challenging political and economic structures and the injustices they perpetuate in Central American society? If evangelical theology and practice and community-building are gradually implanting a sense of empowerment among the poor, does that empowerment stop short of political influence? Can the

Protestant movement have an impact on the inequities of an economic system in which 2 percent of the population own 70 to 80 percent of the land, and in which, as in Nicaragua, unemployment is over 60 percent? Billions of dollars of U.S. aid to Central America in the 1980s were squandered in wars, destruction and corruption. Now, not only are the industrial and transportation infrastructures in worse shape than in the 1970s, but the environment has been severely damaged, illiteracy is greater, and the poverty rate is higher—at about 70 percent throughout much of the region. Can widespread Protestantism in Central America have an impact on developing these countries and reducing political corruption and waste, as many Protestant leaders promise?

The fact that Guatemala has had two evangelical chief executives (the military dictatorship of Riós Montt in 1982, and President Serrano in 1991 to 1992) might lead one to think that evangelicals are most politicized in that country. However, both of those leaders were members of Neo-Pentecostal churches, which tend to support the status quo economy, and both of those administrations ended in violence and corruption and were sobering disappointments for evangelicals.

In Nicaragua evangelical political parties are also emerging, and there they had enough support to win seats in the National Assembly in the 1996 elections. Protestants in Nicaragua are rarely linked to the Christian Right because Nicaragua has experienced a full-scale leftist revolution that has strengthened the more progressive and ecumenical missions. These include the Mennonite Central Committee, the Presbyterian Church USA, the United Methodist Church, and American Baptist Churches USA. The prominence of these historic churches creates a fascinating dynamic in Nicaragua because they support, from a Christian perspective, left-leaning politics in the country. When asked about his political preferences, a Baptist pastor simply said, "I'm a socialist at heart as are all thinking people in Nicaragua" (Pixley 1993). One scholar in Managua succinctly explained the close relationship between the evangelicals and the Sandinistas this way: "when the Catholic bourgeoisie here reacted against the revolution—reinforced by the Vatican—the revolution searched for a replacement church" (Bardeguez 1993). Although more attention has been given to the dramatic political struggles of the Catholic Church in Nicaragua, many evangelicals have been involved in the politics of the revolution and its aftermath, often in support of the Sandinistas. Nicaragua's revolutionary history still invites widespread political participation among all classes and religious groups. More than 80 percent of all eligible voters freely took part in the October 1996 elections (*New York Times,* 22 October 1996, A1).

A nation's political culture and missionary experience provide the context shaping the political impact of Protestants. Leadership development is another requisite for social and political impact, and in this regard, missionaries in Nicaragua have made important contributions. An impressive array of religious leadership institutions have emerged in Managua, encouraged by missionaries, but clearly national by now. For instance, the *Centro InterEclesial de Estudios Teologicos y Sociales* (CIEETS) in Managua, is a seminary founded in 1985 by 85 Nicaraguan evangelical churches. In addition to CIEETS are the *Facultad Evangélica de Estudios Teologicos (FEET),* the *Seminario Teologico Bautista,* and the Antonio Valdivieso Ecumenical Center (CAV). The CAV was founded by a Catholic priest and a Baptist minister in 1979 "to help Catholics and Protestants reflect on this new experience of the revolution" (Campbell 1993). Now it operates two divisions: one for reflection through leadership training, workshops, symposiums, and research; and another for social action and development projects. Another prestigious religious organization in Nicaragua is the *Comité Evangélico Por Ayuda al Desarrollo* (CEPAD) formed after the 1972 earthquake. CEPAD provides services for emergency relief, community development, peace commissions, and credit programs. It works in over 300 communities, and 56 evangelical denominations are members—another example of the interdenominational characteristic of Protestantism in the region. Under the skillful leadership of Gustavo Parajón, CEPAD unites extraordinarily diverse religious groups to assist the poor. Another group is The Foundation for Victims of the War, founded by Methodists in 1987, and now led by Maria del Socorro Guiterrez. The leaders of all these organizations often work together, and, in interviews, they volunteer high praise for each other—indicating a close-knit community. For instance, Maria del Socorro Guiterrez is also President of CAV; and the Secretary General of CIEETS was the first Executive Director of CEPAD. In interviews, the view was often expressed that the many denominations of evangelicals are especially cooperative and congenial in Nicaragua.

We have discussed Protestant leadership organizations in Nicaragua, but what about the church members? Are evangelicals a potentially unified political bloc? If so, are they likely to be political leftists like many of the intellectual leaders, or are they more likely to be withdrawn from politics according to the common image of Pentecostals? How do the political culture and political structures in Nicaragua influence evangelical attitudes toward participation? Fortunately, some suggestive survey data are available to address these questions, which will be supplemented with some early analysis of the 1996 election.

In late 1991 Roberto Zub of CIEETS conducted a survey of Protestants in Nicaragua: 43 questions were given to 248 adults from 24 representative evangelical congregations in Managua, mostly dealing with the 1990 elections and political attitudes. Zub's sample included two denominations that are strongly Pentecostal in their theology (the Assemblies of God and the Four Square Church), plus the more ecumenical Baptist denomination, and three others that fall somewhere in between. First, Zub found that an extraordinary 90 percent of the Protestants said they voted in the 1990 elections, with little variation among the different denominations. With regard to their vote choice, evangelicals were fairly polarized: almost 65 percent of the two pentecostal denominations voted for Chamorro's UNO party, whereas only about 39 percent of the Baptists voted for her. Zub interpreted the Chamorro vote more as a vote against the Sandinistas in 1990 than as support for Violeta Chamorro. The survey also found that, across-the-board, these Protestants were far more willing to experiment among other parties than was the general population. In the national vote, only about 3 percent of the vote went to all the other parties, but among this sample, 10.4 percent voted for parties other than the two major ones. In fact, except for considerable Baptist and Church of Christ loyalty to the Sandinistas, most of these Protestants were not closely linked to any political party. Thus, when Zub asked if an evangelical can be affiliated with a political party, 48 percent said no to such party affiliation. However, Zub went one step further to obtain his most interesting finding when he asked, "Should an Evangelical Party be organized in Nicaragua?" This question produced a great deal of consensus among the Protestants with almost 71 percent answering "yes." Thus, the bare 51 percent who approved affiliation with a party, rose to 71 percent when the idea was raised about forming and directing their own party. Zub noted that this question brought the most effusive responses such as "hallelujah" and "if there is an evangelical government, Christ will reign through it, and they will make a better distribution of wealth and justice" (Zub 1993, 101).

Zub's findings were not without foundation in Nicaragua. In February 1992, the Party of National Justice (PJN) was formed in Nicaragua as the first evangelical party in the history of the country. Its presidential candidate for 1996 was Jorge Diaz, originally a pastor with the *Asambleas de Dios* as well as a medical doctor. His political platform could be termed center-right, although the PJN Declaration of Principles contained strong statements endorsing equality for women. The party also offered approximately twenty candidates for the National Assembly and sixty at the local level.

In November 1992 the *Movimiento Evangelico Popular* (MEP) was formed by Rev. Miguel Angel Casco as a decidedly leftist political party seeking political and economic transformation for a more just society (Casco 1993). In a highly publicized but short-lived move, Casco was even presented as a possible vice presidential candidate for the FSLN.

In May 1996, the *Camino Cristiano Nicaraguense* became a legal entity and put forth as a presidential candidate the radio evangelist Guillermo Osorno Mendoza. Osorno became known for his optimistic claims that (1) his very young party was the third strongest party in Nicaragua with 1,800 candidates nationwide, (2) he would win up to 70 percent of the vote, and (3) God had in various ways specifically called him to the presidential candidacy. Although Osorno fought in the revolution with the Sandinistas, his political ideology in the campaign remained basically unknown because he simply reported that he would "tell the people the truth . . . explain to the people that answers won't come immediately, but gradually" (Osorno 1996). All of these fledgling religiously based political parties have meager resources. The average wage of PJN candidates, for instance, was $300 per month, and candidate Diaz mortgaged his home to finance his campaign (Diaz 1996). These evangelical candidates are not from the upper class; they practice the Pentecostal religion of the poor.

In a crowded field of thirty-two political parties and twenty-three presidential candidates, these groups obviously had an uphill battle in the election. The results of the October 20th voting, in fact, showed that the numerous parties were virtually shut out altogether. During the final weeks of the campaign, it turned into a bitter, polarizing battle between Arnoldo Alemán of the right-wing Liberal Alliance and the Sandinista candidate Daniel Ortega. Without even requiring a runoff vote, Alemán won the presidency with 51 percent of the vote to Ortega's 38.6 percent. Ninety percent of the ninety-three seats of the National Assembly were allotted to the two major parties since all the other parties won only ten seats in the legislature (*Latinamerica Press,* 7 November 1996, 3). Almost 6,000 international and Nicaraguan election monitors concluded that the election was free and fair, although its credibility was weakened by polling places that ran out of ballots, opened late and were generally disorganized (*New York Times,* 22 October 1996, A16). For our purposes, it is significant that the party that came in a distant third in presidential voting was Osorno's *Camino Cristiano Nicaraguense*, with approximately 4.5 percent of the vote.

In conclusion, Nicaragua is a highly politicized and highly polarized society, and its revolutionary history creates a political context of active participation—more than 80 percent of eligible voters participated in 1996. The negative side of this highly charged political environment is the underlying political instability associated with an environment characterized by mistrust instead of compromise or consensus. The positive aspects of Nicaraguan politics include a high level of popular participation, ease of access of new parties (including religious ones), and hope for the future. The immediate challenge is for the Sandinistas and Liberal Alliance to find some way to work together to ease the nation's severe unemployment rate. In the meantime, as scholar Jorge Pixley (1996) predicted, "the evangelical parties will change and grow with political experience. . . . they will form alliances and eventually offer the people a real alternative." These political novices cannot be classified as pawns of the Christian Right, nor as "otherworldly" Pentecostals. In Nicaragua these evangelicals from the poorest segments of society have an amazing sense of faith, not only in God, but also in themselves and in democracy.

Notes

1. Conversion rates are given in virtually every article and book on the topic, however the sources for these figures are problematic. On the one hand, Protestant missionary organizations have a bias to report dramatic conversion rates. On the other hand, some of the critics of the inflationary nature of the figures are Catholic and have a bias toward deriding the rival religion. For example, despite the obvious explosion of Protestantism, Cardinal Obando y Bravo of Nicaragua was quoted in a magazine article a few years ago with his own estimate that only 1 percent of Nicaraguans were Protestant. Many denominational offices do not even have an accurate count of the number of churches, much less members. It seems that the most reasonable approach to assessing the Protestant movement in the region is twofold: Be cautious in citing figures of conversion, "considering the source"; and do not ignore simple observation in the field that indicates the amazing prevalence of Protestant churches. See also my discussion in Hallum (1996).

References

Bardeguez, Jorge. 1993. Interview by author. Antonio Valdivieso Ecumenical Center (CAV), Managua, Nicaragua, 9 November.

Barry, Tom, and Deborah Preusch. 1988. *The Soft War: The Uses and Abuses of U.S. Economic Aid in Central America.* New York: Grove Press.

Campbell, Gary. 1993. Interview by author. Antonio Valdivieso Ecumenical Center (CAV), Managua, Nicaragua, 10 November.

Casco, Miguel Angel. 1993. Interview by author. Movimiento Evangélico Popular (MEP). Managua, Nicaragua, 12 November.

Cortes, Benjámín. 1993. Interview by author. Centro InterEclesial de Estudios Teologicos y Sociales (CIEETS). Managua, Nicaragua, 11 November.

Diaz, Jorge. 1996. Interview by author. Partido de Justicia Nacional (PJN). Managua, Nicaragua, 21 July.

Hallum, Anne Motley. 1996. *Beyond Missionaries: Toward an Understanding of the Protestant Movement in Central America.* Lanham, Md.: Rowman & Littlefield Publishers.

Martin, David. 1990. *Tongues of Fire: The Explosion of Protestantism in Latin America.* London: Basil Blackwell.

Minerva, Otto. 1993. Interview by author. Seminario Biblio Latinoamericano. San Jose, Costa Rica, 26 July.

Nuncio, Enrique. 1995. Interview by author. Campus Crusade for Christ. San Salvador, El Salvador, 19 January.

Osorno, Mendoza Guillermo. 1996. Interview by author. Partido de Camino Cristiano Nicaraguense. Managua, Nicaragua, 21 July.

Pixley, Jorge. 1993. Interview by author. Seminario Teologica Bautista. Managua, Nicaragua, 11 November

———. 1996. Interview by author. Seminario Teológica Bautista. Managua, Nicaragua, 21 July.

Siewert, John A., and John A. Kenyon, eds. 1995. *Mission Handbook: 1993–95.* Monrovia, Calif.: Mission Advanced Research Center, WorldVision International.

Smith, Dennis. 1995. Interview by author. Latin American Evangelical Center for Pastoral Studies (CELEP). Guatemala City, Guatemala, 16 January.

Walls, Andrew. 1987. "The Christian Tradition in Today's World." In *Religion in Today's World: The Religious Situation of the World from 1946 to the Present Day*, edited by Frank Whaling, 250. Edinburgh, Scotland: T and T Clark.

Whitman, Dale. 1995. Interview by author. Christian Missionary Alliance. DeLand, Florida, 20 November.

Wuthnow, Robert. 1988. *The Restructuring of American Religion: Society and Faith since World War II.* Princeton, N.J.: Princeton University Press.

Zub, Roberto K. 1993. *Protestantismo y elecciones en Nicaragua.* Managua, Nicaragua: Centro InterEclesial de Estudios Teológicos y Sociales (CIEETS).

Part V

Evaluation of the Christian Right

12

Growing Up Politically: The New Politics of the New Christian Right

Mark J. Rozell

Soon after the landmark 1994 elections, Christian Right leaders claimed unprecedented success at having helped to elect numerous Republican Party congressional candidates. The leading organization, the Christian Coalition, pointed to the large number of openly pro-life Republicans who had won elections, despite Democratic attempts to characterize these candidates as social extremists. Shortly thereafter, when the Christian Coalition held a postelection press conference in Washington, D.C., to unveil its "Contract with the American Family," modeled after the GOP's "Contract with America," Republican leaders, including several presidential aspirants, eagerly attended the event and praised the leadership of the Christian Coalition's executive director Ralph Reed. The intended message was clear: the Christian Right had joined the political mainstream.

Although the Christian Right cannot claim a great many national policy victories since 1994, the movement at least has achieved legitimacy as a part of the broad GOP coalition. More importantly, the movement can claim a good many successes throughout the country in exerting influence on state and local GOP committees and the policies of state legislatures, local school boards, library boards and town and city councils.

These achievements are even more noteworthy when we consider the standing of the Christian Right only a few years earlier. By the end of the 1980s, it appeared that the Christian Right was in retreat. Rev. Jerry Falwell had disbanded his Moral Majority, and his Liberty University was near financial ruin. Rev. Pat Robertson disbanded his Freedom

Council after an embarrassing run for the 1988 GOP presidential nomination, and extensive news coverage of sordid scandals involving prominent televangelists led to dramatic declines in contributions to
Christian conservative organizations nationwide. As a result, a good
many scholars and popular political analysts predicted the eventual demise of the Christian Right as a force in American politics. And, such
predictions were widely repeated after "Family Values Night" at the
1992 GOP convention—an event that many analysts characterized as
mean-spirited and harmful to the GOP presidential campaign.

But, to paraphrase Mark Twain, predictions of the demise of the
Christian Right were not merely premature—they were wrong. Just as
the movement appeared to be fading fast in influence, Robertson was
building the foundation of a grassroots organization from the impressive list of contributors he had compiled from his presidential campaign
efforts. The purpose of this new organization, founded in 1989 as the
Christian Coalition, was to build a nationwide network of Christian conservative activists who could be mobilized into political action in their
communities.

Whereas the first wave of the Christian Right movement, beginning
in the 1970s, eventually faltered, the "second coming" of the Christian
Right has evidenced greater political sophistication and success (see
Rozell and Wilcox 1995, 1996b). A political movement that once was
splintered, divisive, and engaged in rhetoric and tactics that turned off
voters is now a sophisticated network of leaders and activists who exert
substantial influence. The Christian Right has grown up politically and,
as GOP consultant Ed DeBolt put it, become "more dangerous to their
enemies than ever before" (DeBolt 1993).

This chapter examines the evidence for the growing maturity of the
second coming of the New Christian Right, discusses the electoral and
political strategies of the movement, and speculates about future prospects. The two waves of New Christian Right organizations are emphasized and their constrasting experiences.

The Failure of the First Wave

The New Christian Right became active in the mid-1970s even prior to
the advent of Rev. Falwell's Moral Majority. But it was with the creation of the Moral Majority that the movement attained national recognition as a potentially potent electoral force. Falwell became the
movement's most visible spokesman, and after the 1980 elections, he
claimed that newly mobilized social conservatives had delivered about
four million votes to Ronald Reagan's successful campaign and that he

had built a national network of millions of activists who potentially could reshape the American political landscape. Whether these claims of new Christian voter participation and organizational membership were accurate or not (academic accounts dispute Falwell's figures, and his cronies liked to say that "Jerry never lies; he just remembers big"), it was indisputable that the Moral Majority had made a major impression in a short period of time.

To many Republicans in the 1980s, Falwell's efforts introduced a problem still being confronted today by the party. On the one hand, they wanted the organizational support and the votes of an enthusiastic bloc of Christian social conservatives. On the other hand, the American political culture is very uncomfortable with moral posturing in public life, and many voters expressed their contempt for the Christian Right movement. Opinion polls throughout the 1980s confirmed that Falwell was one of the least popular individuals on the political scene, and a major liability to GOP candidates. Democratic candidates nationwide ran advertisements linking their GOP opponents to Falwell and the Christian Right movement.

Much of this state of affairs could be attributed to the strong rhetoric that Falwell and other Christian Right leaders used at the time. They spoke openly of "taking over" Republican Party organizations and portrayed themselves as being engaged in an intellectual war with secular humanists. And the uncompromising rhetoric they employed often displayed intolerance that made the movement threatening to many Americans.

Moreover, Falwell and other Christian Right leaders at the time did little to build a broadly ecumenical base of support for their organizations. In fact, the Moral Majority and other New Christian Right organizations lacked a broad base even among evangelical Protestants, with each organization appealing to different denominational groups, and with little outreach to religious conservatives among mainline Protestants, Catholics, and other religious traditions (see Georgianna 1989; Green et al. 1996; and Wilcox 1992). Thus, the problem of religious particularism among Christian Right organizations in the 1970s and 1980s undermined the political strength of the movement.

Studies revealed that most Moral Majority chapter leaders were Baptist Bible Fellowship ministers who displayed little tolerance for other denominations. Many such leaders devoted their energies primarily to their churches and religious schools, leaving little time for organized political activity (Green et al. 1996). However, an exception was the Washington state chapter of the Moral Majority—the largest and most successful of the state level chapters. Its director, attorney Michael Farris, understood the need to build a broad-based membership. Assemblies of God pastors served on the board of his state chapter, and for much of his tenure the chair of the chapter was the pastor of an independent Bible church. In that regard, Farris was unusual for an early 1980s Christian Right leader. He recalled that Falwell once told him that "perhaps we need more lawyers and fewer preachers" running the various chapters (Farris 1995). When the Moral Majority began to fall dramatically out of favor, Farris broke from the group and renamed his chapter the more mainstream-sounding "Bill of Rights Legal Foundation."

A final problem was that these social movement organizations made no effective efforts to build at the grassroots level and had few local chapters. Hadden, Shupe, Hawdon, and Martin (1987, 102) reported that their study of the Moral Majority revealed no evidence of a functioning grassroots structure; they argued that "the Moral Majority was primarily an organization for grabbing media attention, built and supported by direct-mail technology."

Thus, the first wave of the New Christian Right failed due to a lack of sound political strategy and organization. With weak coalition building, no effective grassroots structure, the use of extremist appeals, and a heavy reliance on the mass mail fund-raising efforts of controversial leaders, the early stage was doomed to failure. But, in failure, many lessons were learned that proved helpful in the next effort to build a more effective movement.

The Second Coming: Growing Up Politically

The second coming of the Christian Right reveals a politically maturing movement that has learned from its past mistakes. The rhetorical appeals are more moderate sounding; the issue appeals are more broad based; leading organizations express a sincere desire to reach out to as broad an ecumenical base as possible; and the new organizations have built impressive grassroots networks.

It is true that Reed caused a stir several years ago when he compared his tactics to guerrilla warfare and bragged that he figuratively ambushed opponents and left them in body bags. But, in a more recent memorandum to supporters, Reed wrote that "phrases like 'religious war' and 'take over' play to a stereotype of evangelicals as intolerant." He urged his followers to avoid threatening language: "We must adopt strategies of persuasion, not domination" (Taylor 1992, B4).

One useful tactic of persuasion has been the adoption by Christian Right leaders of the rights-based language of liberalism. Some claim that they are a part of a minority whose rights are frequently violated in a secular society. They decry what they perceive as societal bigotry toward people of faith and maintain that they have organized politically simply to protect their rights. They often compare their efforts to those of the civil rights movement in the United States in the 1950s and 1960s.

In conducting numerous interviews with Christian Right leaders, it has become clear that such leaders now understand the importance of adopting rhetorical appeals that do not sound threatening to secular audiences. For example, Anne Kincaid (1993), a former lobbyist for the Virginia Family Foundation (the state-level affiliate of Focus on the Family), said that she had learned the hard way what happens to advocates who use harsh rhetoric:

> I can remember using rhetoric that I don't use anymore, that sounded inflammatory. "Onward Christian soldiers" scared people. So you don't talk that way. Some still talk about witchcraft and the feminist movement. Yes, the Bible says that "rebellion against men is of witchcraft." It's all Biblical tenets, but the layman doesn't understand that. So it makes you sound like you've lost your marbles.
>
> The point is that you have to know your audience. That's not deception. . . . Unless you're talking to a Christian audience, you don't put out all the rhetoric out there that others won't respond to. I learned this lesson the hard way.[1]

Michael Farris (1994) elaborated on the rhetorical approach that he advocates for evangelical Christians seeking to have an impact on the political process:

> Evangelical Christians need to find ways to communicate effectively with different people. They can't just interact among themselves. Many are learning as they interact in the Republican Party, not everyone understands or accepts the lingo that evangelicals use when talking to each other. . . . I've got to understand the other person, if I want to be persuasive. Understanding that person means respecting that other person. I've got to get around other peoples' mental road blocks. That means respecting where that person is coming from. That's the way that evangelical Christians can be more effective. It's a growing up thing. That is, being able to disagree with others but still be respectful of their values. That's the trick. Not all of our spokesmen have been very effective at that.

Both Kincaid and Farris acknowledged that, in order to be persuasive, they had to master the secular language of politics and not merely speak in terms that Christian conservatives understand. They do not perceive such an approach as a compromise because their issue stands remain the same, even though their language is different.

The great difficulty for the Christian Right remains how to credibly mask as moderate-sounding those issue positions that most people consider extreme. The abortion issue provides a good example of the effective use of mainstream appeals. The Christian Coalition State Legislative Policy Handbook advises candidates to "run smarter" on the abortion issue by downplaying the difference between pro-life and pro-choice and instead emphasizing the "subissues" (for example, no taxpayer funding, waiting periods, parental notification, and we could now add "partial birth" abortions). The point is that it is easier to forge a consensus for the conservative positions on the subissues than on eliminating abortion rights in general. The goal of this strategy is to cast pro-choice advocates as extremists for failing to accept "reasonable restrictions" on abortion that are strongly favored by the public. According to the handbook, the pro-life position can prevail if it "is communicated in a reasonable manner" (Christian Coalition 1993, 112).

Robert Marshall, the executive director of the American Life League, is the author of a pamphlet that advises conservative Christians on how to effectively handle questions about a pro-life candidate's views. He cited biblical passages to defend a strategy of presenting to the public only that information that will aid the pro-life cause. For example, he suggested:

> Be hesitant to go beyond what is requested. Don't answer questions that are not asked.
> And when you do talk, you are under no obligation to exhaust your information on a topic.
> And even the Lord did not always answer questions directly.
> Also, it is morally permissible to answer a question with a question. (Marshall 1990, 25).

To some, Marshall's advice may simply amount to a creative biblical interpretation for lying. Nevertheless, the point is that successful candidates and activists of different persuasions must learn to frame their appeals in the best possible light; the Christian Right certainly is not unique in that regard. But, what is telling is the increased recognition within the movement of the need to catch up with other interests in society that have learned this lesson much earlier.[2]

Part of the strategy to reach the mainstream entails emphasizing issue appeals beyond controversial social ones. Some leaders in the movement believe that a key to their long-term success is being accepted as mainstream conservatives who care as much about economic issues as abortion and cultural values. As GOP moderate Bobbie Kilberg commented, "They know that in order to be successful they have to masquerade as just regular conservatives who are interested in tax rates" (Kilberg 1993).

In some cases the masquerade is transparently obvious. When Pat Robertson sought the presidency in 1988, he attempted to offer secular conservatives a reason to oppose abortions: they are bad for the economy. He attempted to calculate the overall loss to the work force caused by abortion and its larger impact on the economy. This tactic was widely and rightfully denounced as a fraud.

A more credible approach has been the more recent effort to argue that higher tax rates are as much a concern to social conservatives as economic ones. Whereas the economic conservatives want lower taxes to produce economic opportunity and wealth, the social conservatives maintain that high taxes are the major reason why many more families must rely on two incomes—a situation that reduces the options available to women.

Often this strategy entails taking controversial social issues out of context. For example, some movement leaders such as Ralph Reed claim that they want *Roe v. Wade* overturned on the grounds of federalism. That is, they wish to strike down the ruling, not because it is immoral, but because it is bad constitutional law that denies the states their proper role in the federal system. Reed and others argue that we should allow the issue of abortion to be decided by the states, guaranteeing a diversity of approaches. Presumably such an approach would result in fewer abortions, although whether significantly so is not certain. Reed and other movement leaders believe that it is more important to make incremental gains on restricting abortions than it is to adopt the purist stance on the issue and continue to lose. They are politically mature enough to understand that fighting the *Roe* decision on the territory of privacy rights may continue to guarantee failure.

The Christian Right has also become better in recent years at building broad-based coalitions. This breadth begins with increased cooperation among religious conservatives of different faiths. As noted earlier, the first wave of the Christian Right failed in part because of its inability to build a broad ecumenical base. The second coming of the movement evidences some success at reaching out to people of different faiths.

For example, the Christian Coalition has recently launched its Catholic Alliance affiliate, with a Washington, D.C., headquarters and the goal of signing up one million Catholics by the year 2000. The Coalition's national lobbying office boasts an ecumenical staff, including a Greek Orthodox, a Jew, and an Episcopalian (Reed himself). According to Reed, the organization's membership also reflects a diverse religious mix, with approximately 25 percent belonging to mainline Protestant denominations, 10 to15 percent associated with Pentecostal churches, half Baptists, and about 5 to10 percent belonging to other churches, especially Roman Catholic (Green et al. 1996, 3).

Farris's latest organization, the Madison Project, a Christian Right group that "bundles" money for congressional candidates nationwide, has backed a Mormon candidate for the House of Representatives. His organization claims a diverse governing board, including a Catholic who also was one of his former campaign coordinators.

Developing a broad base of support also entails building coalitions among members of groups that have no interest in joining any Christian Right organization. The Christian Coalition's training manual lists a number of potential allies who are likely to back causes and candidates supported by the Christian Right: gun owners, home-schooling parents, America First, English First, and antitax groups, among others (Christian Coalition 1993). In fact, the Christian Right is having considerable success in cooperating with secular conservative groups to share membership lists, cosponsor candidate fund-raisers, and join forces to back GOP candidates. A recent survey of GOP convention delegates in Virginia, for example, found that gun owners and religious conservatives formed powerful coalitions to back certain candidates for nomination, even though members of these two groups had very different views on social issues (Rozell and Wilcox 1996b, 157).

Perhaps the most difficult goal for the Christian Right to achieve has been to accept the necessity of compromise in politics. Clearly, many of the movement's leaders now counsel activists on the importance of working within the political system, even if that means that desired change in policy will take years to achieve. To some activists, any compromise on the issue of abortion is immoral and unacceptable. And some activists insist that they cannot support candidates who are not strictly pro-life.

But there is increased evidence that many in the movement are showing increased willingness to make compromises. That may mean accepting a strategy of promoting certain abortion restrictions instead of pursuing total elimination of abortion rights. In an ABC (1993) "Nightline" interview, Pat Robertson explained: "I would urge people, as a matter of private choice, not to choose abortion, because I think it is wrong. It's something else, though, in the political arena to go out on a quixotic crusade when you know you'll be beaten continuously. So I say let's do what is possible. What is possible is parental consent."

Accepting compromise also means backing GOP candidates who are not purists on the social issues, but who have the ability to win elections and ultimately to influence policy. A good example is the effort of Reed and other activists on behalf of Bob Dole's campaign for the GOP nomination. Although columnist Patrick Buchanan staked out the strongest pro-life stand of the GOP candidates, and many of the activists supported him, ultimately in such crucial primary states as South Carolina, exit polling data showed that Dole fared as well as Buchanan among Christian conservatives. Such evidence reveals the willingness of leaders such as Reed as well as a solid core of activists to be pragmatic (Rozell and Wilcox 1996a; Wilcox and Rozell 1996).

Finally, movement leaders stress the importance of staying loyal to the GOP as long as the party does not abandon them. If the Christian Right remains an important GOP faction that helps the party to recruit activists, raise money, and win elections, then the movement may claim the right to influence GOP platforms and policies. Leaders point to their willingness to back such pro-choice GOP candidates as Paul Coverdell and Kay Bailey Hutchison as evidence that they are loyal to the party. They make it clear that they expect, in return, the loyalty of GOP moderates when more socially conservative candidates win party nominations.[3]

The 1996 Elections and the Challenge Ahead

In 1996, despite a lack of genuine enthusiasm for the GOP presidential nominee Bob Dole, the Christian Right actively mobilized its forces to support Republican candidates at all levels. The Christian Coalition mounted its most extensive voter education and get-out-the-vote drive ever. The group claimed that it distributed 45 million voter guides nationwide and directly contacted about 5 million voters (Associated Press 1996, A5). Although this effort could not rescue a long-shot presidential candidacy from defeat, it clearly was an asset to GOP House and Senate candidates nationwide as the party maintained control of the Congress.

But more importantly, the Christian Right can be credited with having had a profound impact on the political discourse of the 1996 elections. Four years earlier the movement's use of "family values" rhetoric to oppose gay rights and promote constitutional amendments to ban abortions and allow public school prayers was divisive, and it turned off a good many voters. But it was clear that the movement had also tapped into a deep well of public concern about the moral direction of the country and has forced public leaders of both parties to address the values agenda.

By 1996 both major parties were seeking to be accepted by the public as best able to deal with values issues in the future. President Bill Clinton took the lead early in the year in signing legislation to require television makers to install V-chips that would enable parental control of programming content. Soon after, as a result of the president's lobbying, television producers and executives pledged to adopt a program rating system. The president succeeded in convincing television executives to agree to provide at least three hours per day of quality educational childrens' programming. Clinton announced support for such policy innovations as requiring school uniforms in public schools and imposing a national curfew on teenagers. The president also framed his views on family/medical leave and banning tobacco advertising to minors in values-based language. At the Democratic nominating convention, numerous speakers invoked the importance of promoting a "Families First" agenda, none more so than Hillary Clinton.

Such Christian Right leaders as Family Research Council Director, Gary Bauer, suggested that these efforts were merely clever political attempts to jump on the values-agenda bandwagon. Whether or not the charge is accurate, the fact remains that by 1996 leaders of both parties had recognized the power of the values agenda and acted accordingly. It was the activities of the Christian Right throughout the 1990s that had changed the nature of the political dialogue in the country.

The GOP presidential campaign clearly accepted the view that it was important to discuss the values agenda without pushing too hard on the controversial positions of the Christian Right. Although the party platform was very compatible with the Christian Right agenda, the public presentation of the convention was much more moderate in tone. Such movement leaders as the Christian Coalition's Ralph Reed urged the strategy of helping Dole by not pushing him to the extremes on the social agenda. And, although this strategy may have been the correct one, and perhaps one that could have paid off for a better presidential candidate than Dole, it nonetheless caused a great deal of concern within the Christian Right that the GOP was backing away from the movement too much. Consequently, if much of the leadership of the movement adopts moderate-sounding rhetoric, accepts compromise, builds coalitions with secular organizations, and builds support within the GOP, there is the real potential for many of its activists to lose enthusiasm for organizations such as the Christian Coalition. As with other social movements, there are elements of pragmatism and purism within the ranks.

Ann Stone, the chair of Republicans for Choice, argued that such Christian Right figures as Ralph Reed ultimately cannot succeed at both mobilizing movement activists and becoming mainstream GOP leaders. As she put it, if Reed and other leaders become too much like the rest of the GOP mainstream, the activist core of the Christian Right will abandon them. She stated: "when Robertson and Reed began saying that they cared mostly about economics and traditional Republican issues, they looked back and saw no one following. Then they would throw in, 'oh yeah, no abortions and gays are bad,' and the troops would follow again" (Stone 1994).

Indeed, many activists are expressing some disappointment with Reed and others who preach pragmatism. When it became known that Reed was working on behalf of drafting a moderate-sounding GOP platform plank in 1996 on abortion, many activists signaled their strong disapproval of his actions, and he retreated. A good many activists who are unwilling to accept compromise have decided that their support should go to more purist leaders such as James C. Dobson, the head of the Focus on the Family organization.

Whereas Reed worked to help Dole in 1996, Dobson openly expressed disapproval of Reed's willingness to compromise and his disappointment with Dole for not being a strong enough voice against abortion. As the vice president of Dobson's Focus organization, Paul Hetrick, commented: "Dr. Dobson is increasingly concerned with some of the way Ralph's been talking about compromise on pro-life. . . . Ralph sets himself up as the representative of millions of Christians, but he's not strongly defending pro-life positions. There is no compromise on killing babies" (Fisher 1996, D2).

There are also limits to how far the Christian Right can go to persuade secular citizens of the rightness of its cause. Although leaders and many activists of the Christian Right appropriate the rights-based language of liberalism to promote sympathy with their plight, the reality remains that what the Christian Right wants is fundamentally different from what civil rights leaders demanded. Whereas the civil rights movement demanded equal treatment under the law—the right to nondiscrimination in employment, housing, and education—Christian social conservatives sometimes advocate policy changes that would require others to live by their moral code.

Although many Christian social conservatives portray themselves as a part of a persecuted minority, it cannot credibly be argued that they are singled out for the kind of discrimination faced by minorities and women in the past (and still to a lesser extent today).[4] It is difficult to make the case that Christians in our society are routinely denied equal employment, housing, and educational opportunities given other Americans.

Most important perhaps, there are significant limits to what the Christian Right can achieve in public policy. To some extent, when Christian social conservatives talk about the need to restore "family values," their pleas find a sympathetic hearing from large segments of our society that would never join a Christian Coalition or watch a "700 Club" broadcast. Large numbers of Americans certainly agree, for example, when Christian conservatives lament the decline in educational standards or the sexually explicit content of popular culture entertainment media. Support for Christian Right policy positions, however, is another matter, as most Americans are deeply uncomfortable with the notion of regulating what people can read in the public schools and libraries and do not support the elimination of abortion rights. A majority of Americans may respond to polls that they are disgruntled with the public schools, uncomfortable with the content of entertainment media, and personally opposed to abortion. Yet, majorities also make it clear that they do not support mandatory teaching of creationism in the public schools, do not want government regulating the content of entertainment media, and do not want to eliminate the option of abortion for others.

It may be that the Christian Right can, at most, continue to be an important part of the broad GOP coalition and hope to achieve incremental gains in policy at all levels of government. The movement will likely continue to exert influence on GOP candidates and platform positions as well as on public policies. But there are clear limits to just how far the Christian Right can go in achieving its objectives. That the movement has succeeded in becoming a part of the GOP coalition and promoting a national dialogue on "family values" is a testimony to the use of effective political strategies. But even the most astute political tacticians would find it impossible in the current climate to successfully promote any ultimate agenda of the Christian Right that would include such goals as the teaching of creationism in public schools and the elimination of abortion rights.

Notes

1. The case of Kincaid is good testimony to the effectiveness of Christian Right pragmatism. Long considered an extremist in Virginia political circles, she changed tactics and became one of the state's most savvy political tacticians. Governor George Allen appointed her the director of constituent relations in his administration, making the state's lead antiabortion voice the statehouse's head of outreach to constituent groups.

2. Not all in the Christian Right are comfortable with what some have labeled "stealth campaigns"—efforts by socially conservative GOP candidates to mask their controversial social views with moderate language. Last year I participated on a National Public Radio program about the Christian Right in local elections with Michael Farris, the former Moral Majority leader nominated for lieutenant governor in 1993 by the Virginia GOP. When I described the real case of a GOP Virginia House of Delegates candidate who campaigned for the party nomination as pro-life, but whenever asked about abortion during the general election responded that he respected current constitutional interpretations, Farris said "that candidate stinks." Farris denounced "stealth" tactics and made the case that pro-life candidates must be forthright with voters.

3. There is much disgruntlement within the movement because of perceptions that moderates do not necessarily reciprocate these arrangements. There is some credibility to this argument given the number of cases in which party moderates abandoned GOP nominees who were closely tied to the Christian Right.

4. I interviewed a leading Christian Right activist in Virginia who, while working as a network affiliate reporter covering politics, was writing speeches and position papers for a conservative GOP candidate for public office. She was fired, she said, "because I'm a Christian." She perceived her dismissal as "anti-Christian bigotry" toward an employee who had backed a pro-life candidate. She did not see the conflict of interest with her job.

References

American Broadcasting Company. 1993. "God at the Grass Roots." *Nightline* transcript. 4 November.
Associated Press. 1996. "Christian Coalition Leaders Trumpet Success with Voter Guide Campaign." *The Virginian-Pilot*, 4 November, A5.
Christian Coalition. 1993. "How to Win with Life." *State Legislative Policy and Campaign Institute*. Chesapeake, Va.: Christian Coalition.
DeBolt, Ed. 1993. Interview by author. McLean, Va., 15 February.
Farris, Michael. 1994. Interview by author. Percellville, Va., 12 August.
———. 1995. Inteview by author. 15 August.

Fisher, Mark. 1996. "The GOP: Facing a Dobson's Choice." *Washington Post*, 2 July, D2.

Georgianna, Sharon. 1989. *The Moral Majority and Fundamentalism: Plausibility and Dissonance*. Lewiston, N.Y.: Edwin Mellon Press.

Green, John, Clyde Wilcox, and Mark Rozell. 1996. Religious Coalitions in the New Christian Right: The Decline of Religious Particularism. Paper presented at the Tenth Citadel Symposium on Southern Politics, 7–8 March, Charleston, S.C.

Hadden, Jeffrey, Anson Shupe, James Hawdon, and Kenneth Martin. 1987. "Why Jerry Falwell Killed the Moral Majority." In *The God Pumpers: Religion in the Electronic Age*, edited by Marshall W. Fishwick and Ray B. Browne, 101–15. Bowling Green, Ohio: Bowling Green State University Popular Press.

Kilberg, Bobbie. 1993. Interview by author. McLean, Va., 15 February.

Kincaid, Anne. 1993. Interview by author. Richmond, Va., 17 November.

Marshall, Robert. 1990. *Prolife Precinct Power*. Stafford, Va.: American Life League.

Rozell, Mark J., and Clyde Wilcox. 1995. *God at the Grass Roots: The Christian Right in the 1994 Elections*. Lanham, Md.: Rowman & Littlefield.

———. 1996a. "It Isn't the Old Christian Right Anymore." *Los Angeles Times*, 29 April, B3.

———. 1996b. *Second Coming: The New Christian Right in Virginia Politics*. Baltimore, Md.: The Johns Hopkins University Press.

Stone, Ann. 1994. Interview by author. Alexandria, Va., 24 June.

Taylor, Joe. 1992. "Christian Coalition Revamping Image." *Richmond Times-Dispatch*, 7 December, B4.

Wilcox, Clyde. 1992. *God's Warriors: The Christian Right in Twentieth-Century America*. Baltimore, Md.: The Johns Hopkins University Press.

Wilcox, Clyde, and Mark J. Rozell. 1996. "Dole's Delicate Balancing Act." *The Christian Science Monitor*, 4 June, 20.

13

Citizenship, Discipleship, and Democracy: Evaluating the Impact of the Christian Right

Ted G. Jelen

The social and political phenomenon generically termed the "Christian Right" has occupied journalistic and scholarly attention for nearly two decades. The various chapters in this volume attest to the enduring character of political activity on the part of religious conservatives and amply demonstrate that the various manifestations of the Christian Right are both cause and consequence of the recurrent activation of issues of personal morality in American politics.

The studies in this volume raise once again the general normative issue of the proper role of religiously motivated participation in democratic politics. Is religion, in any of its many forms, compatible with the requirements of democratic civility? Can religiously motivated citizens be counted upon to "play fair" in democratic political competition, or does religious zeal somehow render suspect the motives and actions of religious activists?

In this chapter, I propose to reexamine these issues and to offer both a criticism and a defense of the activities of the "Christian Right" in contemporary democratic politics. I examine the phenomenon of the Christian Right from "both sides," and hope to do justice to each perspective. In so doing, my account will neither defend nor criticize the Christian Right on the basis of the correctness of its policy positions. To partisans on either side of the debate, such a limitation may seem to beg the important question. Nevertheless, I hope to evaluate the politics of the Christian Right from the standpoint of criteria, which are, to some limited extent, policy-neutral.

Aspects of Democratic Discourse

The extent to which the activities of the Christian Right are compatible with democracy is likely to depend on what the term *democracy* is taken to mean. While a full explication of the nature of democratic politics is clearly beyond the scope of this essay, it is necessary to articulate some essential features of democratic decision making. Democracy, understood by its root meaning as "rule by the people," contains the underlying assumption that human beings are, in some important sense, intrinsically valuable. That is, democratic citizens are valuable in their own right, and not simply as ends to other instrumental goals (see Tinder 1989).

In particular, I would assert that citizens of democracies are entitled to two important prerogatives: autonomy and self-determination. Autonomy means that citizens are entitled to make their own independent judgments about matters affecting them, free from coercion or intimidation. Self-determination is the ability of citizens to participate actively in the formation of their own characters. Self-determining citizens are allowed to choose among those factors that may influence their independent judgments. Thus, choosing whether to marry or whom to marry, choosing among religions (or between religion and irreligion), and choosing among communications media are examples of the choices permitted to self-determining citizens. Indeed, it might be argued that the value of self-determination is the penumbra underlying the diverse set of rights in the First Amendment. One common feature of the rights of free expression, religious freedom, and freedom of association is the empowering of citizens to choose those influences on which they will base political (or nonpolitical) judgments.

From this, it follows that democracy is ultimately a *persuasive* system (Thiemann 1996). That is, authoritative political judgments must be justified, and not simply imposed by public authorities. When, on occasion, public officials fail to justify their policy choices, an important norm of democratic political discourse has been violated. Officials (or for that matter, citizens) can be called upon to offer *justifications* for their political preferences.[1]

In the political realm, it is important to be particularly scrupulous about political justifications, since politics typically does not permit the option of "agreeing to disagree." In the final analysis, political judgments are *public* (applied to everyone) and *authoritative* (backed ultimately by the coercive power of the state). Thus, the manner in which political choices are justified is an issue of cardinal importance in democratic politics.

If an offered political justification is to persuade, it must be located in a shared set of assumptions or premises. In order to attempt to reach agreements, political dialogue often involves a search for the "common ground" on which political opponents can agree (Perry 1991; Greenawalt 1988, 1993).[2] Since agreement on political choices is often (and perhaps definitionally) controversial, the discovery of common ground is often difficult. Several analysts (Perry 1991; Audi 1989) have suggested that the quest for common premises and assumptions requires that certain norms of discourse be observed in democratic politics.

Three particular requisites are commonly cited. First, the justification for a political choice must be offered in terms that are *publicly accessible* (Perry 1991; Thiemann 1996; Greenawalt 1988). That is, if a citizen is engaged in a sincere effort to persuade a political opponent, appeals to particular sources of authority—or premises shared by members of certain subcultures—are illegitimate. Thus, the argument made against preserving natural resources by former Interior Secretary James Watt, who suggested that conservation may not be necessary because the end of the world foretold in the Book of Revelation may be at hand, illustrates how the requirement of public accessibility might be violated. Such an argument was not publicly accessible, since a theology of pre-millenial dispensationalism was not (and is not) the object of anything approaching a consensus of the American public.[3]

Second, public dialogue must be characterized by an attitude of *fallibilism*, or "self-critical rationality" (Perry 1991). Fallibilism suggests that one approach political discourse with an attitude of humility and openness to the possibility of being persuaded. A self-consciously fallible citizen would acknowledge the possibility that one's political judgments were mistaken, and be willing to specify the conditions under which she might abandon them.

Finally, political dialogue would seem to require the obverse of fallibilism, which is *pluralism*. If fallibilism requires us to admit that we might be wrong, an attitude of pluralism requires us to admit the possibility that our opponents might be correct. The value of pluralism suggests that an authentically "civil" democratic citizen should be open to the learning possibilities inherent in political debate, and that the process of intellectual exchange be regarded as genuinely (potentially) fruitful (see especially Mill 1975).

While this account is far from exhaustive or definitive, I submit that the notions of public accessibility, fallibilism, and pluralism capture much of what is often termed "civility" in democratic discourse. Ultimately, civility implies both a respect for one's fellow citizens (including one's opponents) and for one's own moral and intellectual limitations. Such respect demands a commitment to persuade (rather than to coerce) as well as a willingness to be persuaded.

The Case against the Christian Right

In one important intellectual tradition, religious values are regarded as important components of public discourse precisely because such values are thought to provide the common ground within which democratic politics can be conducted. Alexis de Tocqueville (1945) argued that Christianity "ruled by common consent" in the United States, and that whatever disagreements existed between denominations concerned matters of theology and doctrine (the so-called "First Table" of the Ten Commandments). There existed, on the other hand, a societal consensus on the ethical implications of Christianity ("Christian morality is everywhere the same"). Thus, religion provided a commonly shared set of premises within which political discourse could operate.

The notion that the United States is a "Christian nation," or adheres to a "Judeo-Christian tradition" is a very common one. Indeed, Falwell's "Moral Majority" was an attempt to return the United States to a state in which such religious values were embodied into law (Falwell 1980). Analysts such as Peter Berger (1967), Richard Neuhaus (1984), and A. James Reichley (1985) have all argued that, in some fashion, religion (singular) is a necessary ingredient of successful democratic politics (for an overview and critique of this position, see Jelen 1991b).

The implications of such analyses for the Christian Right are obvious. The United States, for various reasons, has strayed from the essential moral framework which Christianity has provided. Often, such accounts involve the belief that secular elites have exercised undue influence in attempting to secularize American politics, and that the political activity of conservative Christians is simply a defensive reaction to this influence (Carter 1993; Reed 1994). Thus, the activities of such groups as the Christian Coalition, the Concerned Women for America, the Eagle Forum, and Focus on the Family are simply a necessary reaction designed to reinstate a preexisting moral consensus.

The problem with such a view is that it is simply empirically inadequate. Indeed, the diversity of religious *and* moral values in the United States suggests that religion is much more likely to be a source of social contention than of social cohesion. First, there does not exist a religious consensus in the United States. Many Americans are quite self-consciously "secular" (Kellstedt and Green 1993; Leege 1995), and others have only nominal affiliations with religious denominations (Kellstedt 1996). Moreover, conflict and prejudice between Jews and Christians—and even between Christian denominations—have often limited the effectiveness of interfaith cooperation (Wilcox 1992; Jelen 1991a; Green 1993). The effects of religious particularism appear to have been particularly severe in fragmenting the political cohesion of religious conservatives during the early and mid-1980s.[4]

Second, it seems clear that there does not exist a *moral* consensus in the United States. Once we get beyond murder, theft, and rape (which could perhaps be proscribed on secular grounds as well), it is difficult to discern the content of a *common* American morality. For example, one of the most noteworthy features of the 1996 Republican National Convention was the virtual blackout on discussing the abortion issue, generally explained by the fact that such discussion is "divisive," and not conducive to Republican electoral success. Indeed, the abortion issue is almost a caricature of a contested (rather than a consensual) moral issue. Similarly, such social basics as gender roles and the morality of homosexuality are also controversial. Such disagreement exists not only between religious and secular people (Hunter's [1991] "culture wars" thesis), but also *within* religious denominations (see especially Segers and Jelen 1997).

The general point to be made here is that religion, defined as either adherence to doctrine or to a set of ethical principles, is not the object of consensus in contemporary American politics. Indeed, the fact that religious elites have attempted to assert that America is a "Christian nation" may indicate (somewhat ironically) that the presumed consensus no longer exists (Wills 1990). As such, religion does not provide the shared set of assumptions on which democratic discourse is likely to depend. The "sacred canopy" no longer exists (if indeed it ever did), and attempts to (re)construct a religious/moral consensus have not been successful.

Moreover, it also appears that the assertion of religious values from conservative Christians may undermine the political frameworks within which American politics is conducted. As Rawls (1993) has argued, in the absence of consensus on substantive principles of morality, there must exist support for constitutional essentials. Beliefs in the processes by which collective political judgments are reached must, according to Rawls, be independent of particular competing substantive conceptions of the good (see also Downing and Thigpen 1996).[5] Thus, for example, although we may disagree on the relative merits of candidates such as Bill Clinton, Bob Dole, and Ross Perot, it is of some importance that we agree that the candidate receiving a majority of the electoral vote is legally entitled to be president.

Aside from small groups of Christian restorationists (Wilcox 1996), I know of no group of religious activists who seek to alter the constitutional structure of American politics. Nevertheless, Christian activists have taken positions that, if adopted, would undermine some of the requisites of democratic discourse described in the previous section. For example, a number of empirical studies have suggested that both evangelical religion, and religiosity generally, are negatively related to support for the free expression rights of nonconformists (see, for example, Wilcox and Jelen 1990; Green, Guth, Kellstedt, and Smidt 1994). Moreover, such a relationship does not appear to be spurious, but may be intrinsic to the nature of certain religious commitments. Indeed, in describing fundamentalist activists, they concluded that "the very motivation for political action reduced the civility of their politics" (Green et al. 1994, 44).

Normatively, such a religiously based set of preferences threatens the discourse requisites of fallibilism and pluralism. To the extent that religious conservatives believe themselves to be operating from an inerrant Scripture, they may not enter into public dialogue open to the possibility of being corrected (see Wilcox 1996; Jelen and Wilcox 1991). The assertion of revealed religion as a justification for public policies seems likely to inhibit, rather than enhance, the search for shared premises from which public deliberation may proceed (Rorty 1994).

It is not clear whether orthodox Christians necessarily violate the requisite of fallibilism when invoking religious justifications for policy choices (see especially Tinder 1989 for a discussion of a Christian-based political tolerance). However, the requisite of pluralism may pose a more serious challenge to the political tactics of religious conservatives. Traditionally, Marxists and feminists have utilized the concept of "false consciousness" to suggest important differences between the expressed preferences of certain classes of citizens and their "real," authentic interests (see especially Berlin 1958). To the extent that the preferences of one's political opponents can be explained "pathologically," one need not confront the content of their arguments.[6]

The tenets of orthodox Christianity contain one of the most complete and comprehensive theories of false consciousness available: original sin. Indeed, the concept of a fallen human nature is essential to most accounts of Christ's sacrificial atonement, and the content of original sin is precisely the attempt to supplant divine authority with human judgments. (In Genesis 3:5, the serpent tells Eve that "Ye shall be as gods" as a result of eating from the Tree of Knowledge of Good and Evil.) When conservative Christians confront arguments from those lying outside the tradition, such arguments can potentially be dismissed as resulting from a prideful, sinful, human nature (see Jelen 1993). Unlike Mill's (1975) characterization of religious thought, one need not make a claim of infallibility to justify silencing one's opponents; rather, the characterization of the opponents' judgment as corrupt may well suffice.

The general point here is that tolerance is not simply another policy preference on which democratic citizens may differ freely. Rather, tolerance is a background condition of democratic politics, designed to enhance dialogue and the discovery of common ground from which particular policy judgments can be made. Tolerance is a requisite of democratic politics, and not merely a possible policy outcome. To the extent that tolerance is inhibited by the preferences of religious activists, dialogue and persuasion are undermined.[7]

Moreover, other policies advanced by leaders and organizations of the Christian Right threaten the requisites of democratic discourse as well. During 1996, a number of state legislatures have passed or are considering laws banning the acceptance of same sex marriage.[8] Arguably, such a ban would constitute a violation of the equal protection clause of the U.S. Constitution, by denying the rights of full citizenship to a particular class of people. Of more direct relevance to the present discussion is the possibility that such a policy would violate the requisites of autonomy and self-determination outlined at the beginning of this essay. Again, democratic deliberation assumes that people are allowed to express and to formulate their own judgments, and to choose among formative experiences and statuses. The right to choose whom to marry, as expressed in *Loving v. Virginia* is not a matter for popularly elected legislatures to decide, but is arguably a requisite for full citizenship. Marriage is, after all, a self-defining and self-determining activity, which will have an enormous influence on the development of one's future preferences and interests (see Sezer 1995 for a fuller account of this point). Moreover, gays who are denied the right to marry are also denied a variety of rights relating to inheritance, property, and travel, and thereby are not full participants in the public dialogue.

Thus, it is possible to argue that the politics of the Christian Right are not compatible with the requisites of democratic discourse. Not only does the Christian Right draw on doctrines which do not form the basis for shared political judgments, but it may contribute to undermining the process wherein political persuasion can take place.

The Case for the Christian Right

The foregoing arguments notwithstanding, it is possible to advance strong policy-neutral arguments in favor of the role of the Christian Right in American politics. At the most basic level, religiously motivated political activity brings unrepresented (or underrepresented) viewpoints into the public dialogue. Indeed, the requisites of autonomy and self-determination would seem to require that religiously motivated (but not necessarily religiously justified) perspectives be taken seriously in political debate. Greenawalt (1988) argued that for many issues (including abortion and animal rights) publicly accessible policy justifications simply do not exist. While such warrants are desirable, there is no reason to exclude religious justifications from public deliberation on issues in which common ground from which policy judgments can be derived are not available.

Moreover, there is no a priori reason not to take such viewpoints seriously. If the notion of falsification means anything at all in the social sciences, the hypothesis that religiously based political activism is the result of psychological or social pathologies has been thoroughly discredited (Wilcox 1992; Wilcox, Linzey, and Jelen 1991; Jelen 1995). The perspectives of conservative religious activists, therefore, cannot be dismissed, and must be accorded a place in the public dialogue if the requisites of fallibilism and pluralism are to be honored by opponents of the Christian Right. While religiously conservative beliefs (and whatever political implications such beliefs may have) are not nearly universally held in the United States (and, therefore, cannot serve as an organizing *framework* for political dialogue), they are widespread, and are therefore deserving of a "place at the table" of political discourse (Reed 1994; Wilcox 1996; Carter 1993).

Aside from enhancing representation, there is some empirical evidence that political participation on the part of religious activists increases political civility. Verba, Scholzman, and Brady (1995) have shown that participation in church affairs has the effect of developing political skills and democratic values. Indeed, such positive socialization is most likely in the egalitarian, "low church" sorts of congregations from which the Christian Right is likely to derive substantial support. Further, church participation enhances the political effectiveness of otherwise politically disadvantaged citizens, and churches are perhaps the only institutions that have such a political "leveling" effect.

Moreover, other research (Wilcox, Linzey, and Jelen 1991) complements this finding. While traits such as authoritarianism, low self-esteem, and anomie were well represented among Midwestern Christian Right members,[9] such traits were *least* common among active members of the organization. Although it is difficult to make causal claims from data gathered at a single point in time, these results are consistent with the "participation hypothesis"; namely, that participation in public affairs has an educative effect on the participant (see especially Pateman 1970 and Bachrach 1967).

In a similar vein, a number of analysts (Wilcox 1996; Rozell and Wilcox 1996; Moen 1989, 1992) have suggested that, as a movement, the Christian Right has become "institutionalized," or has "matured" with the passage of time. Chastened by the political and electoral defeats of the 1980s, it has been shown that Christian Right rhetoric is less particularistic (see especially Reed 1994), less sectarian (Wilcox 1996; Grindstaff 1994), and more likely to appeal to a commonly shared language of "rights" (Moen 1992; Rozell and Wilcox 1996). Moreover, Christian Right activists of the Christian Coalition generation (what Rozell and Wilcox have termed the "Second Coming") have appeared much more willing to compromise and to accept incremental policy gains. While such changes have generally been described and justified on tactical grounds, they are also quite defensible for normative reasons as well. When a religious activist shifts rhetoric on school prayer from a desire to inculcate Christian values in schoolchildren to the language of free exercise, or emphasizes the practical consequences of teenage pregnancy or drug use, she is satisfying the requisite of offering publicly accessible justifications for her policy preferences. As such, contemporary Christian Right rhetoric may well be more "civil" *and* more effective than the failed efforts of the recent past.

Can Civility Be Christian?

As John Courtney Murray (1965, 1966) suggested, the issue of democratic civility poses special challenges for the believer. Christian discipleship is based to some extent on divine revelation. Such revelation would seem to be privileged, if not actually authoritative. God's Word, after all, would appear entitled to make a very strong truth claim. Conversely, for most varieties of Christianity, the acceptance of such truth is typically efficacious only if freely chosen by the individual believer. Moreover, as earlier manifestations of the Christian Right have made clear, the public assertion of values taken to be epistemologically privileged is not an effective rhetorical strategy in a religiously pluralistic society, and has historically occasioned strong countermobilization. Recent changes in Christian Right strategy may well reflect these religious and political imperatives.

Thus, if "civility" (as partially described at the outset of this essay) is the price of participation in public dialogue, the most recent representatives of the Christian Right may have paid it in full. By deemphasizing specifically sectarian or religious rhetoric in favor of more utilitarian or classically "liberal" justifications, organizations such as Christian Coalition, Eagle Forum, and Focus on the Family (among others) may have rendered moot normative concerns about the effects of religious activity in public affairs. However, one more issue remains to be raised: By accommodating its tactics to the norms of democratic politics, has not the contemporary Christian Right surrendered its distinctive religious mission? Has the impulse for compromise and cooperation diluted the Christian Right's very reason for political participation?

I raise two problems with the Christian Right's recently enhanced civility and effectiveness. The specific normative problem is that, in deemphasizing the religious roots of their policy positions, Christian Right leaders may risk sacrificing the uniquely transcendent nature of their message. Ultimately, the justification for particular policy preferences may not be publicly accessible, or subject to modification based on ecumenical dialogue, and requiring Christian Right leaders to act in such a manner may involve restricting the range of their political rhetoric and activities.

For example, consider possible reactions to Dean Hamer and Peter Copeland's book, *The Science of Desire* (1994), in which the authors combine a number of diverse strands of evidence to suggest that there might exist a biological basis for male homosexuality. Such a result, if accepted, might pose a challenge to believers in orthodox Christianity. At worst, such a finding might require religious conservatives to consider the possibility that God (benevolent and omnipotent) might have deliberately created homosexuals, and that homosexuality might well be an ascriptive characteristic. Fallibilism would require that believers leave open the possibility that scientific evidence might entail a reconsideration of the authority of the Bible,[10] while pluralism would require giving these arguments a respectful hearing. Of course, orthodox believers are not defenseless in the face of a work such as *The Science of Desire*. For example, a doctrinal conservative might well argue that homosexuality, like other moral pathologies, is a direct result of the Fall, and does not represent an intentional part of God's design. In this way, religious belief might well subsume a scientific finding. Nevertheless, such an argument might well leave the *political* implications of a biblical view of homosexuality vulnerable to the results of science. If homosexuality is indeed a genetically ascriptive trait, it may be that the fears of social conservatives that adolescents might be recruited into the gay lifestyle (and the implication that, therefore, the freedom of gays to "flaunt" their sexual orientation should be restricted) may well be unfounded. Moreover, the demand that justifications be cast in publicly accessible terms might well rule out appeal to divine revelation or biblical authority, since such religious premises are not generally shared by the American public. Thus, the requirements of democratic civility might well proscribe the most compelling (to the believer) arguments against the book, and limit the range of considerations publicly available to religious conservatives. Given the public accessibility of science, and the lack of such public acceptance of particular religious beliefs, the believer may well be forced to engage in political conversation with one hand metaphorically tied behind one's back.

What this may mean in more general terms is that the requirements of democratic civility[11] may entail a commitment to an epistemological method of rhetorical and experiential trial-and-error in which the efforts of human persons are sufficient to gain greater approximations of "truth."[12] Such a method assumes the essential rationality and benevolence of participants in any such process. Christian Right supporters who accept such a methodology might well be undermining the epistemological basis of their own faith, in which divine revelation is offered to redeem corrupt, sinful humanity. Why, given the cosmology of orthodox Christianity, should interaction (civil or otherwise) between corrupt creatures result in morally or intellectually superior outcomes?

The practical problem may lie in the fact that religious particularism may prove a more intractable problem than some might believe. As noted above, particularism proved to be a formidable limitation on the "old" Christian Right tied to the Moral Majority and the Robertson campaign. More recently, political leaders such as Ralph Reed and James Dobson have deemphasized specifically theological arguments, and have appeared more successful in attracting and maintaining ecumenical coalitions.

Is such a strategy sustainable? Ultimately, of course, such a question is an empirical matter. However, one possible limitation is that support for the Christian Right in any of its forms is strongly related to religious involvement (see especially Leege 1996). Specifically, religious socialization is most likely to take place in a congregation, generally (although not always) within a specific denomination. Finke and Stark (1992) suggested that religious involvement is, to a large extent, a consequence of religious competition. In other words, the general level of public religious observance (such as attendance at religious services) is increased in an environment of religious pluralism. Finke and Stark make explicit use of an economic analogy to suggest that competition provides incentives for religious "producers" to satisfy the desires of the lay members of their congregations.

If this analysis is correct, it may pose two distinct problems for the Christian Right. First, members of some congregations may resist overt political socialization within religious services. Indeed, such a tendency to reject overtly political messages may be strongest in the evangelical churches from which the Christian Right might be expected to draw its strongest support. The individualistic theology (Jelen 1993; Benson and Williams 1980) that characterizes many such churches may impose high potential costs for political leadership on the part of local clergy. Second, to extend Finke and Stark's economic analogy a bit further, congregations ("firms" in a religious economy) may have incentives to engage in "product differentiation," by distinguishing themselves from their closest competitors. The logic of religious competition would seem to suggest that specifically religious organizations may succeed by emphasizing or exaggerating differences between themselves and theologically adjacent denominations. To that extent, the religious basis of Christian Right support may be inimical to the broad, ecumenical message put forth by *political* leaders of the Christian Right. The nature of economic competition (material or religious) is to divide and differentiate; the nature of political competition is to "make 51 percent," which requires compromise and accommodation.[13]

The Volatility Quotient of Religion and Politics

Of course, there is nothing original or paradoxical about the hypothesis that the demands of citizenship and discipleship may, in some circumstances, be radically different. The Christian Right, in both its "old," 1980s manifestation, and in its more recent "ecumenical" incarnation, have enhanced our understanding of democratic politics by testing, to some extent, the limits of democratic and religious discourse. To be "prophetic" requires that the citizen/believer act in the world while transcending it. Can a believer be both authentically Christian and politically civil and effective? Christian political activism poses a stark challenge to both democracy and Christianity, which presents the believer and the polity with both risks and opportunities.

The risks involved in the political activity of the Christian Right relate to the tension inherent in the roles of citizen and believer. Despite the apparent simplicity of the admonition to "render unto Caesar that which is Caesar's," the practice of balancing political and religious roles is somewhat more complicated. Citizens with strong religious motivations may succumb to the temptation to apply the certitude and fervor of religious conviction to the shifting, uncertain plain of temporal politics. In so doing, activists of the Christian Right may undermine the essential requisites of democratic dialogue, and, in so doing, may render unto God that which is properly Caesar's.

Conversely, the religiously motivated political activist may be tempted to accommodate the demands of democratic discourse, at the possible cost of the eternal, transcendent values that Christianity provides. At some point, democratic values such as pluralism and tolerance may indeed defeat the basic motivation underlying the political participation of religious activists. Those who yield to the temptation to engage in political activity "for its own sake" may risk rendering unto Caesar that which properly belongs to God.

If the Christian Right poses risks for both Christianity and democracy, the activity of such people also provides enormous opportunities. From a political standpoint, the political mobilization of religious believers offers the possibility of greater inclusion of citizens and ideas in the democratic dialogue. Religious activity can be a form of "citizen school," in which interpersonal skills and motivations are transferred to the political realm. This is an important notion, since any genuinely publicly accessible political conversation must include the large (and apparently growing) numbers of religious conservatives. Moreover, the introduction of religious perspectives into democratic discourse allows the entrance of transcendent ideas and values into the political dialogue. The presence and visibility of religious activists serves as a reminder that a characterization of politics as simply "the art of the possible" is normatively inadequate, and that political processes are, in the last analysis, inseparable from ultimate values.

Viewed from the perspective of the believer, religiously motivated political activity provides an opportunity for religion to play an authentically prophetic role in the secular life of American politics. An important component of the concept of "evangelicalism" is the spreading of religious values (the "Good News"), and politics is an important public activity through which such sharing may be accomplished. The political assertion of religious values serves as a reminder that religion has a publicly *consequential* dimension, and that authentic religious belief cannot be relegated to a purely private sphere of belief and activity. Christianity, in virtually all of its manifestations, has *public* implications and *public* consequences, and politics is, if nothing else, a public activity.

This analysis thus suggests that there are substantial costs and benefits to the political activity of religious activists, including those of the Christian Right. The question of the legitimacy of such activity, from both religious and political perspectives, seems unlikely ever to be settled definitively. I would have it no other way. Again, the potentially volatile mix of religion and politics poses both risks and opportunities for the individual and the society. Those who seek to fulfill the roles of citizen and disciple should not lose sight of either.

Notes

1. It might be objected that this account of democratic discourse implies a highly individualistic, atomistic, conception of democracy, and that other conceptions of democracy are much more "communitarian" in nature. I begin with an account of the characteristics of *individual* democractic citizens, since many commentators have noted that the contemporary American political culture lacks a publicly shared, publicly accessible basis for political community.

To some extent, more communal accounts of democracy assume either the existence or the possibility of the "common ground" on which the following analysis depends. For example, Rousseau's *Social Contract* (1967) suggests the possibility of a "General Will," which is not only compatible with individual interests, but which *must* exist if genuine individual autonomy is to be achieved (hence, Rousseau's apparently paradoxical comment that some people can be "forced to be free"). Even here, however, the formation of an authentic basis for community requires a certain level of individual freedom and autonomy (note Rousseau's radical egalitarianism, and his condemnation of "partial associations"). While I cannot analyze this issue in any detail here, I would suggest that, in any authentically "democratic" account of communitarian democracy, "community" is, at least in part, the *consequence* of interaction between morally autonomous individuals. While theorists of democratic politics may vary in their definitions and accounts of the requisites for citizen autonomy, I am aware of no democratic theorist who disparages the importance of autonomy itself.

2. If the premises from which different citizens operate are genuinely incommensurable, dialogue (and, therefore, democracy) is clearly impossible. In such a situation, the argument made by Thrasymacus in Book I of the *Republic* (that is, right is simply the interest of the stronger party) may seem compelling.

3. Indeed, Watt's assertion might be regarded as suggesting the political irrelevance of his opponents in the aftermath of the 1980 election, and the lack of any need to persuade opponents in the wake of Reagan's impressive victory.

4. I deal with the more recent manifestations of the Christian Right below.

5. The notion that political processes must be independent of competing substantive outcomes is, in its pure form, impossibly restrictive, since any set of procedures is biased in favor (or against) particular outcomes. For example, the American system of separated governmental powers and federalism is clearly biased in favor of stability and incremental change, and renders drastic policy changes extremely difficult. It is perhaps more appropriate to view the extent of policy-process independence as a continuum, with the constitutional enshrinement of particular outcomes on one end, and a Rawlsian (1971) "veil of ignorance" on the other. Normatively, the extent to which processes are independent of particular policy outcomes is important, since a system in which processes determined outcomes would command no loyalty or legitimacy from the losers of the process (see Guirnier 1994).

6. The tendency to dismiss the arguments of one's opponents by reference to their motives or characteristics is fully reciprocal on both sides of the religion-politics debate. For overviews, see Wald, Owen, and Hill 1989; and Wilcox, Linzey, and Jelen 1991.

7. Clearly, the question of the limits of tolerance is an important one for democratic theory, and is well beyond the scope of this chapter. While this essay is clearly not a treatise on constitutional law, I would suggest that limitations on free expression must be very carefully justified, if the processes underlying the democratic conversation are not to be undermined. Indeed, the persistent attempts by the U.S. Supreme Court to argue that obscenity is something other than speech is a strong testament to the value the Court has placed on the free exchange of ideas.

It seems obvious that the expression of ideas is not unlimited. The circumstances under which ideas can be expressed can often be legitimately restricted. For example, not only am I not allowed to cry "Fire!" in a crowded theater, I may quite legitimately be forbidden to speak at all, if my speech interferes with the ability of other patrons to enjoy the performance. Similarly, there is no legal or normative problem with certain restrictions on the content of speech (for example, "No electioneering within 100 feet of the polling place"). However, such limitations would be normatively pernicious if they contained restrictions on the expression of particular viewpoints. Thus, a "cheering only" rule in a theater, or a "Republican electioneering only" rule within a polling place, would pose quite different issues. To the extent that the intolerance of religious conservatives is based on a desire to restrict the dissemination of particular *viewpoints*, such intolerance may create a *presumption* of incivility. See generally Sezer and Jelen 1985.

8. This flurry of activity was likely motivated by the actions of the state Supreme Court of Hawaii, which appeared ready to declare Hawaii's ban on gay marriage unconstitutional. Were this to occur, under one interpretation of the full faith and credit clause of the U.S. Constitution, other states would be required to recognize the legitimacy of same-sex marriages performed in Hawaii.

9. Since we had no comparable data for other populations, we have no way of knowing whether these respondents were distinctive from the general public.

10. Note that this account assumes that "science" does constitute a publicly accessible warrant. Such an assumption appears to be at least plausible. Many religious conservatives who believe in the Genesis account of creation have adopted a version of the "scientific method" and the label "scientific creationism" (Martin and Jelen 1989). Further, some analysts (Jelen 1993; Grindstaff 1994) have shown that "pro-life" adoption rhetoric has become less specifically religious—and has included more scientific public arguments—over time. While this trend is by no means universal among American evangelicals, there does appear to exist a pronounced tendency for doctrinal conservatives to accommodate the insights and methods of modern science.

11. It is important to note that these requirements are generally drawn from the works of Kent Greenawalt, Michael Perry, and Ronald Thiemann, who present themselves as defenders of a strong political role for religion in democratic politics.

12. Indeed, accounts of liberal democracy appear to require that the notion of "truth" be placed inside quotation marks, to indicate skepticism about the concept.

13. To some extent, groups such as the Christian Coalition may have ameliorated this problem. The studies in this volume by Bendyna and Wilcox and by Berkowitz and Green have shown that, in recent years, the leadership of Christian Right organizations has been exercised by lay people, rather than by clergy. Thus, the imperatives of religious recruitment may not have been as compelling. See also Wilcox, Rozell, and Gunn 1996.

References

Audi, Robert. 1989. "Separation of Church and State and the Obligations of Citizenship." *Philosophy and Public Affairs* 18: 258–96.
Bachrach, Peter. 1967. *The Theory of Democratic Elitism: A Critique.* Boston: Little, Brown.

Benson, Peter L., and Dorothy L. Williams. 1980. *Religion on Capitol Hill: Myths and Realities.* New York: Oxford University Press.

Berger, Peter. 1967. *The Sacred Canopy: Elements of a Sociological Theory of Religion.* New York: Doubleday.

Berlin, Isaiah. 1958. "Two Concepts of Liberty." In *Four Essays on Liberty*, edited by Isaiah Berlin, 118–72. New York: Oxford University Press.

Carter, Stephen L. 1993. *The Culture of Disbelief: How American Law and Politics Trivialize Religious Devotion.* New York: Basic Books.

Downing, Lyle A., and Robert B. Thigpen. 1996. Rawls and Religious Authoritarianism. Paper presented at the annual meeting of the Midwest Political Science Association, April, Chicago.

Falwell, Jerry. 1980. *Listen, America!* Garden City, N.Y.: Doubleday.

Finke, Roger, and Rodney Stark. 1992. *The Churching of America, 1776–1990.* New Brunswick, N.J.: Rutgers University Press.

Green, John C. 1993. "Pat Robertson and the Latest Crusade: Religious Resources and the 1988 Presidential Campaign." *Social Science Quarterly* 74: 157–68.

Green, John C., James L. Guth, Lyman A. Kellstedt, and Corwin E. Smidt. 1994. "Uncivil Challenges: Support for Civil Liberties among Religious Activists." *Journal of Political Science* 22: 25–49.

Greenawalt, Kent. 1988. *Religious Convictions and Political Choice.* New York: Oxford University Press.

———. 1993. "Grounds for Political Judgment: The Status of Personal Experience and the Autonomy and Generality of Principles of Restraint." *San Diego Law Review* 30: 647–75.

Grindstaff, Laura. 1994. "Abortion and the Popular Press: Mapping Media Discourse from *Roe* to *Webster*." In *Abortion Politics in the United States and Canada: Studies in Public Opinion*, edited by Ted G. Jelen and Marthe A. Chandler, 57–88. Westport, Conn.: Praeger.

Guirnier, Lani. 1994. *The Tyranny of the Majority: Fundamental Fairness in Representative Democracy.* New York: The Free Press.

Hamer, Dean, and Peter Copeland. 1994. *The Science of Desire: The Search for the Gay Gene and the Biology of Behavior.* New York: Simon and Schuster.

Hunter, James Davison. 1991. *Culture Wars: The Struggle to Define America.* New York: Basic Books.

Jelen, Ted G. 1991a. *The Political Mobilization of Religious Beliefs.* New York: Praeger.

———. 1991b. "Religion and Democratic Citizenship: A Review Essay." *Polity* 23: 471–81.

———. 1993. *The Political World of the Clergy.* Westport, Conn.: Praeger.

———. 1995. Research in Religion and Political Behavior: Looking Both Ways after a Decade of Research. Paper presented at the annual meeting of the American Political Science Association, September, Chicago.

Jelen, Ted G., and Clyde Wilcox. 1991. "Religious Dogmatism among White Christians: Causes and Effects." *Review of Religious Research* 33: 32–46.

Kellstedt, Lyman A. 1996. "Simple Questions, Complex Answers: What Do We Mean By 'Evangelicalism?' What Difference Does it Make?" *Evangelical Studies Bulletin* 12, no. 2: 1–4.

Kellstedt, Lyman A., and John C. Green. 1993. "Knowing God's Many People: Denominational Preference and Political Behavior." In *Rediscovering the Religious Factor in American Politics*, edited by David C. Leege and Lyman A. Kellstedt, 53–71. Armonk, N.Y.: M. E. Sharpe.

Leege, David C. 1995. "Religiosity Measures in the National Election Studies: A Guide to Their Use, Part I." *Votes and Opinions* 2: 6–9; 27–30.

———. 1996. "Religiosity Measures in the National Election Studies: A Guide to Their Use, Part 2." *Votes and Opinions* 2: 6–9; 33–36.

Martin, Alfred R., and Ted G. Jelen. 1989. "Knowledge and Attitudes of Catholic College Students Regarding the Creation/Evolution Controversy." In *Religion and Political Behavior in the United States,* edited by Ted G. Jelen, 83–92. New York: Praeger.

Mill, John Stuart. 1975. *On Liberty.* London: Oxford University Press.

Moen, Matthew. 1989. *The Christian Right and Congress.* Tuscaloosa: University of Alabama Press.

———. 1992. *The Transformation of the Christian Right.* Tuscaloosa: University of Alabama Press.

Murray, John Courtney. 1965. *The Problem of Religious Freedom.* Westminster, Md.: The Newman Press.

———. 1966. "The Declaration of Religious Freedom: A Moment in Its Legislative History." In *Religious Liberty: An End and a Beginning,* edited by John Courtney Murray, 15–22. New York: Macmillan.

Neuhaus, Richard John. 1984. *The Naked Public Square.* Grand Rapids, Mich.: Eerdmans.

Pateman, Carole. 1970. *Participation and Democratic Theory.* London: Cambridge University Press.

Perry, Michael J. 1991. *Love and Power: The Role of Religion and Morality in American Politics.* New York: Oxford University Press.

Rawls, John. 1971. *A Theory of Justice.* Cambridge: Harvard University Press.

———. 1993. *Political Liberalism.* New York: Columbia University Press.

Reed, Ralph. 1994. *Politically Incorrect: The Emerging Faith Factor in American Politics.* Dallas, Texas: Word.

Reichley, A. James. 1985. *Religion in American Public Life.* Washington, D.C.: Brookings Institute.

Rorty, Richard. 1994. "Religion as Conversation-Stopper." *Common Knowledge* 3: 1–6.

Rousseau, Jean-Jacques. 1967. *The Social Contract, and Discourse on the Origin of Inequality,* edited by Lester G. Crocker. New York: Washington Square Press.

Rozell, Mark J., and Clyde Wilcox. 1996. "Second Coming: The Strategies of the New Christian Right." *Political Science Quarterly* 111: 271–94.

Segers, Mary C., and Ted G. Jelen. 1998. *A Wall of Separation? Debating the Public Role of Religion*. Lanham, Md.: Rowman & Littlefield.

Sezer, L. Kent. 1995. "The Constitutional Underpinnings of the Abortion Debate." In *Perspectives on the Politics of Abortion*, edited by Ted G. Jelen, 131–76. Westport, Conn.: Praeger.

Sezer, L. Kent, and Ted G. Jelen. 1985. Poronography, Feminism, and the First Amendment. Paper presented at the annual meeting of the Northeastern Political Science Association, November, Philadelphia, Pa.

Thiemann, Ronald F. 1996. *Religion in Public Life: A Dilemma for Democracy*. Washington, D.C.: Georgetown University Press.

Tinder, Glenn. 1989. *The Political Meaning of Christianity*. Baton Rouge: Louisiana State University Press.

Tocqueville, Alexis de. 1945. *Democracy in America*. 2 vols. Edited by Phillips Bradley. New York: Vintage Books.

Verba, Sidney, Kay Lehman Scholzman, and Henry E. Brady. 1995. *Voice and Equality: Civic Voluntarism in American Politics*. Cambridge: Harvard University Press.

Wald, Kenneth D., Dennis E. Owen, and Samuel S. Hill. 1989. "Habits of the Mind? The Problem of Authority in the New Christian Right." *Religion and Political Behavior in the United States*, edited by Ted G. Jelen, 93–108. New York: Praeger.

Wilcox, Clyde. 1992. *God's Warriors: The Christian Right in the Twentieth Century*. Baltimore, Md.: Johns Hopkins University Press.

———. 1996. *Onward, Christian Soldiers? The Religious Right in American Politics*. Boulder, Colo.: Westview Press.

Wilcox, Clyde, and Ted G. Jelen. 1990. "Evangelicals and Political Tolerance." *American Politics Quarterly* 18: 25–46.

Wilcox, Clyde, Sharon Linzey, and Ted G. Jelen. 1991. "Reluctant Warriors: Premillenialism and Politics in the Moral Majority." *Journal for the Scientific Study of Religion* 30: 245–58.

Wilcox, Clyde, Mark J. Rozell, and Roland Gunn. 1996. "Religious Coalitions in the New Christian Right." *Social Science Quarterly* 77: 543–58.

Wills, Garry. 1990. *Under God*. New York: Simon and Schuster.

14

Conclusion

Corwin E. Smidt and James M. Penning

This volume has presented thirteen different chapters focusing on the Christian Right in the United States and in other parts of the world. The various chapters present observations, information, and explanations in a comparative perspective in order to enhance readers' understanding of the complexity and richness of the Christian Right movement. To conclude this volume, this chapter will offer various generalizations about the Christian Right drawn from these chapters and suggest avenues for future research on the Christian Right.

Generalizations

Several important generalizations can be drawn from these studies. First, while the concept of the "Christian Right" has sufficient unity to merit its use as an analytical tool, the social reality it incorporates is far from monolithic or unidimensional. The Christian Right, as a movement, is composed of leaders, organizations, activists, members, sympathizers, and distinct constituencies from which potential members are drawn. When discussing the Christian Right, one must always be clear about what particular facet of reality one is referring to. For example, one should not assume that the goals of Christian Right leaders necessarily reflect the goals of most members or sympathizers. Moreover, even when one is engaged in analysis at the same analytical "level," precision is still necessary. As the chapters in this volume clearly illustrate, at the level of organizational structure, the political institutions of

269

the Christian Right exhibit great diversity in focus, agenda, goals, and strategies. Likewise, one must distinguish between the Christian Right's relatively narrow primary base of support (evangelical Protestants) and the potentially larger group of cultural conservatives that constitute its potential base of support.

Second, it is evident that the Christian Right in the United States exhibits considerable continuity with the past, while adapting to a changing social and political environment. There is a tendency in some quarters to view the Christian Right as a recent phenomenon, arising out of the peculiar political and social context of the late twentieth century. Yet, as this volume demonstrates, throughout U.S. history there have been periodic waves of conservative Christian political activity, waves that exhibit sufficient patterns of continuity with each other to warrant their being similarly labeled "Christian Right" activity. Yet, it is also true that the Christian Right in America today is, in important ways, qualitatively different from the Christian Right that was found in U.S. society only two decades ago. Today's Christian Right, seasoned by the political battles of the 1970s and 1980s, and bolstered by a new generation of supporters, is better organized, better led, and more politically sophisticated than the Christian Right of the past. It utilizes the latest technology to communicate with its members and to support favored political candidates and public policies. And, even though there are frequent disagreements among members of the Christian Right over goals and tactics, the movement contains sufficient cohesiveness to make it a major "player" in contemporary American politics. Today's Christian Right may not dominate U.S. politics but it at least has reached its goal of achieving a "seat at the table."

Third, regardless of the country examined, the Christian Right tends to draw its primary support from the same social base—evangelical Protestantism. Consequently, the relative size of the Christian Right in a given society is likely to be largely, though not totally, a function of the relative strength of evangelical Protestantism within that society. This is not to say that all evangelical Protestants are attracted to the Christian Right or that the Christian Right attracts no support from other religious groups. But it does suggest that evangelical Protestants are more prone to do so than those from other religious traditions. And, while the relative size of evangelical Protestantism within a society isn't the sole determinative factor in the vitality of the Christian Right in various national contexts, it is indeed an important contributing factor.

Fourth, the particular institutional structures of the state as well as its party organizational structures also directly affect the vitality of the

Christian Right within a particular political system. Variation in such structural arrangements (e.g., whether there is a parliamentary or presidential system, a federal or unitary system, judicial review or the lack thereof, direct primaries or party caucuses, a centralized or decentralized media system) shape and modify the political opportunities of the Christian Right. Ironically, however, those structures that may contribute to grassroots vitality may not necessarily translate into policy successes for the movement. Moreover, policy success can, at least on occasion, actually diminish grassroots vitality.

Finally, it is clear that important tensions exist with the Christian Right that will directly affect its future vitality and importance. Despite depictions to the contrary, leaders of the various organizations of the Christian Right do not move in lock-step together. Ralph Reed, Gary Bauer, Randall Terry, and Jerry Falwell are not fully united either theologically or politically. Moreover, organizations within the Christian Right movement, as is generally true with movement organizations, frequently must work as much in competition with each other, such as in competing for scarce resources of time, energy, and money among movement members, as they do in cooperation with each other. Nor do the rank-and-file "members" of the Christian Right necessarily follow the calls of movement leaders. For example, calls for moderation (for example, the need for compromise and the achievement of the possible) emanating from leaders of certain quarters of the Christian Right may well serve to undermine not only the enthusiasm and motivational conviction of activists, but ultimately to diminish the size of the movement itself. Furthermore, even the same organization (the Christian Coalition) can vary greatly in terms of its strength and vitality of local chapters; the Christian Coalition is not everywhere to be "feared."

The Future Direction of the Christian Right

What is the future direction of the Christian Right following the 1996 presidential election?[1] If anything, the 1996 election seems to have enhanced the considerable disarray already evident among leaders of the Christian Right over the past several years. Different voices articulating different approaches to politics can currently be heard within the Christian Right movement. For some Christian Right leaders, the time has come to withdraw from political engagement. Some articulate this position because they view the political arena as relatively "ineffectual to accomplish the changes needed within American society (Eberly 1994,

35–36), while others do so because they believe political activity distracts believers from their highest priority—evangelism (Dobson 1996). Other Christian Right leaders have moved more toward what might be called "unconventional" political engagement. This approach involves working outside of partisan politics to pursue specific policy objectives. Militant activists, for example, have used protest tactics and even violence against abortion clinics. Today, a favorite approach among those seeking change is to use state initiative processes to propose legislation or constitutional amendments designed to promote a conservative social agenda. Growth in the use of citizen initiatives has been evident within U.S. politics over the past several decades, and "moral" initiatives have a long political history. However, the November 1996 loss of the Parents Rights Amendment in Colorado may have dealt an important blow to this particular strategy.

Yet other Christian Right leaders are advocating a third approach, partisan change. They call for continued political and partisan engagement, but outside of the current two-party system. Randall Terry, leader of Operation Rescue, has stated, for example, that "the Republican Party is the greatest moral impediment to righteous reform in politics. . . . They've manipulated the 'religious right' to their own ends. They throw us a bone, like the party platform, which the politicians promptly ignore. . . . The Republican Party is marked by betrayal and cowardice. They have lost their heart" (Terry 1994, 24). Given the actions of the GOP, Terry has called upon others to support the U.S. Taxpayers Party. Likewise, Paul Weyrich, President of the Free Congress Foundation, has predicted the formation of a new political party, bringing together elements from both the current major parties. Such a development, according to Weyrich, would simply reflect the failure of both parties to address value questions related to the continued disintegration of American culture, and "thoughtful people are going to conclude that they may as well lead it rather than just be a follower" (Weyrich 1995, 25).

Still other Christian Right leaders have advocated moving toward greater ideological purity within the Republican Party. Gary Bauer, head of the Family Research Council, voices no enthusiasm for any "big-tent" approach within the GOP and calls for continued partisan engagement, but in terms of principled and "ideological purity." This insistence on ideological purity has led to some conflict between Bauer and fellow Christian Right leaders. For example, Bauer has castigated Ralph Reed and the Christian Coalition's Contract with the American

Family because the contract does not call for a constitutional ban on abortion, and he has attacked others within the Christian Right who have expressed support for the idea that Colin Powell would make a fine GOP candidate for President. As Bauer noted, "many 'big-tent' Republicans maintain that they can combine liberal social policies with conservative economic policies and, by some sort of political 'averaging,' claim the mantle of moderate" (Frame 1994, 51). According to Bauer, if Republicans choose to follow such a strategy, they will merely join the ranks of other defeated candidates and parties.

Finally, there are those who call for pragmatism, advocating continued political engagement and GOP partisan support, but in a more flexible, strategic vein. This group includes leaders of the Christian Coalition. Pat Robertson, for example, has indicated that religious conservatives should "begin working as early as 1997 to shape the message of the next Republican Presidential campaign" (Niebuhr 1996, B10). Robertson asserts that he will try to take control from what he called the inside-the-Beltway Republican operatives, whom he denounced as "incompetent and uninterested in moral issues." But, unlike Bauer, Robertson recognizes the need for political compromise and moderation, arguing for the need to "pick someone who is electable."

Thus, it remains unclear just what the nature of Christian Right activism will be or the particular direction it will take. Over the past two decades, the perceptions evident among leaders of the Christian Right have shifted dramatically. The initial hope, perhaps growing out of President Richard Nixon's contention of the presence of a "silent majority," was that a moral majority existed beneath the partisan divide—a majority that could be activated to restore the United States once again to the moral foundations upon which it was founded. Over the past two decades, that image has shifted and has been gradually replaced by other images. Over a decade ago, President Reagan labeled the former Soviet Union the "evil empire." Now some leaders of the Christian Right are beginning to question the moral legitimacy of the government of this country. In fact, Cal Thomas, a national syndicated columnist, recently stated on the "700 Club" that the United States should be viewed as "the new evil empire" (*Church & State*, November 1996, 13). Should such perceptions as that articulated by Thomas come to be held by a significant portion of the Christian Right, a distinctively new era in the relationship between the Christian Right and American politics would be inaugurated.

Future Research

In what direction, then, should future research on the Christian Right go? Discussion at the Calvin Conference pointed in a variety of directions.[2] First, there is a need to better understand how religious beliefs and values become associated with particular political positions. Linkages between such religious beliefs and values and political stands do not occur automatically; they are historically contingent. Accordingly, how is it that certain religious beliefs and values come to be tied to particular political positions? Likewise, how is it that the same religious beliefs and values can be associated with different policy positions in different national contexts? And, how is it that equally committed people, holding the same religious beliefs and values, can move in different directions politically?

Second, there is a need to move toward the specification of those conditions under which the Christian Right movement is likely to be successful or unsuccessful. The specification of such conditions is likely to differ depending upon the type of success examined (for example, electoral success, agenda-setting success, or policy success). Tied to such analyses are more specific questions and issues. For example, to what extent is the broadening of the base of the Christian Right necessarily tied to broadening its agenda? Some might argue that the key to any future success of the Christian Right is dependent upon the movement becoming more pragmatic, exhibiting greater social and religious diversity, and promoting a broader agenda. Others, however, might argue that a simple core, and not a broad, agenda is required, pointing to the Prohibition movement as being successful only after it narrowed its focus.

Third, greater attention needs to be given to the role of women in the Christian Right. Historically, women have exhibited higher levels of religiosity than men, and many activists within the Christian Right are women. In the eyes of many, the ideology of the Christian Right seems relatively hostile toward women. Yet, much of the business of the Christian Right is conducted by women. Why is this so? Moreover, many of these women are highly educated women engaged in various professional occupations. What then moves such women to be part of the Christian Right movement as opposed to other movements with which they might be involved, such as the feminist movement?

Fourth, greater attention must be given to the political interplay between the Christian Right movement and the countermovement it has generated. The actions of countermovements not only shape and modify the actions of movements, but movements and countermovements can come to exist in almost a symbiotic relationship. Resource mobilization, organizational survival, and continued employment within movement organizations on one side are tied, in part, to the "threat" posed by the other side. On the other hand, movements and countermovements need not move to such extremes; one's political opponents can be viewed less as enemies engaged in threatening behavior and more as fellow citizens articulating different solutions to address the same general problem(s). What moves movements and countermovements toward the extremes, and what serves to bridge and ameliorate their differences? What impact do different rhetorical strategies and issue frames have on such matters? How are perceptions of movement members shaped by the language employed by movement leaders?

Fifth, given that Christian Right organizations are now becoming more institutionalized in nature, what should be expected? How does such institutionalization relate to support among its constituents? What strategies are Christian Right organizations likely to employ as they bump shoulders with other organizations and compete for scarce resources? How does such institutionalization affect prospects for policy success?

Sixth, further attention also must be given to how social movement elites, denominational leaders, and party organizational leaders interact. For example, to what extent do leaders within one domain draw leaders from the other domains into their political struggles? What resources, if any, tend to be shared across domains? What prompts such efforts? What effects are associated with the mobilization of "outside" forces and resources?

Finally, increased efforts must also be given with regard to normative assessments of the Christian Right in American politics. While scholars have made important strides in analyzing and understanding the Christian Right empirically, greater efforts are needed to blend the product of empirical research with normative assessment. All too often our normative assessments of the Christian Right are simply a function of the policy goals one pursues or a reaction to particular images which have been promoted. In addition, there is a need for normative assessments which move beyond First Amendment issues. While such issues are obviously very important, other kinds of normative analyses also have merit. For example, do the Christian Right and its opponents share certain common values upon which it might be possible to build increased political civility and mutual respect? What aspects of "the good life" are likely to be more fully realized through the Christian Right than through the efforts of its opponents, and vise versa. And, how may different normative assessments of the Christian Right be related to the use of different normative frameworks?

Certainly, these suggested directions for future research do not exhaust the possibilities. Rather, they simply illustrate the many questions about the Christian Right that remain either largely unaddressed or unanswered by scholars. They are presented here with the hope that others will find such questions interesting and choose to join in the study of the topic.

Notes

1. This section is based on Penning and Smidt (1997).
2. Much of the discussion which follows is taken from a panel session at the conference which addressed this topic. The session was led by James Guth, David Leege, and Kenneth Wald.

References

Church & State. 1996. "Silly Rhetoric: The Religious Right's Gallows Humor." (November): 13.

Dobson, Edward. 1996. "Taking Politics out of the Sanctuary." *Christianity Today*, 16–17 May.

Eberly, Don. 1994. *Restoring the Good Society: A New Vision for Politics and Culture.* Grand Rapids, Mich.: Baker Books.

Frame, Randy. 1994. "Quick Change Artists." *Christianity Today*, 12 December, 50–53.

Niebuhr, Gustav. 1996. "Christian Group Vows to Exert More Influence on the GOP." *New York Times*, 7 November, B10.

Penning, James M., and Corwin E. Smidt. 1997. "What Coalition?" *The Christian Century*, 15 January, 37–38.

Terry, Randall. 1994. "Leader of the Exodus?" *World*, 26 February, 24.

Weyrich, Paul. 1995. "Time for a Third Party?" *World*, 6 May, 24–25.

Index

Contributors

R. Scott Appleby is an associate professor of history at the University of Notre Dame and director of the Cushwa Center for the Study of American Catholicism. He is author of *Church and Age Unite! The Modernist Impulse in American Catholicism.*

Mary E. Bendyna, R.S.M., is a graduate student at Georgetown University. Her dissertation is *Divided We Stand: Catholics and Contemporary American Politics.*

Laura Berkowitz is an instructor in political science at the University of Akron and is associated with the Ray C. Bliss Institute for Applied Politics.

Allison Calhoun-Brown is an assistant professor of political science at Georgia State University. She has written a variety of papers dealing with the politics of black evangelicals.

John C. Green is a professor of political science and director of the Ray C. Bliss Institute for Applied Politics at the University of Akron. He is coauthor of *The Bully Pulpit: The Politics of Protestant Ministers* (forthcoming).

James L. Guth is a professor of political science at Furman University. He is coeditor of *Religion and the Culture Wars: Dispatches from the Front* (Rowman & Littlefield).

Anne Motley Hallum is an associate professor of political science at Stetson University. She is author of *Beyond Missionaries: Toward an*

287

Understanding of the Protestant Movement in Central America (Rowman & Littlefield).

Dennis R. Hoover is a doctoral candidate at Oxford University. His research interests include religion and politics with a specialization in conservative protestant politics, social movements and contemporary political theory.

Ted G. Jelen is a professor of political science at the University of Nevada, Las Vegas. His most recent book is *A Wall of Separation? Debating the Public Role of Religion* (Rowman & Littlefield, 1998).

Lyman A. Kellstedt is a professor of political science at Wheaton College. He is coeditor of *Religion and the Culture Wars: Dispatches from the Front* (Rowman & Littlefield).

Michael Lienesch is a professor of political science at the University of North Carolina. He is author of *Redeeming America: Piety and Politics in the New Christian Right.*

Matthew C. Moen is a professor of political science at the University of Maine. He is author of *The Transformation of the Christian Right.*

James M. Penning is a professor of political science at Calvin College. He is coauthor of *Christian Political Action.*

Mark J. Rozell is a professor of political science at American University. He is coauthor of *Second Coming: The New Christian Right in Virginia Politics.*

Lee Sigelman is a professor of political science at George Washington University. His most recent book is *Black Americans' Views of Racial Inequality: The Dream Deferred.*

Corwin E. Smidt is a professor of political science at Calvin College. He is coauthor of *The New Religious Order in America* (forthcoming).

J. Christopher Soper is an assistant professor of political science at Pepperdine University. He is coauthor of *The Challenge of Pluralism: Church and State in Western Democracies* (forthcoming).

Kenneth D. Wald is a professor of political science at the University of Florida. He is author of *Religion and Politics in the United States.*

Clyde Wilcox is an associate professor of political science at Georgetown University. His most recent book is *Onward Christian Soldiers: The Christian Right in American Politics* (1996).